The Canadian Hiker's and Backpacker's Handbook

Think Globally. Inquire Locally.

The Canadian Hiker's and Backpacker's Handbook

Your How-to Guide for Hitting the Trails, Coast to Coast to Coast

Ben Gadd

Photos by Lonnie Springer

whitecap

This book is dedicated to Ginnie and Stanley Boucher,
who taught me how to walk up mountains.

Edited by Lesley Cameron
Proofread by Naomi Pauls
Design by Chrissy Davey
Photography by Lonnie Springer unless otherwise credited
Printed in Canada by Friesens

This book contains no advertising, either overt or hidden. During the research and writing of this book, the author received no gifts or payments from manufacturers or suppliers of the outdoor clothing, equipment and food described in it. The author did, however, borrow some items he was not familiar with from Mountain Equipment Co-op to try out. The opinions expressed in this book are strictly those of the author.

Library and Archives Canada Cataloguing in Publication

Gadd, Ben, 1946–
    The Canadian hiker's and backpacker's handbook / Ben Gadd.

Includes index.
ISBN 978-1-55285-917-9

    1. Hiking–Canada–Guidebooks. 2. Backpacking–Canada–
Guidebooks. I. Title.

GV199.44.C2G33 2008   796.510971   C2007-905498-6

The publisher acknowledges the financial support of the Government of Canada through the Book Publishing Industry Development Program (BPIDP) and the Province of British Columbia through the Book Publishing Tax Credit.

Cover photo: Hiker in Kananaskis Country in the Alberta Rockies

Contents

Foreword

When I began hiking in the Rockies as a youth, I bought a pair of Hush Puppies desert boots, which were the closest thing I could imagine to real hiking boots. My backpack was an army-surplus poncho wrapped around a flimsy, flannel-lined sleeping bag, which in turn contained a few sandwiches, a wool jacket, an extra pair of socks and a basic first aid-kit—a jury-rigged affair strapped to my back with two over-each-shoulder webbing straps. During that summer I completed many long day hikes and an epic backpack trip, made a first ascent of an unclimbed mountain face (by mistake), and ran afoul of a couple foul-tempered grizzly bears. It was truly the summer of living dangerously, but fate often protects fools, little children, and novice hikers.

A few years later, when I set out to compile the *Canadian Rockies Trail Guide*, I was a bit more savvy but still struggling with my wilderness skills and gear. I bought a "real" pair of hiking boots, but because the selection in Banff was limited, I had to settle for ones that were two sizes too large (the soles parted ways from the uppers by summer's end). And since my tent had to do double duty in roadside campgrounds as well as the backcountry, I bought one tall enough so I could stand up inside. (It weighed a whopping 6 kilos and leaked badly when it rained, but boy was it comfortable once you got it off your back and pitched under a clear, starry sky.) I acquired my first down-filled sleeping bag, but the 5-centimetre-thick, full-length foam sleeping pad was a bit cumbersome to roll and pack (it sat atop my pack like a huge white Twinkie).

Of course, life in the backcountry was simpler then, and there were lots of things we didn't have to carry or contend with. There was no *Giardia* in the streams (as far as we knew), so we didn't boil water or use purification pumps. There were no designated campsites, so we camped pretty much where we wanted (which may have contributed to today's *Giardia* problem). There was no pepper spray, so we relied on our wits and the occasional whistle or hoot to avoid meeting bears (most of the bears were in the garbage dumps anyway). And who could've imagined Gore-Tex rainwear, self-inflating sleeping pads, GPS location devices, and high-tech, shock-absorbing hiking poles?

But we did have the first how-to handbooks on hiking and backpacking. Unfortunately, while these books were useful, they were produced by US authors and skewed to travel in warmer climes. (I couldn't imagine stripping to my shorts and floating with my backpack across the

Sunwapta River.) Why wasn't there a book about the skills and stuff needed for wilderness travel in the North?

Fast-forward a few decades to *The Canadian Hiker's and Backpacker's Handbook*—a comprehensive guide specifically written for wilderness travel in Canada. I can think of no one more qualified to undertake the task of bringing this information to the page than Ben Gadd, venerable guide, naturalist, and denizen of Jasper National Park—Canada's premier trail-accessible wilderness. I have known Ben for a couple of decades, enjoying his wisdom and humour on field trips, day hikes and around the dinner table at his home in Jasper. Though we've never shared a backcountry tent, I've spent many a campground night snuggled up with his *Handbook of the Canadian Rockies*—one of the most complete regional natural-history guides ever published in Canada.

The Canadian Hiker's and Backpacker's Handbook is a worthy companion to his natural history compendium, since it explores every conceivable facet of backcountry travel. (If I'd read his section on boot selection years ago, I might not have become the Imelda Marcos of the Rockies, with a closet full of boots.) And despite its Canadian bias, it is one of the most well-considered books on wilderness travel available in North America today. (It won't help you swim the Colorado River with your backpack, and it's a bit light on rattlesnakes, but otherwise it covers everything you need to know before lighting out for the territory.) And if there is something important not mentioned or with which you disagree, you are welcomed to harass the author at www.bengadd.com. How many authors offer that satisfaction?

In the end, it's about feeling comfortable and at home in that vast, wild landscape that still makes up much of this country. Ever since I was a teenager hiking madly down the trail in my Hush Puppies, it has been about the sheer, unadulterated joy of moving through that landscape. As Ben Gadd says, "Whatever your reasons for wanting to get into the wilds under your own steam, they're good reasons," and "you might as well do so in comfort and safety."

Brian Patton
Co-author of the *Canadian Rockies Trail Guide*

Acknowledgements

Many thanks to Leanne Allison, Ken Berg, Colin Brooks, Paul Dywelska, H. A. Eiselt, Peter Gard, Rob Gardner, Michael Haynes, Karsten Heuer, Taku Hokoyama, Rick Holmes, Jerry Kobalenko, Paul Koberinski, Joel Paquin, Daniel Pouplot, Louanne Ralston, Tony Richardson, Judy Rowell, Angus Simpson and Jeff Whitman, all of whom supplied information about hiking and backpacking in various regions of the country, and some of whom provided photos; Susy Alkaitis and Ben Lawhon of the Leave No Trace Center for Outdoor Ethics; Jim Dennis of Alberta Community Development, who secured an essential photo shoot permit for us; Ed Hergott, Bonnie Curran, Michelle Housley, John Wasch and Sarah Springer, who volunteered their time to take the roles of Reg, Jacquie, Pat, Art and Shannon in the backpacking story; Aaron Springer, Blake Springer, Jan and Lonnie Springer, who made the backpacking-story photo shoot possible (Lonnie's excellent photos grace many pages of this book); trail-guide author Don Beers, who provided the photo on page 2; Rainer Schmid, who took the photo on page 263; Jasper National Park warden Patti Walker, who appears in the photo on page 226, and also her fellow wardens Steve Blake, Wes Bradford and Greg Horne, who checked sections of the backpacking story for warden-activity authenticity; Ed Dominguez, Jennifer Ortt and Bill Fortney of the Seattle Mountaineers, for appearing in some of the for-real backpacking photos (Ed also offered a tip, passed along on page 116); Derek Hammell, Jasper's satirist laureate, for the cartoon on page 139; Neil Haggard, manager of the Mountain Equipment Co-op store in Edmonton, who lent me gear to try out, and Glenda Rowley, manager of MEC Calgary, who arranged for Lonnie to photograph equipment and clothing in the store, plus all the MEC staff across the country who gave me advice about hiking conditions and gear requirements in their areas; Barb and Joe Zimmer, backpackers extraordinaire, who read a draft and made useful comments; Cia Gadd, my wife and backpacking partner since 1965, for appearing in several photos, taking the one on page 262, contributing sidebars and being the best editor ever; son Toby Gadd, his wife Alix, and their son Max and dog Kip for appearing in the photo on page 262; other son Will Gadd for contributing the amusing story on page 148; Lesley Cameron for the copy edit; and Brian Patton for writing such an entertaining foreword.

In a nutshell . . .

If you read nothing else, read this. This is the stuff you really, really need to know about hiking and backpacking in Canada.

Who can do it? Nearly everyone, including people with disabilities. To go for a walk—even if it's technically a ride in a wheelchair—interest and desire are all you need. Whatever your reasons for wanting to get into the wilds under your own steam, they're good reasons. Let's go!

Ability and fitness. If you can't walk very well, whether from lack of experience or lack of fitness, or from age or other physical limitations, go ahead and try anyway. You have nothing to lose and everything to gain. With some medical conditions it's wise to check with your doctor first, of course.

Knowledge and experience. Experience is up to you to acquire, but by reading this book (and I mean the whole book, not just this two-page summary) you'll get the benefit of what many other people have learned about enjoying the Canadian outdoors on foot. The information in these pages will help you to walk easily and well, to assemble good equipment and wear the right clothing, and to feed yourself properly and attend to your bodily needs. It will show you how to walk this country's wild places safely and with little environmental impact.

Walking. Keep the pace moderate, take short steps uphill and down, try using walking poles, stay with the group and be polite on the trail.

Footwear. If you take your time choosing walking shoes and boots carefully, they'll fit correctly and not give you blisters.

Food. You want to walk, walk, walk? You've got to eat, eat, eat. When on a backpacking trip, go for minimum weight, both in the food itself and in whatever you need to cook it, and for maximum nutrition. So what if freeze-dried stuff all tastes like cardboard? This is backpacking. When you're hungry enough, you'll eat anything.

Water. Surface water in Canada is no longer assuredly safe to drink. Bring water you know is safe, or bring the means to make the water you find along the trail safe.

Clothing. Wear layers you can put on and take off according to the weather. Have enough of those layers to deal with whatever the weather gods fling at you.

Pack. Carry a pack that's big enough and fits you well. A large, comfortable pack will work just fine if it's only half-full, but a pack that's too small and/or badly designed will always be uncomfortable, no matter how much or how little you've packed into it.

Shelter and camping. The ideal tent will keep out the bugs, the rain and the wind without keeping in your perspiration, the moisture in your breath and the odour of your dirty socks. Getting a good night's rest in the outdoors can be difficult for a person used to sleeping in a soft bed in the city, but a proper sleeping bag on a suitable pad makes a big difference—and so does a pair of earplugs.

Environmental protection. Most of us go day-hiking and backpacking in national and provincial parks or other protected areas that are administered by people who understand how best to look after them. The rules in such places are sensible and time-tested: stay on established trails and camp in the places provided; keep your campsite clean and pick up litter; avoid polluting the water; respect the animals and don't pick the wildflowers, etc. These considerations should be applied everywhere, parkland or not. In truly pristine wilderness we need to go a step further, practising the principles of Leave No Trace, as explained in this book.

Safety. Avoiding trouble is way better than having to deal with it, so be cautious. Choose outings that are within your abilities. Go with people you trust, and keep the group together. Read the guidebook; bring a map. Carry food and water, and pack the proper clothing and equipment, all of which you may need in case the weather goes bad or the trip takes longer than expected. Learn about the common maladies that befall hikers and what to do about them. Leave word, in case rescue becomes necessary.

"Each one teach one." If you pursue this pastime, you're going to become good at it. Then you can show others what you've learned and take them to places you would like to share with them.

Where to hike. When it comes to great places to go on foot, Canada can't be beaten. This book is not a guidebook as such, but it does describe what it's like to walk in some of Canada's favourite regions for outdoor recreation: the Appalachians, the Rockies, up north, along the coasts and so on.

Hiking by the Mt. James Walker tarn in Peter Lougheed Provincial Park, Alberta Rockies

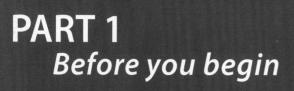

PART 1
Before you begin

I walk in beauty. In beauty I walk.

-Navaho saying

On the trail to Boulder Camp in the Bugaboos, Purcell Mountains, BC

Why we go hiking and backpacking

Keitha & Don Beers

Calgarian Don Beers backpacking in 1958

It hit me in junior high school. Unhappy at being stuck in math class on lovely June afternoons, I would gaze out the window toward the Rocky Mountains. The peaks, the forests, the streams, the cliffs, the trails that led to it all—there they were, so close at hand, so real, so utterly different from algebra. My heart would lift, and I would get an excited, tickly feeling in my tummy as I thought about heading for the high country on the weekend.

A couple of friends and I had recently discovered what would soon become known as "backpacking." In 1959 we called our trips "overnight hikes." Overnight hikers we were, spending single nights in the woods. We carried heavy canvas packs with unpadded straps and no hip-belt. We slept on lumpy beds of conifer boughs hacked from some luckless tree, and we sheltered under a lean-to covered with more of those branches. Our fondest hopes were that it wouldn't rain and that some animal wouldn't attack us in the night. We would lie awake at 3:00 a.m., shivering under our blankets, imagining the swish of paws through the grass. The wind, the sound of the creek nearby . . . these had somehow become animate, perhaps deadly. We loved it.

Back then we were ignorant not only of the true dangers of the Rockies—the weather, mainly—but also of the damage we were inflicting around our camp. We were unaware of the world of mountaineering, with its storm-tight nylon tents and goose-down sleeping bags. But even if we had known of these things, they would have been well beyond our means. A 50-cent weekly allowance and money earned by mowing lawns bought only what was available at the Army and Navy store. But it was enough to get us out there. Wilderness ethics had to wait until we could afford them.

As time went by I began to discover the camping equipment used by climbers. My first purchase was a Swedish white-gas stove in 1964. A proper sleeping bag would have been a better choice, but the stove was much cheaper ($8 rather that $25) and it appealed more to me anyway. I would hold that polished brass in my hands to warm the tank, then the fuel would squirt out the top in fine Freudian fashion. I would light my stove. Five minutes later I would have boiling water for a cup of tea—anywhere I wanted it. Wow!

Ah, the backpacker's obsession with gear. Think of the great toys available today. Shock-corded tent poles that snap together when you shake them out (hard on them, admittedly, but so cool to do), packs that magically transfer the load from shoulders to hips, electronic gadgets that tell you exactly where you are. Just think of all the clever, beautifully made and expensive things that enable city-dwellers to play house in the wilderness—and to do so without making a mess out there.

Yes, it's wonderful. But I don't think it's what camping's really about. I think it's really about the lean-to, the basic stuff, the primitive-looking yet cleverly sophisticated shelter and equipment we humans devised back when we were hunters and gatherers in the forest. More than that, I think camping is about being hunters and gatherers again.

People used to go hunting and gathering all the time. We travelled the wilds in little groups of family and friends, picking plants and knocking off animals. It was a landscape unfenced, unfarmed, unsullied by cities. Like the Navaho, we walked in beauty. We did so nomadically, using temporary shelters we built from whatever came easily to hand. Through most of the 200,000-odd years of our existence as a species, this is how we made our living.

We were very good at hunting and gathering; perhaps too good. Our population began to climb. By 10,000 years ago there were so many of us in the Middle East that we began fighting among ourselves over the right to hunt and gather. Whip-smart apes that we were, we solved the problem by inventing agriculture. Why not just settle down, turn the forest into fields, plant crops and keep animals close at hand to knock off whenever we liked? This worked pretty well, but our beauty-walking days were over.

Agriculture spread worldwide. One tribal culture after another either overpopulated itself into farming or was conquered by the neighbouring civilization. Or they just bought into the idea. We became very proficient at filling our granaries and raising our livestock. Our population grew and grew, doubling and doubling. We invented the town, the city, the nation-state, the cash economy, the division of labour.

Into the industrial age we went, the planet brimming with us. Vocational specialization became truly bizarre. Who among the Inuit of the 1920s, say, would have thought that a good life consisted of spending all day in a single room, taking papers from one pile, writing on them and placing them in another pile? Or nowadays, how many of us truly delight in tapping our fingers on little pieces of plastic hour after hour while staring into a computer display full of accounting data?

I submit that we do this only because we have to; that we are basically unsuited for the world we have made. Famed psychoanalyst Carl Jung might have agreed. He believed that we have "archetypal memories" of our collective past, hard-wired recollections of great days spent gorging ourselves in the berry patches and sticking spears into mastodons. Sure, those were rough-and-tumble times. You could starve, or you could die from a simple ailment. Heaven help you if the sabre-tooth cats got you. But oh, life was fun! And often you walked in beauty.

So here's the point: when we hike and backpack, I think we're re-creating (are you hearing "recreation" in there?) an essential element of that era, the journey taken on foot through wild surroundings. And—here's the really terrific part—when we're tired and dirty we can come home to a hot shower and a soft bed. By golly, we have the best of both worlds.

Few of us actually hunt and gather on our simulated foraging ventures these days. The gathering we can do at the supermarket and at Canadian Tire; the hunting we mainly forego, although as post-tribal peoples we are inclined to hunt one another, but that's a topic for another book. True hunting and gathering is tightly restricted or prohibited entirely in many of the places we like to go for recreation, as well it should be, because in our modern hordes we'd hunt and gather too much. The wildlife would be gone and the wilderness would be wrecked.

However, we still get to do the roving-around part, patrolling the commons—meaning national and provincial parks and Crown land, mostly—with family and friends. We put on our packs and head into the wilds. We walk in beauty once again.

And it brings out the best in us.

For example, when I pitch my tent in a backcountry campground, I note with initial displeasure the arrival of the folks popping up their digs beside me. Yet a few minutes later we're getting acquainted, and midnight may find us all sitting happily around the fire and telling each other things that we haven't told our best friends. Judging from the recorded activities of cultures untouched by the world's population explosion, that's what we used to do when we were a rare and thinly distributed species. We valued each other a great deal. An encounter was typically an occasion not for a fight but for a party.

Nowadays we live in crowded, hyper-competitive cities. We act accordingly hyper and competitive. When we get ourselves out of those surroundings and onto the trail, though, things are different. Having hiked for an hour and seen no one else, what do we do when we meet another person? We both smile and say hello. Perhaps we make a little small talk—"Nice morning, eh?" "Sure is!"—before moving on. One doesn't do that when passing strangers in downtown Toronto.

Some of us live for the difference between Toronto and the great outdoors. I'm one of them. Maybe you are, too.

But never mind this squishy-science rationale. There are lots of other good reasons for going hiking and backpacking. Maybe you just like the feeling of putting one foot in front of the other. Walking is very good for our bodies, no question about that. It's good for our minds, too, especially when the cares of the world are on our shoulders. It can produce spectacular results when we're mulling over a problem. Many great ideas have been brought home from a walk in the woods.

Given an empty space big enough to be worthy of the label "wilderness," we recover something that urban-dwellers lost long ago: the night. Human-generated light is a form of pollution. But in the middle of Jasper National Park, after the long Canadian twilight, the sky becomes truly dark. On a clear night you can see at least 3,500 stars instead of the 30-odd that are bright enough to be visible against the glare of a lit-up city. Watch the Jasper heavens for 15 minutes and you'll see the streak of a meteor. Watch for a few nights and you'll find yourself wanting to learn the constellations.

For some of us—Al Brawn, for example, Canada's dean of outdoor-pursuits educators—the wilderness is a spiritual place. It humbles us and opens our hearts to the oneness of things.

Experiencing wildlands in good style helps to put the world right. To quote from Al's writings about backpacking:

Will you follow in the footsteps of St. Francis?

Will you be part of the solution and not part of the problem?

Let me show you the way; walk with me. [1]

If you're walking, you might as well do so in comfort and safety. That's the philosophy of this book. Sure, you can wander the Canadian backcountry with only a bit of sausage and a crust of bread for supper. That's the way John Muir tramped the Sierras, wrapping up in his blanket to fall asleep under the stars. You might have a marvellous, transcendent experience in so doing. But more likely your experience will involve low blood sugar, waves of mosquitoes and hypothermia. Canada is not balmy California.

And that's why we Canadians need a how-to book of our own about hiking and backpacking, one that can be used from coast to coast to coast. Up until now we have relied on books written mainly for American and British readers. No longer. This book was written with Canadian geography, weather, wildlife, vegetation, clothing, equipment, units of measure and attitudes in mind (although, of course, I hope that it's also useful to people from other countries who want to learn about hiking and backpacking in our part of the world), but a lot of what you'll find in these pages is applicable anywhere.

It's a rather personal book. I've learned a lot about this activity in my 47 years of doing it, including many years as a backpacking guide, and I'd like to pass the salient points along. It's not that other ways aren't worth investigating, but I'm trying for a concise job here, so minimal ink has been expended on everybody else's way of doing things. Take it from this know-it-all: never rely on a single source of information.

And I might as well 'fess up right now to the fact that this book is biased toward western Canada. Actually, it's worse than that. It has a Canadian Rockies bias. This is what happens when you spend most of your time plodding the trails in the same mountain range. But it's a good mountain range to have plodded, with lots of variety in topography, elevation and climate, and what works in the Rockies works nearly anywhere in the country. Still, I've tried to broaden the scope to include info specific to the dripping woods of coastal British Columbia, the blackfly capitals of eastern Canada, the fogs of the Maritimes and the midnight sun of the North. Be forewarned, though: when you're wondering whether or not to pack a mosquito head net into the Torngats, good local knowledge beats the printed page every time.

---

1   The quote is from Al Brawn's *Eco-backpacking*, University of Calgary Faculty of Kinesiology, 2001, page 3. St. Francis is the patron saint of animals and the environment.

So here's an invitation to help make this book better. This is the first edition. It's bound to have errors and omissions in it, and I take full responsibility for any you find. If enough people buy this there will be a second edition, and it could contain your contribution, duly credited. Fame awaits! Contact me through www.bengadd.com if you have something to offer.

Walking: The basics

Sure, walking is a no-brainer. A chicken can do it with its head cut off. Nearly all of us got up off the floor and onto our feet before the age of two, and we've been walking for many years. But North Americans generally don't walk more than a few blocks at a time—we drive everywhere—and surprisingly few of us really know how to walk comfortably and efficiently for any distance uphill and down dale.

Let's see if this applies to you. Do you like to walk rather quickly, stopping every now and again for a rest? Do you like to take long strides, even when going uphill? Do you push yourself, shrugging off the pain as part of the experience?

Heck, we all do at times. There's a measure of joy in feeling one's heart beating strongly and one's lungs working hard. But beyond a certain point—and especially when you're walking with others—it morphs into competition. That's fine on the track, but in the wilderness? Not for me. Instead, I'll go for the greater joy of moving along smoothly and well, letting my body carry me through landscapes I love in a way that lets me focus on what's around me, not on my oxygen debt.

The key to comfortable walking

As Woody Guthrie used to say of life in general, "Take it easy, but take it." This applies perfectly to walking. Rather than running and resting, keep a moderate, steady pace.

Of course, if you're very fit a "moderate" pace can be pretty fast. But is it *too* fast? Here's a good way to judge: if you're breathing too hard to carry on a conversation with your companions, the pace is probably excessive. In which case, ease off the throttle a little. Be able to talk as you walk. Stand more upright. Take shorter steps. (Your heels will thank you for that: fewer blisters.) Most importantly, walk a long time—at least half an hour—between rests. This will allow your body to warm up nicely, find its rhythm and keep it up, which on a long hike is the whole idea.

Hey! What about folks who can't walk?

This book is mainly for people with the physical ability to take to the woods on their own two legs. But did you ever stop to think of how many hikers passing you on the trail might be travelling on legs that aren't actually theirs? Feet, knees, legs, hips—you name the skeletal part, and these days an artificial version seems to be available. Many kinds of injuries, amputations and congenital conditions that once kept us housebound can now be overcome with cleverly engineered spare parts and a strong desire to get outdoors. After a serious hit to your drive train, becoming mobile again may make all the difference to your health and happiness. So, as my athlete of an elder son would say, "Get after it!" If you do, much of this book will prove useful.

But what about people who have no other way to see the woods except by wheelchair? The good news is that there are now wheelchairs designed just for this. For some examples, go to www .landeez.com. Outdoor adventures in a good all-terrain (AT) chair will build skill and confidence, along with arms of steel. Many trails are navigable by AT chair, especially if the person in the chair goes with hikers willing to give a push, shove or carry here and there.

What if you have to be pushed or carried all the time? No hope of self-propulsion? Well, if at all possible you should get out into the wilds anyway—and not in a car. I once guided a university student who had little use of his muscles but could navigate the outdoors in a special low-slung wheelchair with lots of places to grip it. His classmates told me that they took him everywhere in that one-of-a-kind conveyance. I saw them manoeuvre him through the moraines of the Athabasca Glacier, which is rough terrain for anyone, and with pleasure for all concerned. For some astonishing examples of what can be done, check out www.cordclimbs.ca, the website of cord (Climbing Over Restriction and Disability Society). This organization is dedicated to getting people into the wilderness no matter what.

To me, the world's roadless places are also its most beautiful places. Wilderness demands considerable effort both in getting there and in learning to become comfortable there. But we go anyway, because we find something we need out there. For a person who can't walk, imagine how much greater the reward will be.

It's a fact: by pacing yourself properly you *will* get where you're going, and you *will* get there just as soon as if you run and rest, run and rest. The time spent resting will have been used in walking. Not only that, you'll feel less tired at the end of the day.

Going slowly at the start is especially important. The muscles in your legs need a few minutes to warm up before they reach proper efficiency. You might want to stretch before beginning the walk, as runners do.

Another reason for a gentle start is that many people find themselves somewhat choked five minutes into a hike, coughing and finding it difficult to exhale. These are signs of exercise-induced asthma, which is becoming increasingly common in Canada. As a guide I see it often. It manifests quickly on a chilly morning, becoming really uncomfortable for those affected when the group has started at a trot in cold air. Soon everyone will stop to rest, and that's when an attack can become more serious. Anyone leading a party of hikers should keep the asthma problem in mind. Perhaps one of the people you're responsible for has the condition and is unprepared, having foregotten their medicated inhaler. Now what? (See the item on first aid for asthma, page 292.)

After walking for some time, any group will need a rest break. Or perhaps the party would enjoy stopping to take in the view. By all means, do. You might want to eat a snack and drink some water, too. Many experienced hikers insist on taking a short break every hour or so and a longer one mid-morning and mid-afternoon. Just remember that after a rest long enough to cool your body you'll need to start gently again.

Walking uphill

In addition to adopting a moderate pace, **stride length, foot placement and foot angle** are all crucial to uphill walking, especially if your pack is heavy.

A high-stepping, long-striding chap when I was young, I have since learned the value of operating the human machine more wisely. Long strides under load put a lot of strain on your heel tendons. Big uphill steps cause high-pressure heel-rubbing in your boots. For me the result has been soreness and blisters. On steep sections I now back off and take shorter steps, watching for the little flat spots on the trail that will hold my feet more comfortably. My body thanks me. As well, when my pack is heavy I've learned to climb the hills *with my heels flat on the trail*. This has proved to be very important, because it makes better use of my leg muscles and avoids straining my tendons and ligaments. Here's

Whyte Museum of the Canadian Rockies

Conrad Kain (left) with Albert McCarthy and William Foster after their first ascent of Mt. Robson, 1913

The guide's lesson about walking

The following anecdote is told of Conrad Kain, the great Austrian-Canadian mountain guide (first ascent of Mt. Robson in 1913, etc.). It may or may not be true—I couldn't confirm it—but it's worth passing along anyway. While in his teens, Kain was taken for his first climb by a local guide, a much older fellow. Together they started walking up the trail.

Young and full of energy, Kain grew impatient with the guide's slow pace. Kain knew the trail well, so he asked the guide whether it would be all right to go ahead, meeting at the start of the steep, roped section of the ascent. The older man said, "Yah, yah, Conrad. You go ahead."

And he did, practically running up the path. He would grow breathless, sit down for a short rest, then get up and keep charging along. While resting he could see the guide far below him on the switchbacks.

During one such rest—and they were becoming more frequent—Kain realized that the guide was gaining on him. Yet the guide wasn't hurrying, just plodding steadily along.

Hmm . . . Yes, it was the tortoise and the hare. Eventually the young man lay beside the trail, gasping, as the old guide stood before him, saying gently, "Conrad, Conrad. How are you going to climb the mountain when you don't even know how to walk?"

why flat-footing your 20-kilogram pack up a long grade makes better sense than going tippy-toe: when you raise your heel, your calf muscle has to do the job. The calf muscle's tendon attachment to the heel bone is pulled hard. Also, the toes must bend, which puts a lot of stress on the ligaments in the foot.

When running, raising your heel at each step is essential, but this is not so when walking slowly with a heavy pack. Yes, you must raise a heel to take a step forward, but you can let your big thigh muscles, with their very strong tendons, do the work *first*, letting the heel rise only when the weight has been transferred to the other leg.

The thigh muscles straighten the whole leg, using the strong hip, knee and ankle joints to raise the load up the grade. Straightening the whole leg offers a mechanical advantage as well, like that of a car's scissor-jack when it's well extended. If the foot is held flat to the trail as the leg is straightened, the heel is not raised and the tendon stress is much reduced. You raise your heel *after* you take that forward step, when the weight is on the other leg.

Walking uphill—the easy way

Walking uphill—the hard way

While I've emphasized the keep-your-heel-down aspect of this technique, others emphasize the fact that when your leg is straight, your weight and the weight of your pack are balanced over your knee. No force is required at this point in the step, so your muscles have a momentary rest. This kind of step is therefore known as the *rest step*. (When I learned the term many years ago, it was applied more strictly to high-altitude mountaineering, in which you literally stopped to rest with each step, taking a breath or two while your leg was straight.)

Regardless of what you call it, here's how to make use of the rest-step principle. When you take a step upward, *keep the heel behind you flat on the ground*. Rather than pushing your weight up on your rear foot, which requires that you forcibly lift that heel, just roll your weight forward onto your uphill leg and raise your weight mainly by straightening the uphill leg, continuing to keep the uphill foot flat on the slope. As your downhill leg comes forward and that heel lifts up, it will have much less weight on it.

At first it may feel awkward to keep your heel down and your foot flat as you take an uphill step, especially when the trail is steep. Your ankle must flex forward more than it's used to. Some stretching is required. But with a little practice the calf-muscle tendon and the ankle-joint ligaments will accommodate nicely, and you'll be gaining elevation more easily than before.

Combine this technique with short steps and you'll see very good results. Also, keeping your boot flat on the trail puts the entire sole on the ground, instead of just the forward part, so you get better traction. And the sole wears more evenly, instead of mainly at the toe. Worn tread at the toe makes for slippy footing, so you wind up replacing your boots sooner. The rest step actually saves you money.

As you walk uphill, look ahead for foot-sized flat spots in the trail. Even in very steep terrain, there will be flat rocks to step on, or the upper surfaces of rounded rocks, or level spots formed behind roots. These allow you to ascend as if using a staircase. The lower the risers, the better.

When the way becomes very steep, try **switchbacking** rather than going straight up. That is, angle up and across the width of the trail until you come to the edge, then angle upward the other way until you come to the opposite edge, and so on. This can reduce the steepness considerably.

If the trail's too narrow for switchbacking, step up sideways. This isn't something you'll want to do for more than 10 or 20 metres at a time, but it eliminates the need to bend your ankles so far forward. On a long stretch of extremely steep trail, you can alternate the direction you face while sidestepping, using one leg as the uphill leg, then switching to use the other.

Finally, use walking poles to get your upper body involved in the work of moving uphill with a load on your back. If you haven't tried this yet, you're in for a pleasant

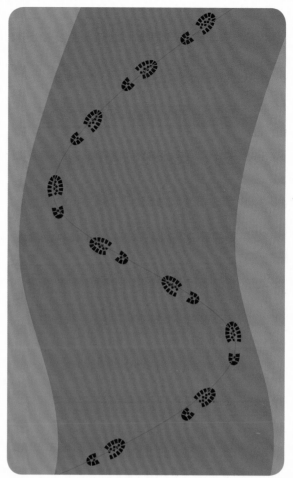

Switchbacking up a steep but wide trail

surprise. Your arm muscles provide auxiliary power that can make a noticeable difference in effort. (See page 16.)

Walking on flat ground

Here's where a long stride can be put to use. After a lengthy uphill grind it feels terrific to hit a level stretch along which you can stretch your legs out and make some time, using your calf muscles and raised heels to kick you along.

But it's not a good idea to take steps that are *too* long. Doing so is tough on your joints—particularly the knee joint—and somewhat hard on that sensitive heel tendon. You're coming down hard on your feet, too. If they slide around in your boots even slightly, the friction and heat can build up and cause **sheet blisters,** large patches of separated skin on the soles of your feet. There isn't much you can do about sheet blisters—a large patch of moleskin under your foot may help a little—so it's important to avoid them in the first place.

Longer steps make your pelvis swivel more, a motion that must be taken up by your lower spine. That's a body part infamous for trouble. When I walk with too long a stride, my back complains in the evening. The next day I'll take somewhat shorter steps.

Walking downhill

There's a trick to this, too, and it's one that saves your knees. (The older I get, the more my knees need saving.) Most mountaineers have learned it, because they undertake lengthy, very steep descents.

Beginning hikers have a tendency to take overly long steps downhill. This hammers the knee joints, heavy pack or no, and it certainly is tiring on the thigh muscles. You get that feeling of "rubber legs" when you've overdone it. More than once I've seen someone walking backward down a plunging trail, trying to give their exhausted thigh muscles a rest.

Here's how to handle a steep downhill grade with maximum efficiency and minimum pain. As with going uphill, take small steps. In addition, let your lower leg straighten fully before weighting it. Try the following on a steep slope. Stairs are ideal if you want to practise this move.

1. Extend one leg to take a step downhill. Make it a short step.
2. Allow that leg to swing out straight. Now step onto that leg.
3. Do so while it's straight, not bent.
4. Repeat, extending the other leg, letting it swing out straight and smoothly transferring your weight to it.

"What?" you may be saying. "Put all your weight on a *straight* leg? That can't be right." But it *is* right. Your knee joint is designed to take a lot of weight, as long as it's applied to the joint in the correct sector of its arc of motion—that is, the centre. This is the "dead point," where weighting the joint puts the least stress on the cartilage and ligaments.

Weighting the joint near, but not over, the dead spot generates considerable stress, just as lifting with your back slightly bent does. You want your back straight when lifting, and you want your knee straight when you hit it with the force of your body weight plus that of a loaded pack. Further, you want to keep that weight moving, so the joint isn't weighted for long.

Practise this sequence. On each (short) step downhill let your lower leg swing forward until it's straight before you transfer your weight to it. The weight-shift should be a smooth motion, with only a momentary transition at the dead point. Note that you shouldn't over-straighten ("hyperextend") your leg, extending it backward beyond the dead point. Landing on a leg bent slightly the wrong way is very hard on the joint.

One last tip: Set your foot down as flat as possible on the slope ahead of you. When you walk downhill it's natural to set your weight onto your heel first and then roll forward onto the toe, but the more of your heel you can set flat on the trail, the better grip you'll get.

Again, it's important to take short steps. Striding downhill with long steps makes you pound hard and repeatedly on the back of your boot heels, which quickly wears away the tread there. All too soon you have no lugs left, your feet are slipping out from under you in steep, gravelly spots, and you're falling onto your bum—hard, owing to the weight of your pack. Not good. Protect your posterior and your tail bone. And your wrists! Many a wrist has been broken by the automatic stiff-arm one does when falling backward. Get the maximum rubber onto the trail on steep downhill sections. Just as you saved money by saving the tread on your boot toes by walking uphill properly, so you'll avoid premature boot replacement by walking downhill properly.

This method of descent has been aptly described as the **mountaineer's shuffle.** You move down a steep slope with many short, quick steps, keeping your feet as flat on the trail as you can. You reach the bottom of the mountain with your knees intact, legs not rubbery and no bruises on your behind.

Positioning your feet

Humans shouldn't walk like ducks. It's inefficient, because it puts your foot at an angle to the line of travel. Watch an experienced hiker. Chances are, that person's feet will be pointed pretty much straight ahead, not sharply angled to the side.

Having said that, there are times when duck-walking is the only way to go. For example, angling your feet outward when going flat-footed up steep climbs may come naturally to you. And even on level ground, those of us who have a history of spraining an ankle by turning it inward may want to keep a little outward angle on our feet. Of

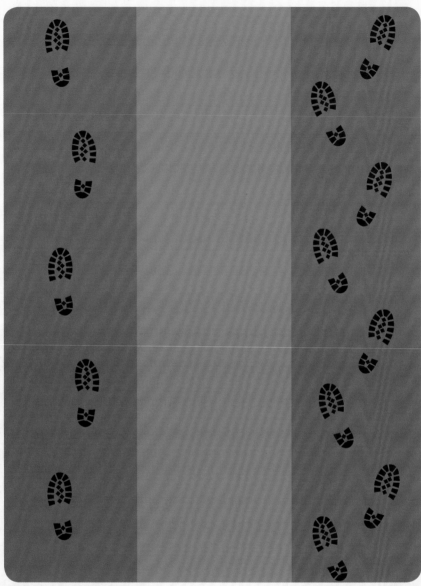

Feet pointed straight ahead:
Most efficient walking

Feet pointed to the side:
Less efficient, but comes naturally
on steep grades

course, you'll not want to be walking pigeon-toed at speed, providing an all-too-easy opportunity to roll that bad ankle under.

Should you use walking poles?

George Orwell had it right in *Animal Farm:* "Four legs good, two legs bad." Walking poles, also called **trekking poles,** give us those four legs and offer some real advantages to hikers and backpackers. (Note that I'm referring to paired walking poles, not single **walking sticks.** Paired walking poles are used in much the same way that cross-country ski poles are used, by placing them alternately at each step. Single walking sticks are popular with some hikers, but since they're used only on one side of the body, they don't provide all the advantages of paired poles.)

Ben Gadd

At times like this, you'll really appreciate your poles!

- With poles you use your arms on uphill sections, resulting in a noticeable boost in power. Climbs become easier.
- Using the arms gives a more complete workout when you walk, strengthening your upper body as well as your legs.
- Poles can take some of the load off the knees on downhill sections, helping to avoid soreness and possibly preventing injury.
- Poles provide stability, helping to check slips and falls.
- When you're faced with crossing a creek on stepping stones or a log, poles make all the difference in balance and safety.
- When walking in wet brush, you can tap the shrubbery ahead of you with your poles and shake off much of its moisture before you contact it.
- When backpacking, a walking pole can be used to help support a sagging tarp or tent.
- When walking anywhere, a pole can be used to fend off a vicious dog.
- If you sprain your ankle, develop a really bad blister or otherwise require a cane, you have two of them on hand.
- Waving a pole to attract someone's attention can be more effective than waving your arms, especially if you tie a handkerchief to the end of the pole.
- If you're the know-it-all in your group, a pole is handy for pointing out peaks, wildflowers, wolf poop, etc.
- You can do "All for one, and one for all!" and other silly things with poles. See the photos on page 199.

Walking poles do have some drawbacks, however. Chief among them is the constant attention required to place them at each step. This takes some getting used to. Poles can also be troublesome on narrow trails, especially those deepened by horses. There's no room for poles beside your feet in such trenches; you have to hold the poles up and work them along the sides of the trail. Thick trailside vegetation causes problems in placing poles, and so do boulders. Poles do help to prevent falls, but they can also trip you up—believe me! I've taken more than one pole-induced tumble in my time.

The metal tips of walking poles make an annoying clicking sound on rocky surfaces. For that reason, I use rubber tips on my poles. They slip on over the metal tips, so if you need the metal tips for any reason you can simply remove the rubber ones. There are times when rubber tips slip—on icy trails, for example, or on a thin layer of mud over rock—but in general they grip adequately.

Correct way to slip your hand through a walking-pole strap. Note that there is a left pole and a right pole, as indicated by the different strap overlap on each.

Rubber tips also cause less trail damage. Metal tips dig into the trail surface or into the soil beside a narrow trail, leaving poked-up ground along and beside popular routes. Rubber tips are wider than metal tips, so a rubber-tipped pole digs in very little. Neither does it scratch the lovely lichen-covered boulders one finds along many trails.

Sharp tips can do damage to humans, too. Keep your poles close to you while other hikers pass by. If you're coming up on a pole-user from behind, you may wish to announce your presence before you get within range of being accidentally whacked.

So, unless you really need metal tips—if you're hiking in winter, for example—it's a good idea to put on rubber tips. It saves the environment and it avoids annoying other hikers. Ask for rubber tips when you buy your poles. Perhaps the clerk will throw in a set for free. Buy extra sets, because you can wear out a pair in a single season of active hiking.

If you want to save money on walking poles, ignore the expensive adjustable-length ones and go with a pair of old ski poles. This is what I use. Just be sure they have straps; some ski poles don't. Pull the baskets off and there you go—although you should really locate rubber tips that fit over the metal ends. Rubber tips intended for walking poles will often work. If the pole shaft is too thin to hold rubber tips, fatten it up by wrapping duct tape around it.

Getting the proper pole length is important. With your hands properly in the straps (see illustration on page 19) and standing normally, the angle of your forearm should be about level to the ground. Too long is better than too short.

Fixed-length poles have some disadvantages. They can't be made shorter for use as canes (see the fictional story on page 230), and they won't collapse and fit into your luggage. On the other hand, fixed-length poles can be lighter than adjustable poles. They're stronger, and they have no clamps to slip. It's a rare pair of adjustable walking poles that doesn't eventually give you slippage trouble.

Here are some hints for using walking poles:

- Believe it or not, there's a left pole and a right pole. Well, the poles are the same but the strap arrangement is subtly different for each hand. On the right pole, where the two parts of the strap emerge from the grip, the upper half-strap should angle slightly to the right and the lower half-strap should angle slightly to the left. On the left pole, the upper half-strap should angle slightly to the left and the lower half-strap should angle slightly to the right. Each strap should have been installed with a half-twist in it so that the loop bulges out to accept your hand easily. If the strap hangs flat off the pole, no half-twist, then it has been mounted incorrectly.

- How long should a strap be? On a bare hand, it should be long enough to allow the palm to rest comfortably in the centre of the grip. If you set your straps just a tad long, they'll also be comfortable when you put your gloves on and you'll have no need to readjust.

- Insert your hands into the straps correctly. Insert your hand through the strap from below, as you would for a ski-pole strap. Bring your hand up through the strap, reaching past the top of the pole. Then close your hand downward over both the grip and the strap, so that the strap lies between your palm and the grip. If you have the correct hand on the correct pole, your thumb will be resting on the half-strap that emerges from the grip *below* the other half-strap. (See page 19.) Getting all this right makes a difference in comfort and blister prevention.

- On flat sections of trails and stretches that slope gently downhill, where you're walking quickly with little effort, you may want to place a pole at every other step instead of at every step. This is less tiring for your arms.

- On gentle downhill sections, if you have adjustable-length poles you can make them long, to go with the long strides you'll probably be taking.

- Further, you may enjoy the feeling of carrying your poles occasionally through such sections, holding one pole in each hand, balancing the poles horizontally, with the tips pointed ahead so you can see that they don't poke anyone. Or walk with both poles in one hand. Either way, you can let your arms swing by your sides for a change, instead of working the poles constantly.

- If you get knee pain when you're going steeply downhill, try this trick. It can do wonders. Adjust the length of your poles to make them short enough to use them as a pair of canes. You place your palm flat atop a pole with your arm straight, and use the pole to brace your knee at each downward step.

- To avoid leaving your poles behind at a rest stop (I have done this more than once), put a small carabiner on your pack and clip your pole-straps to it as soon as you take the pack off. It's pretty difficult to forget your poles if they're attached to your pack.

Trail etiquette

If you abide by the following guidelines—some of which are actually formal regulations in some national and provincial parks—the other trail users will appreciate it. So will the environment. (See also Leave No Trace, page 270.)

- Walk single file when passing people coming toward you. Don't force approaching hikers to step off the path. Rather, give them room and greet them with a smile. If there's something worthy of mention—perhaps you saw a bear within the last kilometre—you might want to mention it.

- Stay on the trail. Walking two or three abreast on a narrow trail damages the vegetation on either side. Over time, the trail becomes wider. Walking to the side of a muddy stretch just makes the mudhole bigger. Walk on through the mud and complain to the powers-that-be about the condition of the trail. Perhaps they'll have repaired that mudhole by the next time you come by.

- When someone is gaining on you from behind, step aside and let that person pass by.

- When you're the one gaining, say, "Hello," or give some other greeting as you approach. The person you're catching up with will probably realize that you wish to pass and will step aside for you. If not, ask politely, e.g., "Mind if I go by?" When you've passed, thank them for their consideration.

- If faster members of a party get ahead of slower members (this is a bad idea; see page 283), then give the slower members not only time to catch up but also time to catch their breath. There's nothing more demoralizing for a slower person than to go all-out to catch up, only to have everyone run off as soon as they arrive. A group should walk at a pace that's comfortable for its slowest member. The best way to do that's for the slowest member to walk first in line. (They probably won't want to—no one likes to be singled out—but perhaps they can be prevailed upon.)

- When you stop, step aside so that other walkers can pass by. No one should have to force their way through a group of babbling hikers inconsiderately plugging up the path. Many trails are wide enough to keep you off the trailside vegetation while making room for others. If it's a narrow trail, you'll have to place your feet carefully as you step off the tread.

- Don't cut switchbacks. A switchback is the zig or zag in a trail that zig-zags up a slope, providing an easier gradient for walking than going straight up. Well-graded switchbacks are a pleasure to walk, and they prevent erosion. However, too many people figure they'll save time by not following each switchback to the end. They head steeply up or down the slope to the next leg, thus "cutting" the switchback. Because such shortcuts are steep, water quickly erodes them, producing gullies. Cutting switchbacks is irresponsible and it seldom saves much time. Please, please, DON'T CUT SWITCHBACKS!

Don't cut switchbacks!

- I'm a mountain-biker as well as a hiker. If we cyclists wish to continue enjoying our sport on public lands, we must behave properly when encountering people on foot. If you're cycling on a trail, make sure you have a bell on your bike. When approaching hikers, slow down. If approaching from behind them, ring the bell to let them know that you would like to pass. Give the hikers time to step off the trail, and as you go by, thank them. Being suddenly forced off the trail by an inconsiderate mountain-biker is quite unpleasant and even dangerous. This is the main reason that mountain bikes are being banned from so many trails. That and the penchant some mountain-bikers have for cutting switchbacks and charging down mountainsides where there are no trails. These are clearly no-nos.

- Horse parties, which, from a hiking perspective, ruin and pollute trails shared with hikers, also demand the right-of-way. This is an unfair fact of life. Horses are just too large to move neatly off the trail when passing by or overtaking people on foot, and whenever horses leave the trail they rapidly do a lot of damage to the vegetation, so we have to get out of their way. Thus, it, uh, behooves the riders of these beasts to appreciate it when we surrender the path. They should smile and say "Thank you" as they go by, and most of them do.

- Keep your dog leashed in the wilds. No doubt your dog is very well-mannered and wouldn't think of chasing wildlife or attacking other dogs, but please set a good example anyway and keep your pet on its leash. If it poops on the trail, pick up the dropping as you would in town or, at the very least, use a stick to flick it off to the side so hikers won't step in it. (See also page 266.)

Preparing yourself

The good news is that hiking and backpacking aren't Olympic events. A high level of cardiovascular fitness and body strength is not required. You need merely walk with a pack. Given adequate preparation nearly everyone can enjoy a trip on foot into the wilds—even those with fairly severe physical limitations.[2]

So how much preparation is adequate? Start by assessing what sort of shape you're in. Take a short walk. If you've been inactive too long, your body will tell you so. Your heart will pound on a moderate hill and your lungs and leg muscles will ache. There's a message here: get up and get going. But do so carefully, and not by flinging yourself into a one-week backpack before you're ready for it. You may pay a heavy price in sore muscles, nasty blisters, or maybe even a tendon or ligament injury that will wreck your whole summer.

Here's a conservative approach to getting fit that should result in gain with no pain. Start early in the spring by walking easy paths. Choose routes without a lot of elevation gain or loss. If possible, walk on bare-earth trails or loose-surfaced ones, which are easier on your feet and legs than hardened paths. Do carry a day pack—your body needs to start getting used to that, too—but carry very little weight in it at first (just water, snack, rain jacket and other essentials).

Walk a few kilometres the first time, more the next, and so on, giving yourself one to three days between each hike for your body to build fitness. If you plan to hike with walking poles, use them at this stage, because they'll build strength in your arms and upper body. Wear the boots or shoes you intend to wear on the trips you hope to do later on. Add a little weight to that pack (not too much, yet) as the days go by.

Bring **blister pads** with you on these training walks. The new gel-type pads by Band-Aid and Dr. Scholl's work well and are available in most drugstores. Apply a pad immediately if part of your foot starts to complain. Wear the pad only for the duration of the hike, taking

---

2   If you always find yourself trailing the group, you're going with folks who are too fast for you. Better to seek out others who walk at your pace. And those others are out there, hoping that you will find them, because they, too, need companions.

it off afterward to let the skin dry and toughen. If that spot gives you trouble next time, put on another pad and repeat the process until your hide can handle whatever your boots or shoes are doing to it. If blistering continues to be a problem, you may need different footwear. (See page 33.)

When you can do 10 kilometres without feeling sore the next day or getting blistered, you can safely begin adding more weight to your pack and steeper, longer hills to your outings. Use the pack you intend to carry on longer trips. If it's new, this is an opportunity to do the adjusting now, on your pre-season walks, instead of making everyone wait while you do it on the first day of an overnight trip.

Start with only a couple of kilograms in your large pack. You might want to reduce the distance, to give your back and shoulders time to strengthen. Gradually increase the weight along with the distance and the elevation gain. When you can handle 10–15 kilometres up hill and down dale with a full load of 20 kilograms on your back and no soreness, then you can hit the trail with confidence, knowing that you're ready.

How long will it take to reach this point? Let your body be your guide. It will inform you—the next day—whether you've overdone a training walk or not. A young person who is unfit but not overweight may be able to go from couch potato to trail-cruiser in a couple of weeks. An older person in the same situation may require a month or more.

Being overweight adds time to the equation, of course. Chances are that plenty of walking will produce enough muscle and skeletal strength to deal comfortably with the amount of fat you already carry on your frame, plus the extra weight of your pack. That is, you don't have to be lean to be a backpacker. But it helps. And what better excuse to shed some belly, eh?

While in training physically, you can also be sharpening your mental skills. Bring along a map and a GPS unit, and practise using them. (See page 117.) Update your first-aid certificate, or attend a course if you don't have this valuable training. Learn to identify wildflowers and birds. Take an interest in weather forecasting or in the geology of your favourite hiking area. In short, gain whatever knowledge and skills you might put to good use in the wilderness, even if it's only to increase your on-trail enjoyment.

How can you do your training in the city? Just fine. Never mind the inquisitive looks of others as you stomp along in your boots and your big backpack, your walking poles flashing smartly. If your city offers

no hills of any consequence, do what the backpackers of Toronto do: climb and descend stairs in tall buildings. This offers the advantage of really steep training. Just be careful not to overdo it before your body's ready—particularly when going down the stairwell flights. It's all too easy to injure your knees. Above all, don't run down the stairs. Beyond the age of 40, doing this is quite likely to give you painful joint problems. Walking down flights of stairs correctly, however, is actually good for your knees, building strength and thickening cartilage. Do so by using the mountaineer's shuffle described earlier.

If you have knee problems and want to treat those joints with extra care while building fitness, the exercise machine of choice is the bicycle. Indoors on a stationary bike or outdoors on roads and paths, cycling is easy on the knees and great aerobic exercise. Do a lot of "spinning," as cyclists call it: using a lower gear than you think you need. This will quickly build muscle while protecting your knees. If your image of bicycling is two rock-hard tires on a rain-slick street in traffic, you'll be glad to hear that a modern full-suspension mountain bike is wonderfully comfortable, easy to control and as skid-resistant as a bicycle can be. Try a decent mountain bike. It will take you gleefully along the many bike paths found these days in any major city in Canada.

In general, the best thing is not to have to do any training, because you hike and backpack a lot and are always fit. You can put on your pack and go, whenever, wherever. Of course, this is Canada, and in most of the country the climate precludes summertime-style hiking in the winter. (See pages 322 and 324 for basic info about winter hiking on the West Coast and in the Okanagan area.) Still, in the cold months we can go cross-country skiing and take multi-day trips on skis or snowshoes that will keep our bodies strong year-round.

PART 2
What you need

A Book of Verses underneath the Bough,
A Jug of Wine, a Loaf of Bread—and Thou
Beside me singing in the Wilderness—
Oh, Wilderness were Paradise enow!
—Omar Khayyám/Edward Fitzgerald

Heading for the top among the limestone peaks west of Calgary

Clothing and footwear

Whatever shall we wear to the . . . storm?

Something good, I hope. Gaston Rebuffat, the Swiss guide who wrote *On Snow and Rock* back in the 1960s and taught my generation to be mountaineers, said of clothing and gear, "In the mountains, the very best is just good enough." Given the amount of hiking and backpacking that take place in mountainous regions—or in tough environments generally, in a country of tough environments—Rebuffat's wise words apply just as much to hikers and backpackers as to climbers.

Sure, you could wear shorts and runners for a backpack through the warm Ontario woods in July and survive almost anything the gentle climate of the Niagara Peninsula could throw at you. But try that in the Alberta Rockies or on the West Coast Trail and you're taking your life in your hands. The rapidly changing weather there can kill you at any time of year. So in places such as this, please heed the old Scout motto: "Be prepared!" You can always take off something warmer than required and stow it in your pack, but you can't put it on if you don't have it with you. When the storm hits, you want to be properly dressed.

Let's cover this subject from the ground up, starting with footwear.

Ben Gadd

After four hours near the treeline in these conditions, whether you're still smiling or hypothermic will depend largely on what you're wearing.

Boots and shoes

Your footwear can make or break a hike. For day hikes with a light pack, below-the-ankle footwear works fine and feels great. I have a pair of **approach shoes,** tough, grippy shoes intended for rough terrain. They give me excellent footing, especially on rocky trails, and I often wear them on day hikes.

Grit, small rocks and bits of vegetation tend to find their way into these shoes, though, and like most low-cut footwear they're made of thin materials that get wet easily. However, these disadvantages are no problem when I know I'll be back at the car at the end of the day.

For backpacking, though, I prefer above-the-ankle boots. This isn't because of the extra support they give. You can sprain an ankle in a boot almost as easily as in a shoe.

The real advantages of boots are as follows:

1. They protect your feet better than low shoes do, so you get less toe-stubbing and fewer pokes from sharp rocks—more painful while lumbering along under a heavy load.
2. Boots are warmer in wet cold conditions.
3. Low shoes let in more grit than boots do.

Bottom line in the boots-vs.-shoes debate: shoes are for warm days in warm places with light loads, and boots are for chilly days in chilly places with heavy loads.

Having been through every hiking-footwear fad since the early 1960s, I can offer some seasoned advice on choosing boots. For summer backpacking you'll need something light in weight, warm when required, comfortable after 20 kilometres and not falling apart after 200.

In the mountains, and in other parts of the country where you may encounter temperatures in the low single digits in July, real leather still rules, and the more of it in the boot, the better. Lined leather (leather outer layer plus an inner layer of leather or some other soft, smooth material such as Cambrelle) is best.

Boots made with fabric panels instead of a full leather outer are light and airy on hot days, but when conditions are cold and wet, fabric-panel boots are far chillier than good ol' one-piece, lined leather uppers. Lined leather is thick and warm. Yes, leather takes longer to dry out, but not all that much longer. In the meantime, your feet are comfier than they are in thin boots.

Break in your boots, or they may break you in

One of my guided clients wound up doing two backpacking trips with me in the Canadian Rockies with sandals on his feet. The poor chap developed such terrible heel blisters on day one of each trip that he had no choice but to wear the sandals he'd brought for wading creeks and lounging around in camp. Fortunately the weather during each trip was good (no snow), and he was agile enough to avoid spraining an ankle, breaking a toe or lacerating his feet on the quartzite. Still, I worried about this guy the whole time. By failing to properly break in his boots, he put the whole trip—and, of course, his personal safety— at risk.

Boots that are touted as waterproof rarely live up to their promise. After a day of rain on the trail your feet will almost certainly be wet anyway, despite what's written on the box. This is because the outer surface of the boots will be entirely wetted, regardless of waterproofing. If there's a waterproof barrier in the boots, typically of Gore-Tex or some similar waterproof/breathable membrane, when it has "wetted out" it won't pass water vapour very efficiently in such conditions. The surface is essentially sealed. This means that your feet will become damp in their own sweat. If there's no waterproof barrier in the boots, your feet will get wet from rain soaking through.

So either way, at the end of a rainy day you'll be camping with wet feet. In a place with cool evenings, soon they'll be *cold* feet, too. The idea is to be *warm* and wet, not cold and wet. You'll need some insulation between your skin and the chilly, soggy outdoors. Lined leather boots give you that. Additional sockage supplements the lining, which we'll discuss later.

Gore-Tex may not be magic in boots, but **Gore-Tex socks** offer a lot of comfort. They delay the soggifying process, and they help to maintain warmth by allowing very little air movement through them. See page 47 for info on waterproof/breathable socks.

Time was when the better boots had **sewn-on midsoles,** indicated by a line of heavy stitching around the edge of the sole. Cheaper boots were made with stapled-and-glued-on midsoles, which sometimes came apart, as did the early versions of the one-piece **injected soles** that have since become practically universal. Boots with sewn-on soles are still available in some stores, and they have one clear advantage: they can be resoled easily. The one-piece models cannot. However, modern one-piece soles wear so well, and boots are made with such thin leather these days, that by the time the sole is worn out the upper is too.

All this tech-talk aside, nothing about a boot is more important than the way it fits. I have delighted in ugly, heavy boots that have been very comfortable, and suffered in spiffy, feather-light boots that have fit badly. I've learned that if a boot is the least bit uncomfortable while trying it on in the store, the discomfort will probably magnify on the trail. So be sure to get the proper fit in the shop.

Shopping for boots is tricky. You may want to bring this book with you—or at least copy the pages from this section—to guide you. Also, wear the socks you plan to wear on the trail. For me this means two pairs: a pair of light socks worn next to the skin, turned inside out, plus a pair of heavier socks worn as an outer pair, the right way out. (Find out why on page 45.) And if you're shopping for footwear that's going to do the job under the load of a heavy backpack, wear such a pack while trying out boots.

Look for the following attributes in whatever models catch your eye:

1. *Boots that won't blister your heels.* A flexible boot that fits closely over the upper part of the instep will do the job. In a well-designed boot, the pressure of your instep against the tongue will lift the heel of the boot with minimal lag. This is vastly important. The heel of the boot should lift up *as your heel lifts up,* so there's little or no motion between your heel and the heel pocket of the boot. No motion means no rubbing and no blisters.

    The opposite occurs in a stiff boot with a tight heel pocket and an instep that fits too high over the top of your foot. In this case, the heel of the boot is still on the ground as your heel rises within it. There's motion between the two and you'll end up with blisters.

When you're trying on a pair of boots in the store, take a few long forward steps. If there's no heel-rubbing, the boots probably have the right geometry through the instep. If the heel rubs at all, keep looking.

Ideally you shouldn't have to tighten the laces very much to get the proper heel-lifting effect. A thick, well-padded tongue helps—especially one that extends above the top of the boot, which also ensures that the laces tie across the tongue, not across your socks, even if the tongue should slip down somewhat.

2. *Boots with back seams that don't press on your tendons.* Heel pockets are too deep on some boots, meaning that the heel pocket bulges out too far at the back of the boot. The seam above such a heel pocket rubs your heel tendon (Achilles tendon) as you move your foot forward with each step. This can cause heel tendonitis, a painful and persistent condition that has afflicted me several times. To test for a boot's tendonitis potential, hold your booted foot out in front of you and point it. In an ankle-height boot, does the top of the boot in back press fairly hard on your heel tendon? In an above-the-ankle boot, does the leather on the back fold inward and press on your tendon? If so, this pinching will get worse on the trail.

3. *Boots that won't give you sheet blisters on the bottoms of your feet.* Length and especially width are important here. Wearing your usual socks, with the bootlaces snug but not tight, your feet should be cradled nicely, not slopping about from side to side or front to back. Boots that are too wide and/or too long will allow your feet to slide inside them. This will leave your soles tender at the end of the day, and by morning the outer layer of skin may be sore, leaking clear fluid and separating. You've got sheet blisters. Walking with sheet blisters is not as painful as walking with heel blisters, and sheet blisters usually clear up in a few days, but who needs them?

4. *Boots that bend in the right place.* Ever try on a pair of boots, wear them for a few days, then find that one or both have developed a fold that crunches down on your toes and blisters the tops of them? A shoemaker may be able to hammer that fold out for you, but it's better not to leave the store with boots that fold

improperly. Bend the toe sharply to see where the fold comes. You shouldn't feel it against your foot. If your feet are both the same size and shape, the fold should occur at the same place on each boot. If not, the boots may differ slightly in size or thickness or eyelet spacing and may give you trouble later on. Identical folding on each boot is an indicator of good-quality construction.

5. *Boots that won't jam your toes.* The better outdoor-equipment shops have a short ramp in the shoe department, so you can test boots on an incline. Walking up the ramp, check for the heel-lift business mentioned above in item 1. Walking down the ramp, check for interior foot-slippage—especially *forward* slippage that brings your toes into contact with the ends of the boots. If you can force your foot forward into the end of the boot, that's what you'll be doing all the way down a steep trail with 20 kilograms on your back. This hurts, and it can produce blackened toenails that eventually fall off. Buy your boots with enough toe room in the front to prevent this. Women backpackers seem to suffer from jammed toes more than men do. Perhaps it's because some women tend to buy their boots too small, choosing daintiness over comfort. Don't let aesthetics make your decision for you. Get yourself footwear that's large enough to do the job, and wear those comfortable clodhoppers with pride.

6. *Boots with no lumps and bumps inside.* Here's where cheap boots often fail to make the grade. You're trying on a pair, and they fit well, but you notice that one boot has a lump over your little toe, or a bump under the insole, or something that presses on an ankle bone. Not good; try another pair. If there's something wrong with the construction in every pair you try, meaning poor quality control at the factory, then give up on that model and look for one with better workmanship. Pay more if you have to. You won't regret it, whereas you will certainly regret accepting boots that cost $40 less but have this niggling little knob in them that's driving you crazy 70 kilometres from the trailhead.

7. *Boots with the right flexibility.* There was a time when we all went backpacking in stiff mountaineering boots. The blisters of that era were magnificent. These days a good backpacking boot is stiff torsionally but flexible longitudinally, meaning that it resists

Boots with good design features

bellows tongue

lace locks

lace hook on the centre
of the tongue

double rivets
on hooks

multiple lines of
stitching

sturdy metal
hardware

insoles (also called foot
beds) that stay in place

soles that don't stick out
beyond the uppers

low heels

sole material that doesn't
mark or squeak

speed lacing

twisting between the toe and the heel, but it flexes at the toe as you walk. Try a few pairs in the store to see which are too stiff (hardly any toe flex), which are too floppy (too much torsional flex, and the toes bend as easily as they do in running shoes) and which are just right.

8. *Boots with good design features:*
   - Multiple lines of stitching (the centre holds; things don't fall apart).
   - Lacing that runs through sturdy metal hardware that will last, not plastic rings or leather/fabric loops that will eventually break, rip through or tear off.
   - Speed lacing, meaning cast bronze rings that allow the laces to move smoothly through them horizontally without bending the laces much, which makes the laces easy to tighten and produces less wear on them.
   - Lace locks: a pair of hooks at the instep that pinch the laces as you pull them tight, allowing different tightness above and below the lock.
   - Double rivets on hooks, especially on hooks around the upper instep, which are subject to more stress.
   - A lace hook on the centre of the tongue to keep it from slipping down (nothing seems to stop a tongue from sliding over to the side on some feet, although a lace slot on the tongue can help).
   - Insoles (also called foot beds) that stay in place and don't bunch up in the toe. Pull an insole out of one boot and look for a line of adhesive on the bottom, or Velcro, or plenty of front-to-back stiffness to hold the insole in place.
   - A bellows tongue (the tongue is sewn to each side of the slot in the centre of the boot) to keep water out.
   - A sturdy pull-on loop at the back of the boot. Look for a beefy leather or nylon-webbing loop and extra rows of stitching here, to keep the loop from tearing out.
   - Low heels, which make it less likely that you'll turn an ankle under and sprain it.
   - Soles that don't stick out beyond the uppers, for better edging on side-slopes. Soles that stick out will lever against your foot and make it slip sideways downhill.
   - Sole material that doesn't make black marks on the floor or squeaky sounds on polished surfaces.

Do you know how to tie your shoes?

Of course you do, but can you tie them correctly? Lots of people tie their shoes improperly, and so the laces come undone frequently. Or they require extra knots-on-top-of-knots to stay tied.

Tied properly, the bow knot we use on our shoes and boots is essentially a square knot (also called a reef knot) with a quick release. Tightened well, a square bow knot should stay tied all day. If this is the kind you tie, congratulations.

In a granny bow knot the second part of the knot is tied with a twist in it and is not really square. The bows lie along the length of the boot tongue, not across it as they do if you've tied a proper bow knot. After a while the granny bow knot loosens. You have to stop and retie it. Sound familiar? Feeling embarrassed? Don't be. You're not alone. A lot of us were taught incorrectly how to tie our shoes when we were little, and we've been doing it wrong ever since. The good news is that it's never too late to learn to tie a proper bow knot. It's not rocket science.

Start as per usual, crossing the laces whichever way you normally do and pulling them tight. Then, for the second part of the knot—the part where you take one of the laces and bend it into a bow, tucking it under or wrapping the other lace around it—do something different: use the *other* lace than your usual choice to tuck under. Or wrap the bow the *other* way. When you pull the knot tight, it should look square and symmetrical, with all the laces on each side emerging next to each other and parallel. The bows should lie naturally across the tongue, not along it. This knot will stay tied much better.

For the ultimate in staying power, make each part of the knot with an extra wrap of the laces. Trickier to tie, but the result holds even better.

Alternatively, just forget this whole knot-tying business. Do what I do and secure the laces with a toggle, like the one used to close the drawstring on a stuff sack. Using toggles is quicker than tying, they never come undone and they don't loosen. I have toggles on all my boots and shoes, because we Canadians take our shoes off when going indoors, and toggles make this much quicker.

To install a toggle, lace up the shoes and slip both the lace ends through the toggle in the same direction. Put the boot or shoe on and snug the toggle down until you get the same tightness as you would with a bow knot. Now make a knot in each lace that will keep the lace from slipping out of the toggle. A simple overhand knot will do, tied loosely for now in case you want to adjust it. Tie this knot in each lace about 5 centimetres away from the toggle. Don't make a single knot that ties the laces together. You don't want a loop that will catch on things and trip you.

Move the toggle up against the knots. Loosen the laces enough to take the boot off. Is there enough lace between the toggle and the boot to allow you to get into and out of the boot easily? Is the distance to the toggle the same for each lace? If so, fine. Add a loop or two to each knot to make it fatter, so it definitely will not pull through the toggle (use the lace *beyond* the knot for this, to keep the knot in the same place), tighten it well, then cut off the end of the lace close to the knot. If you need more space between the toggle and the boot, or the laces are uneven in length, move the knots and try again.

Most bootlaces are made of

Shoe with toggle

nylon, so when the knots are in the right positions and the ends of the laces have been cut off, you can melt the ends to prevent them from fraying. A disposable lighter works well for this, or you can heat up an old kitchen knife to red-hot and use it to cut the lace by melting it through.

And, of course, there's always the fashion angle. For this you'll need the $500 three-tone boots with the fluorescent colours, the ski-boot buckle "system," 11 seams per boot, at least four different materials in the uppers, plastic strips sewn on here and there that advertise the manufacturer, heels with LEDs that flash as you walk—and don't forget the wireless digital pedometer chips.

Not. As with gear in general, a simple, elegant design is better than a complex, problem-prone design. Other things being equal, go for plain black or brown boots with one-piece leather uppers, smooth and sleek as a weasel slipping through the grass.

Be aware that ill-fitting boots can harm your feet. For example, I can't wear the ankle-top boots that are so popular for light hiking. For some reason these always irritate my heel tendons. It happens insidiously, painlessly at first. Then one morning my right heel hurts as I begin to walk, a sure indication that I have developed Achilles tendonitis, and some damage has been done.

A trip to the doctor will provide a diagnosis, but I've yet to meet a physician who has recognized the cause or suggested the only cure that works: going about in very low shoes for a couple of months, thereafter wearing boots only of the above-the-ankle type. I know I'm not the only one with this problem; other hikers have told me that ankle-top boots give them trouble, too.

Other examples of footwear issues include boots that are too short, jamming one's toes to the point of blackening the nails, which then fall off; boots with heels that are too high, increasing the chance of turning an ankle under and spraining it; boots that develop deep wrinkles that press inward on ligaments and tendons, injuring them; boots with rough interior seams or layers of thick material that overlap inside; or boots with badly installed lacing hardware, so that metal studs and even sharp metal edges press against your foot.

The last word about boots: *break 'em in before they break you in.* Any new pair should be worn for several hikes, including one of at least 10 kilometres, before committing to them.

Taking care of your boots

I've been through at least 20 pairs of hiking boots in my life. A few pairs have been discarded or given away as hopelessly uncomfortable or badly made, but the ones I've worn out all ended their careers in much the same way: they developed folds that became cracks that became holes. At the same time, the fronts of the soles became rounded and smooth, making for insecure footing while ascending steep slopes. The same thing applies to the heels, which round off and slip on the descent.

There's not much you can do about wearing out the tread on your boots in these days of non-replaceable injected soles. And worn soles are a matter of pride, a badge of honour. All those kilometres on the trail . . .

Fortunately you can extend the life of the uppers by slowing down the cracking of the leather. Cracking is accelerated by repeated wetting and drying, which stiffens leather. And daily wetting and drying of your boots is to be expected in Canadian backpacking, because our climate is northern and moist. Dew is common, making trailside vegetation wet in the morning, yet by early afternoon the way is often dry and has been for several hours. Then comes the afternoon rain shower. Thus, in Canada boots usually start the day by getting wet, then they dry out, then they get wet again. Given such tough conditions for boot leather, how can you keep it flexible for as long as possible?

The answer is to use **wax waterproofing.** By this I mean a beeswax-paste compound such as Atsko's Sno-Seal. There are other wax waterproofing compounds on the market that are liquids, and there are liquid waterproofing compounds that aren't wax-based, but I've found that beeswax paste works best.

Of course, no waterproofing agent will have any effect on boots that are made of plastic except to goop them up. Surprisingly, though, wax waterproofing is fairly effective at sealing fabric boot panels and making them stronger.

Boot manufacturers will recommend various treatments for their boots, sometimes specifically warning against wax waterproofing. However, regardless of what they say, if the material is any kind of leather you'll probably get the best results from beeswax.

I put the wax on hot, as a liquid. The makers of Sno-Seal don't recommend this method of using their products—they'd like you to just rub it on—but hot-waxing lasts a good bit longer than rubbing-in. I've been applying hot-wax waterproofing to my boots and shoes for many years to good effect, without any apparent damage. It's up to you which method to use. You may prefer to follow the manufacturer's advice.

My routine is to remove the laces from the boots and clean off any dirt with a stiff dish-washing brush. Then I melt a goodly glob of wax waterproofing on my backpacking stove. I do this by opening the can and placing it in a double boiler, outdoors for fire safety and protection from fumes. If you heat the can directly over the flame, it can quickly get hot enough to produce ignitable vapour. Even if you're using a double boiler, you should keep the lid of the can close at hand to slip over the opening and put out a fire. I keep a pair of leather work gloves nearby, too, in case I have to handle the hot can.

I spread the heated liquid over the leather with an old toothbrush. The leather soaks it up eagerly and I use lots. When no more will go in, I warm the boots with an electric blow-dryer (a heat gun from the hardware store works better than an ordinary hair dryer) until the surfaces go from glossy to matte. Done.

Whether the boots are hot-waxed or cold-waxed, you'll find that they take longer to get wet than untreated boots, and when they do get wet, they dry more quickly than untreated boots. Cracking is much reduced, even though wax tends to stiffen the leather somewhat—a paradox explained by the fact that leather loaded with wax is stiff from the wax, not because the leather itself is dry and stiff. Further, waxed boots resist abrasion and cuts better than unwaxed boots. Hiking through rocks can leave deep scars on unwaxed boots. Waxed leather slips over rough edges rather than catching and cutting. Waxed boots will get marked, but when you rub the marks they mostly go away.

New leather boots need waxing. Ignore the claims on the shoebox about the virtues of the leather and its factory treatment: "Congratulations on purchasing Godzilla's Own® Backcountry Bashers! They're made of Super Titanium Bull Moose Leather, waterproofed with Walrus Oil and guaranteed to last through dozens of trips into the volcanic shard-lands of Mt. Kilimanjaro! In the rain!"

Uh, sure. But just to be on the safe side, go ahead and wax them boots up.

This will have an effect on their appearance. It will darken the leather, it will slickify the fuzzy surface of any split leather in the boot, and it will turn any fabric panels into dust-traps. Still, your boots will now have a better chance of actually getting up and down Kilimanjaro without too much damage.

How often should you waterproof your boots? Do so as soon as they're out of the box, then at least once each year, at the start of the hiking season. Wax them more often if you notice them getting wet more quickly.

You should dry leather boots with care. The fastest way is to use artificial heat from a heat lamp or an electric dryer (electric boot-dryers are available). But you need to remove the heat before the boots are completely dry, or you'll hasten cracking of the leather. If you have a couple of days to let the boots dry, it's better to just set them in a dry but cool place and let them lose their moisture slowly. Wadding newspaper in the toes evens out the process.

Should you dry your boots by the fire? This is risky, because the heat is intense. It keeps changing as the fire burns higher or lower and the wind shifts. I once wrecked a pair of boots this way. I don't recommend it.

On the trail, you can walk your boots dry in a couple of hours, which is probably too fast, but the sweat from your feet may slow down the process inside sufficiently. In camp, set wet boots in a sunny, breezy place. Boots don't dry well inside a tent overnight—it's too moist in there. Set them just outside, under the fly.

Will rattlesnakes and scorpions and black widows get into your boots overnight if you leave them outdoors? Should you shake your boots out in the morning, like they do in the westerns? This is not required in most of the country. But who knows what you'll find overnighting in your footwear around Osoyoos, BC, which bills itself as "Mexico North"? Of course, wherever you are, when you decide to get those smelly boots out of your tent, be prepared to wake up quickly if you hear gnawing sounds.

Camp shoes, wading shoes

On a backpacking trip, ain't it nice to get your boots off at the end of the day and just lounge around camp in something lighter, more comfortable and—especially—not sweaty and stinky? For some backpackers, camp shoes or sandals are a must, even though they can add nearly half a kilogram to a pack.

Camp shoes I can forego, but like everyone else I do need something to protect my feet in the rocky, glacial stream crossings one encounters on Canadian Rockies backcountry trips. For this, sandals are an inferior choice. As stream-crossing shoes, sandals do little to shield my bare toes from those brutal stubs that occur when my feet have gone numb. And sandals are chilly in a treeline camp after sunset. The solution is to pack wading shoes that cover your feet. The lightweight neoprene slippers sold as "surf shoes" or "paddling booties"

Paddling booties make good wading shoes

fit the bill nicely. Generally cheaper than expensive Teva-type sandals, neoprene slippers are intended for canoeing, kayaking and coastal wading, but they work equally well for camp shoes. At 300–400 grams per pair, they're lighter than most sandals, too. This compares with an advertised weight of 255 grams for the Technica PacMoc, perhaps the ultimate camp-shoe-cum-wading-shoe and designed specifically for backpackers. Another choice: the light plastic "holey" slip-on shoes so popular with kids these days.

Socks

When it comes to choosing socks for hiking and backpacking, you'll find a big, and potentially overwhelming, selection on the rack. Thick, thin; short, tall; wool, cotton, synthetic or a combination. In my experience, the best combo fabric is wool plus some sort of synthetic (polyester, acrylic, polypropylene). Look for about 10 percent synthetic. Wool is soft and provides warmth when wet, while the synthetic portion gives extra wear and adds stretchiness, making the socks easier to put on after washing has inevitably shrunk them a little.

Good socks pull on easily and fit well. No wrinkles, no lumpy seams, no bunched-up fabric around the little toe, no overly stretched fabric around the heel. They retain these qualities through many washings, never becoming rough to the touch or losing their stretchiness. They wear evenly and you won't find holes in the heel long before other spots become worn.

Cotton socks are rougher on the feet and colder when wet than wool socks. They also wear out quickly. All-synthetic socks wear longer than cotton or wool, but they're not as soft or as warm, and they're more likely to cause blisters. However, synthetics have the advantage of drying more quickly than either cotton or wool. Wool's main problems are itchiness and allergic reactions. If you've had trouble with wool, consider socks made with SmartWool. This stuff is merino wool, which is very soft and agrees with nearly everyone.

Incredibly, most socks are designed to be smooth outside, so that they look nice, and rough inside, where the pattern of the knitting places many threads at right angles to the motion of the foot in the shoe. This creates more friction against your foot than against the inside of the boot. Further, the seams are typically made rough-side inward. That's also where you'll find any dangling threads.

The better brands of hiking socks generally have less roughness, and they're made with extra thickness on the bottom and at the heel, plenty of stretchiness around the tops and other well-thought-out features. Yet, despite this good work, nearly all sock manufacturers currently insist on making the insides of their socks with zillions of little loops, like terrycloth. These loops are hyped as being extra-comfy, pulling sweat away, etc., but on my feet they produce more friction and give me hotter foot-soles than smooth surfaces do.

I've even gone so far as to test this theory, wearing such a sock inside out on one foot (smooth side against my skin) and the usual way on the other (loopy side against my skin). Guess what? The right-side-out sock produced more friction. Okay, maybe it was just something about my feet that caused this. So, in the interests of fairness and objectivity, I asked a willing group of backpackers to try this, too, and every one of them reported the same thing I had noticed.

A couple of sock manufacturers must have carried out similar (although probably expensive and high-tech) research and come to the same conclusion. The Wigwam company and Wrightsocks are now both producing two-layer models in which the inner layer is purportedly smooth, not loopy. I've just discovered these and plan to test them as soon as I can. Mountain Equipment Co-op (MEC) carries both brands.

In the meantime I'll continue with my guerrilla approach to beating the loop-makers: I wear two pairs of socks, the inner one inside out. The inner pair is thin, the outer one thicker. This combination can be a bit warm on a really hot afternoon, but otherwise it's very comfortable and noticeably less blister-inducing than a single heavy pair worn right-side out. Perhaps foot motion within the boot is partly taken up by the two layers sliding against each other, and the extra cushioning helps.

How long should hiking socks be? For over-the-ankle boots, you might want your socks to reach just below the calf muscle, a size shown on most socks as "medium" or "crew." If I'm wearing shorts and hiking on a loose-surfaced section of trail from which grit gets flung up into my boots, there's enough sock sticking out to roll the outer layer down over the top of the boot and keep the dirt out. (See also the item on gaiters, page 62.)

How often should you wash your socks in the wild? Let your nose—better yet, your tent-mate's nose—be the judge of when to wash. Wool takes longer to get smelly than synthetics do. For most hikers, washing out socks in plain water every two or three days will suffice, no soap required. A little liquid detergent kills bacteria.

Washing socks in the creek or the lake introduces yucky between-your-toes stuff into the ecosystem, and anyway you can lose your socks in the creek while trying to wash them, so wash and rinse your socks in a pot. Fling the used water well away from the creek. You can dry wet socks on the back of your pack as you walk. I always seem to manage okay with just two sets of socks (four pairs) per trip. I certainly haven't heard any complaints.

Whether wet from washing or wet from wearing in the rain, socks dry too slowly in cool, showery weather. How to deal with the cold, soggy things? You have a few choices, none of which involve holding your socks over your stove, which wastes fuel and endangers both fabric and fingers. And forget about drying wet socks inside your tent at night. There's too much moisture present from your breath.

Hanging them outside will do the job on a warm, dry, breezy night. Be sure they're well-secured, so they don't blow away in the wind. But what if it rains while you're sleeping? And what about a heavy morning dew, which will wet them all over again? You could try hanging them under your tarp. Sometimes this works, if you don't tuck them up under a seam on the tarp where moisture will soak through to them, but most often they still won't be dry by morning. This isn't the best choice, then.

Instead, if it's morning and you have to hit the trail with wet socks, just put 'em on and walk. Tucked into lined leather boots, wet socks warm up quickly and aren't much of a discomfort. If the way is dry, the boots and socks soon will be, too.

If it's evening and you're camping in the rain in wet socks, and you really want them dry by morning, try this radical action: wring them out well, then put them back on and wear them in your sleeping bag. That's right: wet socks on your feet, inside your sleeping bag. Your body heat will dry them. Really. Your feet will be cold for a while, then they'll warm up. By morning the socks will be dry. The end of your bag will be damper than usual, because not all of the moisture will have escaped, but if you follow my advice about pitching your next camp with enough time left in the afternoon to let everything dry out before evening, then the bag will dry, too.

A friend suggests that you needn't actually keep wet socks on your feet in your sleeping bag. To avoid the chill of that initial cold period, try taking the socks off and slipping them into the end of the bag. They may dry out just fine that way, but they'll dry faster on your feet.

In really nasty conditions—day after day of rain—you can get a lot of comfort from **Gore-Tex socks,** or some other sock with a waterproof/breathable membrane in it. You wear this kind of sock over your regular socks. Thin and not intended for warmth or cushioning, waterproof socks won't keep your feet dry when your boots are soaked, because wet boots don't allow moisture to move out. Your feet will be damp in their own sweat. So what's the use? The use is that additional moisture won't get into your socks, and additional moisture is cold. So the net result of wearing Gore-Tex socks is less-soggy insulation and warmer feet. Remarkably warmer feet.

I also like my Gore-Tex socks for walking in good weather along trails overhung with dewy vegetation in the morning. My boots get wet, but my socks stay dry long enough for the vegetation and the boots to dry out, at which point I remove the Gore-Tex socks.

The downside of Gore-Tex socks is that they're frightfully expensive.

Underwear

Plain old cotton undies work fine for most hikers, most of the time. Cotton fabric readily passes sweat outward, so it stays drier than polyester underwear, which provides better digs for bacteria.

However, cotton is inferior when it's wet, meaning cold on your nethers, and in hot weather it may chafe. Try a combination cotton/polyester weave, which is what I usually wear. Pricey pure-polyester underwear made especially for hikers has very flat seams, chafes less than cotton or cotton-poly and dries much more quickly after washing. However, it starts to smell sooner than cotton or cotton-poly does, so you have to wash it more often.

You shouldn't wash your undies in the creek. Anything that's been on your crotch should be washed at least 30 metres away from any water body, and the used water should be flung even farther away. This helps to prevent the spread of giardiasis (page 100) and other bum-borne intestinal ailments.

Women wash their underwear more often in the backcountry than men do. Women wash everything, including themselves, more often in the backcountry than men do, and women carry more spare underwear. It's light, guys. You can do the same. Dark-coloured undies make passable swim trunks when you'd like to swim in places where skinnydipping is out. A dark or brightly coloured bra can make do as a bikini top for women.

Speaking of bras, what's the best type for backpacking? A soft, supportive bra is good. Hiking with a large pack is a slow-paced activity and doesn't usually cause the uncomfortable breast-bounce that running can, but some women find that the chest-strap found on modern backpacks—most of which are designed by and for men—is a pinchy piece of gear. Yet for most people a chest-strap is very effective at keeping a backpack's shoulder-straps comfortably situated. It's well worth spending time fiddling with a chest-strap's up-and-down and tightness adjustments and trying out different bras before a trip.

I carry lightweight polyester **long underwear** on backpacking trips, even in the warmest part of the summer, not so much to wear during the daytime—although I have done so when crossing high passes on chilly, windy days—but to wear in my sleeping bag. Longies weigh very little and offer a lot of comfort on cool nights. Worn alone under rain pants, they ease the clamminess, and if the weather becomes unseasonably cold and damp they make all the difference, night or day. I wouldn't be without long underwear for a coastal backpack.

Undershirt and shirt

There are lots of choices here. For an undershirt, I usually wear the same Stanfield's cotton-poly V-necks I've worn day in and day out for many years, familiar and comfortable, thick enough to prevent sunburn through my outer shirt and provide a little warmth when I need it, yet not overly hot. The V-neck sheds body heat better than a crew-neck design.

You may wish to wear a sturdier tee-shirt as your undershirt, one presentable enough to be worn as your only shirt on a hot day. For this purpose, try to find one with a tight weave and fuzzy thread, to keep the sun from getting through and burning you badly. Dermatologists advise fair-skinned people to wear sunscreen under their tee-shirts.

As the innermost layer, my undershirt is the last thing on my body to get wet, meaning that it rarely gets wet at all, so the cotton is not a liability. Cotton has a major advantage over polyester in that it doesn't stink after only a few hours of sweating in it. Some manufacturers of polyester underwear treat the cloth chemically to slow microbial growth—the source of the odour—but Patagonia, a leader in outdoor clothing, doesn't treat any of its synthetic products with antimicrobials, saying that the chemicals used aren't environmentally friendly and perhaps not good for you.

A new wrinkle . . .

Consider all the seams, folds and other pressure-causing strips of material you may have between your skin and a tight hip-belt on a heavy pack. There's the top band on your underwear, the folds in your shirt if it's just jammed into your pants, the top band on those pants, your belt, the folds in a jacket, etc. If these wrinkle, or if they overlap to the point of stacking, you may suffer.

So get those wrinkles out, eh? It's worth taking a little extra time when dressing to smooth your clothing. Carefully tuck in a shirt for minimal wadding over your hips. The same goes with pulling the fabric of your jacket one way or another around your waist to keep folds from gathering under your hip-belt.

Check the alignment of the various items as you put your pack on. Perhaps underwear with a higher or lower top band will help. So will a thinner belt, or no belt at all, if your pants stay up without one. Some backpackers wear suspenders just to get that belt off their pelvic bones.

Over my undershirt, I used to wear an ordinary but tightly woven cotton-poly collared shirt for the same reasons of comfort and familiarity. However, in the last few years I've gone over to a Supplex nylon shirt. This fabric repels rain better, dries faster and is wonderfully tough, with a good sun-protection factor (SPF). It rustles a little, but not much. It takes a long time to smell bad, washes easily and dries quickly. You'll probably be happy with any shirt that offers those same attributes, regardless of the material. Not so good are plain cotton and cotton-flannel shirts, which get wet easily and stay wet a long time, and any shirt that isn't woven tightly enough to prevent mosquitoes from getting their little noses through it. Look for sleeves long enough to cover your wrists and upper hands, even when your pack is on and some of the fabric is bunched under your arms.

Whatever you choose to wear on your upper body, please don't let popular fashion dictate its length. Exposing your navel and upper butt may be fashionable at the mall, but on the trail it leaves bare skin vulnerable to insect attacks or rubbing under a backpack. Thank heavens this flesh-exposing fad seems to be coming to an end. Buy your undershirt and shirt long enough to tuck well down into your pants.

Pants

You know those pants with the zip-off lower legs? I used to think they were stupid. Surely the zippers wouldn't work properly. And who needs short pants in the Canadian Rockies anyway, where the weather is always the long-pants variety?

Ah, but then someone gave me a pair of zip-leg pants and now I'm hooked. They are, in fact, perfect for the Canadian Rockies, where you normally start and finish the day in long pants but can enjoy shorts in the afternoon. There's no need to nip into the woods and change—just zip off the legs and zip them back on later. With the better makes, either lower leg zips to either upper leg. The ones with an additional zipper in each lower leg allow you to slip them on without having to take your boots off.

Other characteristics you should look for in a good pair of backpacking pants include the following:

- Materials: all or mostly synthetic, and not very heavy. Pants made of Supplex nylon are tough, lightweight, shed rain, dry quickly and don't feel like plastic on your legs. *Not so good:* cotton jeans and corduroys, yucky when wet and cold.

- Construction: sturdy, of course. A double seat will extend the life of the garment, as will double knees. Look for extra seams at stress points such as pockets. *Not so good:* fashionable but useless straps and flaps. One pair of pants I bought recently had a small nylon-cord loop of no apparent utility sewn to the leg in exactly the right position to get caught on the little lever that adjusts the seat of my car. The pants were otherwise good, so I just cut the loop off.

- Fit and cut: loose enough for easy leg movement, but not so loose that they go swish-swish between your thighs all day long. You should be able to take long upward steps easily without binding around the knees.

- Length: long enough to reach down to your instep, covering your boot-tops and helping to keep grit out. *Not so good:* pants with knit cuffs on the legs. These direct grit, leaves, twigs, stickers and snow right into your boots.

Shirt and pants with good design features

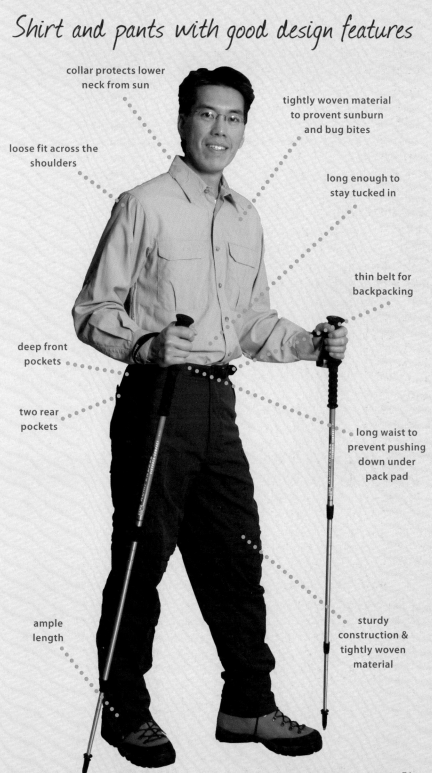

collar protects lower neck from sun

tightly woven material to provent sunburn and bug bites

loose fit across the shoulders

long enough to stay tucked in

thin belt for backpacking

deep front pockets

two rear pockets

long waist to prevent pushing down under pack pad

ample length

sturdy construction & tightly woven material

- Pockets: no need for more than the usual four, two front and two back. For some reason backpacker's pants always seem to come with big "cargo" pockets on the legs, into which you're supposed to put maps, guidebooks, etc. Cargo pockets can be handy, but when loaded they rub on your legs, which is annoying, and they catch on trailside vegetation. Fortunately most cargo pockets are easy to remove by just carefully cutting the stitching.

- Deep front pockets: to hold your handkerchief and your pocket-knife, two items to have instantly available on the trail. A well-designed front pocket has a short line of stitching at the base of the pocket entrance, creating a coin-catching lip. Having two rear pockets instead of just one is handy. I keep a comb in one and use the other for pocketing bits of trash I pick up along the trail. *Not so good:* mesh pockets, in which keys and other pointy items become entangled and difficult to remove, and front pockets from which everything tumbles out when you're sitting on the ground. This is how you lose your favourite pocket-knife. *Also not so good:* pockets that close with Velcro. Yes, nothing can fall out, but you always have to force your hand in, *scriiiiiitch*. If you need to have at least one pocket that closes securely, look for pants that come with a back pocket that zips.

- Front fly closure: a snap closure is not comfortable to work with cold fingers, and a button eventually pops off. What works best for pants is a flat hook-and-eye closure. Properly sewn on, this is easy to work and won't tear off.

- Belt for backpacking: anything thin, so it doesn't create a ridge under your pack's hip-belt. I use a belt of flat nylon webbing, which also has the advantage of drying more quickly than leather does. A friend of mine always wears suspenders. This is not only because he wants to avoid pain under his hip-belt, but also because he starts the season overweight and loses weight as the days go by. With suspenders, the waist size of the pants doesn't matter much, as long as it's big enough in May so he can use the same pair all summer!

Staying warm

Fuzzy synthetic fleece[1] pullovers and jackets have largely supplanted wool sweaters as the next layer over your shirt. That layer is likely to get wet, in which case synthetics have clear advantages: they repel rain better and dry more quickly than wool. I like to bring a thick fleece jacket with me, one that takes quite a while for drizzle to soak through. The principle here is one discovered by mammals quite a while ago, when fur was invented: a dense coat of hair is a great thing to have in place between you and the weather. (More about this in the discussion of rain gear, page 55.)

When buying fleece, you might want to be a good conservationist and opt for fleece made from recycled plastic. Most manufacturers indicate on their garments which ones are made of yarn spun from

Fleece jacket with good design features

zips up to cover throat

generous cut

full front zipper

zip pockets

---

1   As used these days, the term "fleece" includes the fabric we used to call "pile." Both fabrics are essentially similar, being made of loops of yarn. In the original pile garments of the 1960s the loops were on only one side of the fabric; the other side was like the underside of pile carpet. Thus the name. In true fleece garments, the loops are on both sides.

old pop bottles and such. This fabric is just as good as that made from un-recycled yarn, and it's no more expensive.

I'd rather wear fleece that zips than fleece that must be pulled over my head. A zipped jacket is easier to get on and off, and you can open it if you're overheating. A stand-up collar provides adjustable wind protection for your throat, and zip pockets will keep your gloves from falling out. A zip breast pocket is a handy place to stow sunglasses temporarily, and a couple of pockets inside the jacket can likewise be put to good use.

Like a sweater, a fleece jacket is wonderfully breathable. Fleece doesn't get sweaty or clammy, and it's comfortable over a wide range of temperatures—as long as the wind isn't blowing very hard. Strong wind penetrates fleece, but to overcome this problem you can buy fleece with a layer of tightly woven synthetic fabric stitched over it. Jackets made with this combination are popular, as are jackets made from two woven layers with a thin layer of insulation between. Such designs are warmer and more water repellent than plain fuzz, but they're also less breathable, meaning sweatier and clammier, and they're a whole lot more expensive.

"Wind-stopper" fabric is the most expensive of all. It puts a breathable membrane such as Gore-Tex between two layers of fleece. Like all such semi-permeable membranes, these garments breathe with a death rattle and not at all when the material is wet. So, all told, I like plain fleece the best, adding an outer layer for rain and wind protection when the need arises.

A thick fleece jacket is usually enough to get you through a summer evening in the Canadian Rockies, and it's overkill in southern Canada in July, but it's still wise to pack an extra layer of something warm, just in case. Just in case of what? Well, your main jacket could get wet. It might be swept away down a river or wind up at the bottom of a lake, or be blown over some precipice. Unseasonably cold weather could roll in. Someone else might need that spare jacket. Or—and this is the main reason I always carry an extra piece of puff—you might really want a pillow.

That's why I make my extra jacket a **down jacket.** This makes a great pillow when stuffed into a little flannel backpacker's pillowcase or a stuff sack–pillow combination (see page 194). A light down jacket weighs very little, and it feels great to throw on over my fuzz on a frosty mountain morning in late August. Or during the long July twilight at treeline, as you sit and watch the sun sinking into a sea of peaks, gliding down at a low angle as it slides northwestward for what seems like hours, lighting up the undersides of the clouds before taking the day's warmth with it over the edge of the world. Oh my goodness, we live in a beautiful country.

Staying dry—or if damp, at least comfortably so

Worn over fleece, a waterproof, windproof jacket provides the extra layer we humans think we need on rainy days. I say "think we need" because an impenetrable outer covering is perhaps less important than we assume. Read on.

Humans are uniquely un-furry among mammals, not counting naked mole rats and Mexican hairless dogs, neither of which hails from Canadian latitudes. Since our own species came out of Africa only 70,000–100,000 years ago, arrived in Europe much later and is a slow reproducer, we haven't had enough time to evolve the sort of pelage we need to survive properly at northern latitudes. Mountain goats, grizzly bears, bighorn sheep, wolverines—these critters have been here for enough generations to sport thick, dense coats that work well for them year-round in rain and snow, cold and wind. Rain takes a long time to soak through the heavy fleece (real fleece) of a bighorn sheep. Wind has a hard time reaching the skin, which is warm enough to dry the wool that lies above it. In anything but a full-on storm, not much water gets through and whatever does is soon evaporated back out again.

This is a wonderful combination for our climate. Sure, your average Rockies bighorn looks uncomfortably hot at times, panting away on a summer afternoon beside the Icefields Parkway, but it survives, even though it can't take off its coat. We humans can emulate such critters. Sailors have been doing so for a long time, working in the drizzle under layer upon layer of wool sweaters that provide much the same comfort as the material did on its natural host. A thick fleece jacket is merely the modern analogue. Why, then, the need for a waterproof over-jacket?

In point of fact, in all my years of tromping about in the Rockies I have worn mine surprisingly little. It's not that I haven't been glad to put it on in a downpour, and that's why I always carry it with me, but I'll bet I haven't spent more than five percent of my hiking time inside a rain shell. I've worn that jacket more often to boost the warmth of fleece or down when the evening has become chilly. Out on the trail during the day, my jacket comes out of my pack only when the rain is really coming down and/or the wind is really strong. Otherwise I prefer to be a sheep, letting my fuzzy fleece get wet on the outside. It

Rain jacket and rain pants with good features

zipper reaches high
enough to protect
throat

deep hood to keep
rain off face

taped seams

armpit zippers
for ventilation

exterior pockets
with zips

sleeves long
enough to cover
hands if necessary

the longer the
better

side zippers for
pulling pants on
over boots

has to become quite soggy before it's wet on the inside. I've walked for hours in light rain with only my fleece on, perfectly comfortable under it, not sweating and clammy as I am whenever something waterproof goes on over the fleece.

Why the sweaty and clammy? Don't we all use Gore-Tex-type jackets, and isn't Gore-Tex supposed to prevent this? Yes, it does—as long as (1) you're not sweating very much, because Gore-Tex and its imitators aren't nearly as breathable as plain fleece, and as long as (2) moisture beads up on the jacket, leaving plenty of tiny dry spots for the perspiration vapour to come out. However, if the rain continues for an hour, or if you haven't treated your jacket with water repellent spray for the last couple of trips, the beading will stop, the surface will "wet out" (the exterior fabric becomes soaked), and your $400 typhoon-buster might as well be a $30 polyurethane-coated jacket that doesn't breathe at all, ever.

So why not just use the $30 job? It's lighter as well as cheaper. That's what I've generally done: opted for an inexpensive, non-breathable jacket. It packs small, weighs little and does the job. Recently, though, my son Will has given me a very lightweight rain jacket made of a new Gore-Tex fabric, almost as light as the cheap urethane job and better when it's *not* raining, because when I'm sitting in camp it doesn't condense inside like the coated model does. Will is a world-class athlete who runs up and down mountains, throwing off heat like a Roman candle wherever he goes. For him, Gore-Tex over fleece is too warm. Fleece alone is too warm. In rainy weather Will prefers a waterproof/breathable jacket worn over his shirt, and that's enough. If you have his kind of energy, that combination might work for you, too.

The only negative I can think of for light rain jackets is the same as for any light jacket: they're not very strong. If you're going to be walking in brush or thrashing your way through the rocks, you'll want tougher fabric. A rain jacket need not tear all the way through to leak.

It's important to note that *waterproof/breathable clothing is terrific in weather that's cool, rainy and windy all at the same time.* I once spent several very long days outdoors above the treeline in those conditions, for which my deeply hooded Gore-Tex jacket and rain pants were wonderful. The fabric would get rained on lightly every hour or so, but never enough to fully wet it, so it stayed permeable and non-sweaty. The breeze was strong enough to get through my fleece, which without the jacket acted like an air-conditioning unit as the moisture evaporated, brrr. Backpacking in the North and along the coasts can present situations like this.

Regardless of what kind of fabric your jacket is made from, you'll probably like it more if it has the following features:

- All seams taped for waterproofness.
- The front-zipper type rather than the pull-over type, with "pit zips," which are zippers that run from armpit to elbow, good for ventilation.
- Exterior pockets for your hands.
- Interior pockets to hold your gloves.
- Deep hood with a drawcord to snug the hood around your face when the weather gets really nasty, plus a bill on the hood to keep some of the rain off your eyeglasses.
- Long enough to cover your bum.
- Sleeves long enough to cover your hands completely, so you can walk along in the rain without getting your hands and/or your gloves soaked.

Rain pants are a comfort in this country, where storms tend to be windy and the rain gets up under a simple over-garment such as a **poncho.** I often slip my rain pants on in the morning, for walking along a brushy trail wet with dew. For rain pants, expensive waterproof-breathable material is usually a waste of money. This is because (1) in most parts of Canada rain pants needn't be worn for more than a couple of hours at a time, so about the time they're getting clammy you can take them off, and (2) rain pants wet out quickly by rubbing against wet trailside brush, so the breathability soon ceases to function anyway. Unless you're hiking the West Coast Trail or some other notoriously drippy place, you may prefer to save money and buy rain pants of plain coated fabric.

Be sure that you can get your rain pants on easily over your boots. Wear your usual hiking boots when trying on rain pants in the store. Some models are cut wide enough to slip over boots, but most are narrow in the legs, with zippers along the sides that do the trick. If the legs are wide enough, such zippers need reach only from the knee down, so you can unzip and step right in with minimal hassle. However, most rain pants are cut slim through the knee and require full-length zippers. Don't unzip such pants entirely, such that they come apart into a front half and a back half. You'll be trying to zip the two halves together on your body in a squall, with everything flapping around. Leave the top of each leg zipped. If the full-length zippers on rain pants are also two-way zippers, you can unzip each side at the top and be able to reach into your pants pockets, which is a handy feature.

Should you carry an **umbrella** on a rainy day? A small, lightweight umbrella works great in an all-day drizzle when there's little wind to blow rain underneath it or turn it inside out. If you're hiking with walking poles, though, you'll have to figure out a way to attach the umbrella to your pack. See the illustration for a method that works for me.

Laugh if you will, but this actually works quite well!

Gloves

There's no need for mittens or ski gloves in a Canadian summer, although my wife loves her boot-wax-treated leather mitts and knit liners so much that she uses them year-round.

For most of us a pair of lightweight gloves will do. Knit gloves weigh next to nothing and may get you by even on mornings with a trace of frost. But they tear rather easily, a problem in the Alberta national parks, for example, where I'm always hauling heavy food bags up bear poles with the steel cables Parks Canada provides. For that sort of thing leather is way better than yarn. Snag a knit glove on a wire-end and you've got a hole in it that's only going to get bigger.

My favourite kind of gloves for summer are made of wind-stopper fabric (two layers of thin, tightly knitted fleece with a waterproof/breathable membrane between them) and palms of pigskin, which are tough enough for hauling and can be repeatedly wetted and dried without stiffening. Such gloves are fairly good in the rain. This isn't because the membrane keeps the inner layer dry. It doesn't. Wind-stopper gloves get sopping wet. But even so they keep my hands a lot warmer than knit gloves do, which when soaked—and they soak easily—allow too much air movement over the skin. Wind-stopper fabric prevents that, and it dries more quickly than knit fabric.

Hat

Okay, maybe that pith helmet is just *you*, and that's all there is to it. Such is the fashion factor in choosing headwear, even for the trail. And that's great. Hat-watching makes for good backcountry entertainment. I've seen everything out there from, yes, people wearing pith helmets (popular with Japanese hikers in the Rockies for a couple of years) to fake coonskin caps (briefly popular with British army troops in Jasper National Park when on leave). All that aside, what makes for a sensible backpacker's cap? Consider the following desirable qualities:

- Keeps the sun and rain out of your eyes and off the back of your neck.
- Protects your nose and the tops of your ears from sunburn.
- Doesn't stick out so far in back that your pack keeps hitting it.
- Warm on a chilly day.
- Not too hot on a warm day.
- Stays on in the wind.
- Doesn't get soggy in the rain.
- Can be worn under the hood of your jacket.
- Dries quickly.
- Can be carried in a pack without being damaged.

Surely there must be something out there that meets all these requirements? Actually, there isn't. A ball cap comes close, when worn with a bandana tucked under it to cover your ears and neck (there are commercial versions of this sold as "safari" hats), but to meet all requirements, you're going to have to carry more than one hat. Which is what I do. I have a favourite Filson waxed-canvas hat that scores high on most of the criteria above, plus a light ball cap for wearing under the hood of my parka in the rain and as backup in case I lose the Filson in the wind, despite the chinstrap I've sewn onto it, and also a little fleece cap that does dual duty as evening wear and something to cover my balding head in my sleeping bag.

Bug protection

Calling the mosquito "Canada's national bird" is an exaggeration only in the size of these beasts. Nearly any place in this country can be home to hordes of them, the two exceptions being the far, far north and the west-coast seashore, neither of which is typically very buggy. Elsewhere, any spot of water that has lain for a few weeks in summer will breed the things. Add a nearby creek or river to produce blackflies, throw in some hoofed creatures to attract horseflies and deerflies, and you're looking at a bad day on the trail. Unless, of course, you're properly clothed for the event.

Note that it's "properly clothed," not "chemically treated." DEET-based repellent will keep the bugs from biting, but who wants to slather on this smelly solvent? It's better to put some fabric of the proper sort between you and the humming multitudes.

Begin with lightweight, closely woven material for your shirt and pants. Nylon or cotton/poly with a high thread count is impervious to mosquito probosci, while most plain cotton fabrics aren't. For your shirt, look for sleeves that can be closed tightly, a collar you can fold up and button, and bug netting behind ventilating flaps or other openings. The same goes for those grommetted openings in the crowns of some hats. Such insect doorways should be screened. For your pants, tightly woven synthetics are good. Look for enough length to allow the lower ends to reach well down over your boots, working up and down as you walk and thus keeping blackflies from crawling up. Pants with elastic cuffs and drawstring cuffs aren't as effective against bugs as you might think. Such pants ride at or above your boot-tops, leaving a gap there that can be exploited. For sitting around in camp with your knees drawn up, which pulls your pantlegs up to expose your ankles, tuck those pantlegs into the tops of your socks.

The neck—especially the back of the neck—is a preferred attack point for biting insects. The combination of a buttoned-up collar and a bandana is reasonably protective, but it makes for hot hiking. Sometimes the best approach is to protect everything from your shoulders up with a head net. This item provides excellent ventilation and weighs very little. Lee Valley Tools (www.leevalley.com) sells a clever, lightweight, inexpensive, folding sun-hat-plus-head-net combination that keeps the netting off your face.

Lee Valley also sells a clever defence against deerflies and horseflies: a strip of fly paper that's also adhesive on the back. You stick one of these deerfly patches onto the back of your hat, where deerflies and horseflies often land between flesh-seeking sorties. There they stay, trapped, awaiting whatever revenge you have in mind. The downside is that the person walking behind you has your fly collection in constant view.

Finally, let it be known that there is a way for you to walk through hot, buggy country in shorts and a tee-shirt—even shirtless—without the need for DEET. You put on a **bug jacket** and **bug pants.** (For complete protection, wear **bug socks** and **bug gloves** as well.) These are all featherlight over-garments of very finely woven nylon mesh, with no-see-um netting over the face and drawstrings at the waist and cuffs. Not even a mosquito proboscis can get through, yet the breeze can. Well, sort of. Ventilation is way better than it would be through regular clothing, but the fabric does impede airflow somewhat. And the feel of the material on your skin takes some getting used to. However, it's better than being bitten.

Bug jackets and bug pants also offer some protection against ticks. However, nothing except bathing in DEET will keep a persistent tick from finding its way through any gap, even one snugged shut by a drawstring. Without DEET, you just have to assume that ticks will manage to get on board. So check your body for them at least once a day, more often when dealing with the small ticks that can carry Lyme disease, and pick 'em off before they attach. (See page 307 for more on ticks.)

Gaiters

We are speaking of zippered fabric tubes that you slip onto your lower legs, over your pantlegs. Someone from south of the 49th might blanch at seeing Canadians hiking in Banff National Park wearing shorts and snow gaiters. "Whoa—is it really going to snow that deeply around here in *July?*" Probably not. (Note "probably.") But regardless of the weather, when you're wearing shorts you may wish to put on your cross-country ski gaiters to cover your boot-tops so trail grit and stickers don't get in.

If you'd like to save weight and sweatiness, though, buy a pair of really short gaiters, the kind that cover your boot-tops but don't go much higher up your leg. It helps if they're made of uncoated fabric, which breathes. If you wear two pairs of socks, you can get by without any gaiters at all. Just roll down the outer pair of socks over your boot-tops. Grit will get between the two layers, but it won't be terribly bothersome, and you can shake it out in the evening when you take your boots off.

Gear

Now that you're dressed, and assuming the credit card is not maxed out, let's pick out a pack, a tent, a sleeping bag, a stove, a cookset—aye, we're into the gear. It's wonderful. It's clever and very sophisticated. It's also expensive. (For getting by on the cheap, see page 138.)

My advice about gear is to acquire the best you can, because it will work better, weigh less and last longer than lower-quality stuff. But there's no need to fork out for the high end in everything, or to snap up whatever's being touted as the latest and greatest. I've learned my lesson on this. When I'm thinking about investing in some whiz-bang new item, which always costs more than the model that preceded it, I wait a couple of years to buy. If it's still around, it was a good idea and the glitches will have been worked out of it. If it's not around, I'll be glad I didn't waste my money on it.

But let's start with that monkey on your back.

Choosing a pack

I have a closet full of packs. I mostly use only two, though: one for day hikes and mountaineering, the other for backpacking.

Backpacks first. There have been three major innovations in backpack design since I started hiking in the 1950s. The first was the curved, body-fitting aluminum frame with the bag secured high up on it. My wonderful 1964 Kelty pack moved the weight forward on my body, so the pack didn't pull back on my shoulders. I no longer had to walk hunched over and in some degree of pain all the time. And the shoulder-straps were actually *padded*. Dick Kelty also pioneered the second innovation, the hip-belt. This took most of the weight off my shoulders. Yes, yes!

The third big improvement was Greg Lowe's clever redesign of the internal-frame pack in 1967. Lowe reduced the weight of the frame to a couple of aluminum stays, used the hip-belt to advantage and added a chest-strap to pull the shoulder-straps together, thereby making the pack more comfortable for us round-shouldered types. Further, the side-straps on this kind of pack could be pulled in to make it slim and small, so you could haul lots of gear far into the wilderness and then use the same pack for day-hiking from your camp.

Most people use updated variants of the Lowe design these days, although external-frame packs are still around, and for some backpackers they offer the most comfort under heavy loads. They're heavier than internal-frame packs, though, and external frames are more easily broken.

Regardless of what kind of pack you choose, here's some key advice for getting one that's light, fits you well and doesn't cost a lot of money: *a simple, no-frills, well-made pack is best.* It's also likely to be among the less expensive ones in the store. With most backpacking items, the more you pay the less you get—in weight. But with packs it's the opposite. Expensive backpacks are tricked out with fancy suspensions, extra compartments and pockets, additional straps and whatnot, all of which add to the weight on your back before you've even put anything in the pack. The more you pay, the more you have to carry. Go figure.

When you're shopping, look for the following:

- A pack that's large enough. For your average weekend trip, you'll probably be carrying a sleeping bag and foam pad, all or part of a tent, all or part of the cooking gear (stove, fuel, cookset), food, extra clothing and a number of smaller personal items. For this you'll need a pack with a capacity of 70–80 litres. For a week-long trip you'll need more room for the additional food, perhaps as much as 90–100 litres. If those numbers seem large, be aware that with pack size it's better to err on the side of excess. *A large, under-loaded pack is more comfortable to carry than a small, overloaded pack.*

- Simple suspension. Pack manufacturers are always advertising the virtues of their latest "suspension system," meaning that between your back and the weight you're carrying there are numerous straps, attachment points, buckles, rings, fabric loops, metal slats, plastic rods, etc., etc. All of this will require initial adjustment, which takes time and can be frustrating. It may also need readjustment later on. Sway is usually present and difficult to get rid of (see below). The fact that pack designers keep introducing complex suspensions, then changing them, suggests to me that they haven't got it right and never will.

The alternative is the tried and true KISS ("keep it simple, stupid") approach, and several pack-makers actually employ this principle in their suspensions. On some models the tops of the shoulder-straps are simply sewn to the pack. There is no back-length adjustment; you try the various pack sizes available and buy the one that fits you. I'm not easy to fit, having a long back and the posture of a vulture, but this kind of pack is perfectly comfortable on me, doesn't sway and never gets out of whack. Whenever I've caved in to someone's pleas of "Ben, Ben, you've *got* to try this new pack!" and headed out for a few days with the latest and greatest whiz-bang suspension, I always wish I hadn't.

- Simple, single-compartment pack bag. My favourite backcountry pack is a great big empty sack that I can fill from the bottom up and unload from the top down. Simple, strong, reliable and versatile. All those internal pockets, external pockets, zippers, strap-on points, "daisy-chain" loops are more bother than they're worth—few bells and whistles on a pack are really useful, and they all add weight. For example, the pack illustrated is as plain as they come. It can hold everything needed for a week in the wilds, and it weighs 2.3 kilograms. A competing brand offering the same stowage weighs 3.2 kilograms, nearly a kilogram more. Some of that extra kilogram is heavier padding, which you might appreciate, but most of it's in the form of gizmos.

Many packs are made with at least two compartments, typically arranged one above the other, the lower one accessible through an outside zipper. If you carry your sleeping bag as the lowest item in your pack (see page 172) it has to go through this zipper. Just stuffing it into the compartment won't do, though, because the pack cloth alone won't keep a sleeping bag dry. A sleeping bag needs to be carried in its stuff sack, and getting that plump sack through the zippered opening can be a pain, especially when your fingers are cold. Then you have to yank the zipper closed. Eventually it will break.

Conclusion: it's better to just drop the stuff bag in from the top—you won't need that sleeping bag until after supper anyway—and let it get tamped down well from the weight of the stuff above. If you own a two-compartment pack, you may be glad to discover that the divider between the two compartments can be removed easily. If not, this is what seam-rippers are for.

Bags for pack frames usually ride on the upper two-thirds of the frame. On most models your sleeping bag and/or sleeping pad get strapped to the bottom of the frame, under the pack bag. The advice above about internal-frame pack bags applies equally well to external-frame pack bags.

- Drawstring closure at the top. A zipper closure on the outside of a pack can be convenient, because you can open your pack like a suitcase and extract whatever you want from any part of the bag. However, zippers snag on soft items such as shirts and sweaters, and no matter how heavy the zipper it will eventually split, presenting you with a serious equipment failure to deal with. Better to have a bomb-proof marble-sack of a pack bag, meaning one with a drawstring closure. The natural order of packing puts things you need most often near the top anyway, where they're easy to retrieve through the drawstring opening.

- Extension sleeve and collar. Most drawstring-closing packs actually have two closures: the main one, which is found at the top of the bag, and another one at the end of a sleeve of material that folds down inside the pack when you don't need it and pulls upward when you do. The sleeve provides a more weatherproof closure on any size of load, and it covers a load that extends upward beyond the main closure. Third use: if you have to sit out the night somewhere with no tent or sleeping bag, but you do have your pack, then you can slip your feet into the pack and pull the sleeve up over your legs. Mountaineers do this for warmth on their bivouacs.

- Side-straps for flattening the load. A pack that's thinner front-to-back is more comfortable than a pack that's thicker, because a thinner pack rides closer to your centre of gravity and pulls back less on your shoulders. Three straps per side are enough to compress the load. Side-straps can also be used to hold your tent poles, which you slip down between the straps and the pack. The same goes for your walking poles when you're not using them.

- Pockets at the bottoms of the sides to keep those poles from slipping out.

- Cushy hip-belt and shoulder-straps, preferably of dual-density foam, which is softer on the inside, next to your body, and stiffer on the outside, so the padding holds its shape.

- A large head-flap compartment with a strong zipper to hold items that you need to reach in a hurry. The head-flap is the part at the

Backpack with good design features

large head-flap compartment

detatchable head-flap that can be used as a waist pack

side-straps

no back pocket

pockets at the bases of the sides

overall shape is narrow, tall and flat

extension sleeve and collar

simple suspension, easy to adjust, and sway-free

drawstring closure at the top

built-in foam back pad

cushy hip-belt & shoulder-straps

top of the pack that straps down over the rest of it, keeping the rain out. The bigger the better for this item; the head-flap on my pack always seems to be full to bursting.

Many external-frame packs have **side pockets** sewn onto them that provide extra space and let you reach frequently needed items easily. These are handy and don't adversely affect a hiker's centre of gravity. Since they're sewn on, they don't wiggle around.

Side pockets are optional on many internal-frame packs, attached by means of the side-straps. Pockets like this may be impossible to affix tightly, and anything that flops as you walk wastes your energy. For quick-access items, it's better to have a big head-flap on your pack than floppy side pockets.

It's handy if the head-flap is detachable, with its own nylon-webbing hip-belt, so you can wear it as a waist pack. If not completely detachable, at the very least the head-flap should be mounted with adjustable straps, so it can be made to sit flat over a large load rather than tilting inward toward your neck. The zipped opening is often positioned along the front of the head-flap, and if that opening is tilted downward things will fall out when you unzip it.

- No back pocket. If the idea is to keep a pack slim, then why would you want a pocket on the back, which makes a pack thick? Well, maybe to hold one of those big bladder-style, sucky-tube water containers that are popular these days. But putting any weight out there on the back of a large pack—especially water, which is dense, heavy stuff—will cause the pack to pull backward on you. And whether or not you drink from a bladder, if a pack has a back pocket sewn onto it, you'll surely end up putting stuff into that pocket just because it's there. So don't have the pocket. If you're looking for something for your water bladder, look for a pack with a pocket *inside* the pack bag to hold it, preferably near the top, in the centre, against your back.

- Strong materials, good hardware and careful craftsmanship. You don't want your pack coming apart on its second trip. Look for heavy fabric and extra lines of stitching at points of stress, taped or hot-cut seams and a beefy zipper on the head-flap pocket. The straps and buckles should work smoothly; you should be able to adjust the length of the shoulder-straps and the hip-belt with easy tugs as you wear the pack. The hip-belt buckle should click into place smoothly. It should stay clipped when you put pressure on it by leaning over, and it should undo easily.

Finally found a model you like? The next thing is to get the proper length. Packs can have lots of adjustments—too many, in my view—but regardless of adjustability you still need one that's approximately the right length to begin with. The distance between the hip-belt and the shoulder yoke has to be neither too long nor too short.

To find the right length, first try on a pack that's long enough to keep the shoulder-straps *above* the tops of your shoulders. With the hip-belt snugged up around your middle, the back-length adjustment (if there is one) about in the centre and the shoulder-straps pulled in far enough to keep the bag close to your back, there should be a gap of a couple of centimetres between the tops of your shoulders and the underside of the straps. This may sound strange, but bear with me.

Now load the pack up. Have the salesperson put weight into the bag, preferably about 20 kilograms of whatever the store has available for this purpose. (*Store managers:* if you haven't done so already, you might want to have some sandbags made up just for this purpose. Fill strong plastic bags and put 'em into stuff sacks.) Cinch the hip-belt tighter, to keep the pack from slipping down your hips. Shorten the shoulder-straps a little more if you have to,

A well-fitted, properly loaded pack. Note that the hiker has a little forward lean.

trying to reduce sway. Nearly all multi-day packs have **sway-straps** that connect the tops of the shoulder-straps to the top of the pack, near your neck. Tighten these up, too. The shoulder-straps should now rest lightly on your shoulders, taking a little—but not much—of the load. If the straps still stand off your shoulders, the pack's too long for your back. If the straps put a lot of weight on your shoulders, the pack's too short for your back.

This is not yet a reason to reject this pack. See if the distance between the hip-belt and the place where the shoulder yoke is attached can be made shorter or longer. If that's the case, and you like the pack you're trying out, perhaps it can be made to fit with this adjustment.

Some packs also have an adjustment for the horizontal spacing of the shoulder-straps, but most don't. If the shoulder-straps are set too far apart they'll pull backward on the outer edges of your shoulders. This causes muscle fatigue and soreness, and the straps may keep slipping off. The chest-strap can be used to pull the shoulder-straps together somewhat, but for women this can cause boob-pinch. If the shoulder-straps are too close together, they pinch the trapezius muscles at the base of the neck, which is also uncomfortable.

Women, who are generally wide across the hips, short in the back and narrow across the shoulders, have had to make do for too long with packs designed for men, who are generally narrow across the hips, long in the back and wide across the shoulders. So if you're a woman, finding a comfortable pack isn't easy. However, some pack manufacturers do produce models designed especially for women. Yay! These are worth searching out.

When you have your possible purchase fully loaded up and reasonably well adjusted to fit you, and it feels comfortable, you still need to wear it around the store for a while. If possible, go up and down stairs. As you walk, look for three important make-or-break qualities:

- The pack shouldn't sway from side to side. Sway is not only annoying, it also wastes energy. You're moving the pack this way and that, work that should be going into propelling you up the trail. Generally speaking, the more complex the pack's suspension is—the more rings, rods, straps and buckles there are around the yoke and the hip-belt—the more sway you're going to get. With some suspensions there's no way to get rid of it. Don't buy such a pack.

- The pack shouldn't move forward and back with each step. Some packs develop a peculiar motion as you walk, alternately bumping your back and pulling away from it, even when the shoulder-straps and sway-straps are pulled tight. This will definitely annoy you and waste effort. Again, it seems to be a function of the suspension. In a pack with the upper ends of the shoulder-straps sewn directly to the fabric, there's minimal play in the whole system. (Since there's no back-length adjustment option, selecting such a pack requires care. It either fits you or it doesn't.)

- Finally, the pack should let you stand nearly straight while wearing it fully loaded. Have the load distributed properly, with most of the weight up near the top and close to your back. If the mock weight is sitting in the bottom of the pack, you should ask the salesperson to put a couple of stuffed sleeping bags or empty boxes under it, to shift the weight higher, up where it ought to be located when you're ready for the trail. Pull in the side-straps to make the pack slim. Now look at yourself in a full-length mirror. If you're quite noticeably bent forward, the pack's still pulling back on you. Your shoulders will feel the strain. Something ain't right. Pull the sway-straps tight.

If that doesn't help, it may be the shape of the frame. Nothing can be done about this with an exterior-frame pack, but most interior-frame packs have bendable metal **stays,** which are two flat pieces that run inside the fabric from the hip-belt to the top. These pieces are formed into an S-shape, so that the curve of the pack follows the curve of the average human backbone. Perhaps this is not the exact curve of your backbone. Fortunately, stays can be bent to the right shape.

Many packs are made with the tops of the stays bent sharply back, away from your neck, something that has never made sense to me. It serves only to increase the length of the anti-sway-straps, thereby inducing sway, and it makes the pack pull back on you. I always straighten these bends out, and you may need to as well.

See if the salesperson is willing to bend the stays to fit your back. She or he should be; this is the last step in your decision-making. If adjusting the stays makes everything perfect, you should buy the pack.

No, wait! Stop! What about the colour? Is it exactly the right shade of blue? Does it match your trekking pants? What about the logo? Is this the same brand you saw in that cool ad in the magazine? No? Well, for heaven's sake don't buy it. After all, it's not how good you are, it's how good you look. Isn't it?

Should I buy accessories that attach to my pack? You can get all kinds of clever pockets and doodads that hang from your waist belt, your shoulder-straps, the side-straps, the head-flap. You can get the aforementioned side pockets, a pocket for your water bottle, a pocket for your camera, a pocket for your binoculars, a pocket for your map and guidebook, a case for your sunglasses . . . the list goes on. My advice? Avoid all of these. They flop. They detach and get lost. They get crushed when you set your pack down without moving them out of the way. A water bottle or water bladder carried on the outside of your pack in the sun merely ensures that your drinking water heats up. All this impedimenta? It makes you look like you're headed for the battlefield, not the wilderness. "KISS," eh?

What about day packs? The better day packs are simply smaller versions of the better backpacks. My usual day pack is larger than those I see most people wearing. It has plenty of room for lunch, a water bottle, a jacket and other essentials. Like a full-size backpack, this day pack has an internal frame and a padded hip-belt. It has been made long and skinny to allow enough distance between the hip-belt and the shoulder-strap yoke to actually transfer the weight from shoulders to hips. There are side-straps—great for carrying skis—and it has ice-axe loops for mountaineering use.

A word of caution about day packs, though. Lots of them are designed in the old European rucksack style. They look cute, especially the ones made of leather, and they'll certainly do for holding your purse, sweater, books and whatnot while strolling around campus or going to work. But packs like this aren't very comfortable to carry for any distance.

The design to avoid is short and bulbous-looking, narrow and thin at the top, wide and thick at the bottom. The hip-belt, if there is one at all, is a narrow strap whose only purpose seems to be to get caught in the car door. There's no frame, sometimes not even a layer of padding down the back to offer some protection for the lumpy objects that get lobbed into it. Nix.

If you're going backpacking, should you carry a separate day pack? This is seldom necessary. Your backpack will work just fine as a day pack by pulling the side-straps in to make it thinner. However, suppose that you're hostelling through Europe, staying for a day or two here and a day or two there. Your big backpack—maybe it's a travel pack—with your sleeping bag and so on can be left at the hostel while you're out exploring the town with a small pack in which to carry essentials. For this you want the lightest day pack available, commensurate with reasonable strength, and it exists: a sleeping-bag stuff sack with shoulder-straps. A US company called Oware makes one (www .owareusa.com). These things are so simple that I'll bet you could buy a stuff sack and make one yourself.

Other possibilities are a large shoulder bag or its cousin the sling pack, meaning a pack with only one shoulder-strap. Slings are currently fashionable. If worn with the strap across the chest, bandolier-style, both hands can be free for use with walking poles. The same thing works for shoulder bags generally, as long as the strap is long enough. But they do flop around.

Lastly, let me make a quick pitch for waist packs, also called "fanny packs" in North America. (But not in Britain, where they're called "bum bags." In Britain, "fanny" is a rude term for the female nethers.) When you need something for carrying the absolute minimum—small water bottle, light jacket, snack, camera—then a waist pack will do the job. There are no shoulder-straps at all, just a wide hip-belt that takes the whole load. In addition to a small waist pack, I have a large, 15-litre-capacity one. It's terrific for skiing, because it keeps the weight low. One other advantage of a waist pack is that you can wear it when your back or neck is sore.

How can you keep your pack dry in the rain? This is not a stupid question. Pack cloth is heavily coated on the interior side and fairly waterproof at first, but soon it starts to leak from abrasion of the coating as things in the pack rub on it. So don't count on your pack to keep the contents dry. For that you'll need some kind of pack cover. The cheapest one is just a very large plastic garbage bag, the type for holding leaves you've raked up in the fall. You slip one of these over the pack and cut a slit in it for the shoulder-straps and hip-belt. Bring an extra bag, though. They tear easily.

For longer service, buy a proper pack cover. These are made of tent-fly material, which is light but not as light as a plastic garbage bag. And much more expensive, of course. There are various sizes, so be sure to choose one that's large enough to cover your pack when it's filled to the max.

To make sure that your sleeping bag doesn't get wet, even if you fall into the river, slip a plastic bag into the stuff sack to line the sack with the plastic bag before you stuff in the sleeping bag. Once it's stuffed, flatten the sack under your knees and seal the plastic bag tightly with a twist-tie or a knot. Fold the end into the stuff sack, then pull the stuff sack's drawstring tight.

How should you maintain your pack? It will get scuffed and dirty. A jam container will leak inside it. A ground squirrel will nibble a hole in it. The waterproof coating will wear off. Holes will appear at the lower corners. Zippers will go. A strap will tear out of its attachment point. But you can at least keep it clean.

To clean your pack, make sure no articles remain in any cranny or pocket—aha, that's where my compass went!—then handwash the pack in the bathtub with mild detergent. As with your tent, don't put your pack in the washing machine. The straps are likely to get snarled up, perhaps in the mechanism. For other maintenance, I carry a big needle, thick thread and a small piece of sturdy nylon cloth for

Ben Gadd

A cheap tent will cost you later . . .

making in-the-wilds pack repairs. A decent seamster can do wonders with a pack you'd thought was a goner.

Choosing a tent

You're way back in the wilderness and way up high. It's midnight and the rain has been drumming down on your tent for two hours. The whole campground is glistening with water. You have to get up to pee. You grab your flashlight and unzip the door. As you wiggle out, a pool of water that has somehow collected on the tent fly drains out over you. Ach! You rush over to the biffy. Ahhhh . . .

You get back into the tent. That's when you notice the drip. No, there are two drips, one for you and one for your companion, each positioned directly over the centre of a sleeping bag. The wet spots are growing fast. Immediate action is required. You remember that there are some extra plastic garbage bags in one of the packs, which had to be left outside covered with a tarp because the tent had no room inside for them. Maybe that plastic could be spread over the top of the fly.

You yank open the tent zipper again. What the . . . ?! The zipper jams partway. You wrench it open. It comes off its track. The shaking you've given the tent has turned the drips into streams. Your tent-mate is yelling at you. That's when you notice the puddle of water at the end of the tent, muddy and thus indicating that it's getting in through the floor. And the rain is turning to snow . . .

Friends, if you're going to carry a tent into the wilds at all, make sure that it's a *good* one.

The basic design of a dependable, easy-to-erect backpacker's tent hasn't changed much since the free-standing tent was introduced by Eureka in 1959 (they called it the Draw-Tite tent). Before that, one must look back to World War II for major advances, when zippers andnylon fabrics came into widespread use, replacing cotton walls and button-up doors.

Question: why have there been so few truly ground-breaking innovations over the years? Answer: there's no need for them. The currently popular basic design—a tent of uncoated nylon and mosquito netting with a coated floor, zip entrance, fly of coated nylon, external frame of light-alloy poles—works very well. Tents are like bicycles: the more you spend, the less you get. The less weight, that is. Forking out about $600 will get you the lightest of all, a Stephenson Warmlite, which is a gossamer thing of beauty, with a total weight of 1.25 kilograms for the two-person model.

But even this tent has trade-offs. To save weight on poles, it's not free-standing, meaning that you have to guy it out from stakes stuck into the ground or by using trees, shrubs and rocks as anchor points. The profile is low, especially at the back. It's like camping in a culvert. This is typical of the reduced convenience and comfort you get when going with ultra-light gear. You really do pay more and get less. For me, saving weight is important, but it's not the only thing. Sure, a backpacking tent has to be light, but I'll carry an extra kilo for adequate room in my tent, ease of assembly and an additional margin of strength and weatherproofness. Here are the criteria I had when I was shopping for a new tent a few years ago:

- Free-standing design, meaning that only a few stakes are needed and none has to hold against a lot of pull in windy conditions. Free-standing tents are easier and quicker to pitch than staked-out tents, especially on a hard, rocky tent pad that doesn't accept the stakes very well. Another advantage is that while you're packing up, you can pick the whole tent up and shake it to remove dirt sticking to the bottom. You can set the tent on its side or end to brush off any remaining bits. If you open the door and point it downward as you shake, material that has got inside will fall out—along with those earplugs you left in a corner.

- Tall enough, at least at one end, so that you can sit up straight without touching the ceiling.

- Long enough so sleeping bags don't touch the wall at either end. A sleeping bag tends to get wet where it touches, because condensation inside doesn't escape readily at such spots.

- Wide enough for the number of intended sleepers. The sides of the sleeping bag(s) should not touch the walls of the tent. Two-person models are tight for two and comfortable for one. Tents sold as three-person tents make good two-person tents.

- The fly must not leak! The coated fabric must be completely impermeable and stay that way for a long time, despite wear from rubbing against the tent poles. All seams in the fly should be factory-taped for waterproofness. In any event, it's wise to carry a small sponge to sop up any leaks that may occur.

Eight-legged invasion

Seldom do we find ourselves outwitted by arthropods, but that's what happened to me once at a favourite backcountry campground in Jasper National Park. I pitched the tent, spread out my sleeping bag in it, zipped the netting shut—not many mosquitoes around, but even one in the tent is an annoyance—and went to make supper.

Later, when I crawled into the tent for the night, I noticed that something else had crawled in with me: a small wolf spider. Wolf spiders are venomous and have attitude, so I put on a glove and tossed it out. Hmmm . . . might there be others in the tent? Yup. I found three more of the same, one of them in my sleeping bag. How the heck did they all get in? The netting had been closed. Oh, well; out the door with them. That was that. I drifted off to sleep.

I awoke at midnight. There was just enough light to see something moving on the netting by my head. I switched on my headlamp and saw several more wolf spiders on the mesh, two of them inside. How could that be?

I checked all the netting for holes but found none. I checked the corner of the door, where two zippers came together. There was just the smallest of gaps—but here was another spider, wiggling through it.

This was giving me the creeps. How did these tiny-brained critters know exactly where to enter my tent? And why were they doing so?

I pulled the zippers tightly together, then systematically went through everything in the tent: clothes, sleeping bag, sleeping pad, empty stuff sacks, etc., etc. I found yet more spiders, a couple of them squashed under the pad. I caught all the live ones and removed them, unzipping and re-zipping the door as quickly as possible each time. Even so, I had to flick a couple of would-be intruders away from the opening. Ye gods!

Eventually I was satisfied that there were no more spiders in my tent. I put a piece of tape over the place where the zippers met and ignored my bladder all night. No way was I opening the door again.

Next morning, the first thing I heard was one camper asking another, "Hey, did you find a bunch of spiders in your tent?"

Clearly, some kind of arachnid shindig had occurred that evening, and our campsite just happened to lie in the middle of it. We packed up and moved on. When we unpacked the following evening, we all discovered yet more spiders in our belongings.

Tents with good design features

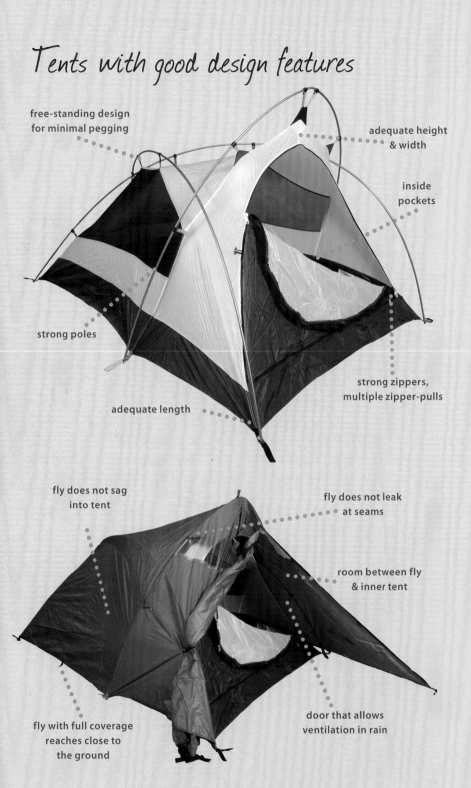

free-standing design
for minimal pegging

adequate height
& width

inside
pockets

strong poles

strong zippers,
multiple zipper-pulls

adequate length

fly does not sag
into tent

fly does not leak
at seams

room between fly
& inner tent

fly with full coverage
reaches close to
the ground

door that allows
ventilation in rain

- The fly should cover the entire tent, right to the ground. Otherwise rain will splash up on the interior tent walls and wet them through. The lower 20–30 centimetres of the interior walls should be made of waterproof material anyway.

- The fly shouldn't touch the inner tent, or condensation under the fly will leak through the inner tent ceiling and walls. A wet fly loosens and droops inward. The more room between the fly and the inner tent, the better.

- No flat places on the fly where water will pool and eventually begin to leak through a seam, or where interior condensation will gather and drip.

- The fly colour should be tan, for cheery interior lighting.

- The poles should be strong, made of a well-tested aluminum alloy such as 7001 T-6, or made of carbon fibre, with pole-joint ferules inside the poles instead of sleeves outside the poles. Outside sleeves generally indicate inferior quality. Poles should be joined by elastic cord and they should snap together smoothly. It makes for better packing if the sections are short enough to fit crosswise

The knife-thrower

Many years ago I was guiding a large group of junior-high-school students—the hormonally challenged—in the mountains west of Calgary. A kafuffle erupted one morning and I went over to investigate. There was a hole in the side of one of the tents and a teacher standing there with a large knife in his hand. Yikes!

Turns out the knife belonged to one of the kids. He'd been throwing it around, trying to make it stick in this and that, and it had caromed off something into this particular tent, in which another kid was still sleeping. (Here's your wake-up call! Thunk!)

That evening the group convened after supper. The knife-thrower was summoned forward. For his action, he was presented with a small wooden bird figure, painted yellow. It had been carved that day, especially for the occasion. Henceforth, on all such camps held by this school, the "Golden Turkey" awaited anyone demonstrating sufficient stupidity.

in your pack, within the tent's stuff sack, instead of separately down the side.

- A door on each side instead of just at the front. Side doors allow each person to enter and exit without having to crawl over another person.

- Door that can be kept open for ventilation in the rain without water getting into the tent.

- Large panels of bug netting in the tent sides, door(s) and in the closed end, so that air flows freely through with the door(s) closed.

- Netting should be effective against no-see-ums as well as mosquitoes.

- You can enter and exit in the rain without having to brush against wet fabric.

- Zippers should be strong and long-lasting. Tents are discarded mainly because of failed zippers.

- Zippers should close snugly at the ends, leaving no gaps through which bugs can enter.

Ben Gadd

Tarp bivouac, okay when the bugs are few and the rain comes without much wind

- Three different zipper-pulls in a door, so that it can be opened from top, bottom, or partway along. If one pull fails, it can be left shut and another can be used to work the zipper.

- Floor with as few seams as possible, and these should be factory-sealed.

- Inside pockets, for holding small items at night.

- Interior loops in the front and back, for hanging flashlights or stringing a line. No loop in the centre, as this can funnel drips into the interior.

- Orange or white guy lines, which are plainly visible when you're walking past the tent. Too many tents are sold with dark-coloured guy lines, which are difficult to see at any time of day or night. People stumble over them. But they're easily replaced with brightly coloured cord. I also put little flags of white grocery-bag plastic on my guy lines.

- Decent stakes. Nix on the cheap plastic ones; they're difficult to drive. The better stakes are of strong aluminum alloy, square or round in cross section, about 15–20 centimetres long, with a hook at the top to hold the tent-loop or line securely. In normal ground these stakes insert easily by just pushing them in with hand pressure. In hard or rocky ground they can be wiggled about and/or tapped in with a rock. There's no need to carry a hammer.

- Repair sleeve. The better tents come with a short length of aluminum tubing in the pole bag. The buyer may wonder what this is for and may be tempted to throw it out. Don't. Keep it with you to field-fix a broken pole. Slip the broken ends into the tube and secure them in place with duct tape.

Is there a tent out there with all these desirable features? Of course not. But there is endless variation in design, and some models come close. Take your time when shopping. Hit all the stores; check out mail order.

Tent-floor shapes can be rectangular, trapezoidal, hexagonal, octagonal or asymmetrical. Profiles can be prism-like, culvert-like, domed or squared-off. You can get single-walled tents made of Gore-Tex or some other waterproof/breathable material to save the weight of a fly. You can get very light tents in which the body is made entirely of mosquito netting. You can get tents that set up by clipping the body of the tent under the fly after the poles have been set up, which is great for trips on which you're likely to be setting up and dismantling camp in the rain. You can get tents in which the body and fly are sewn together, further speeding set-up time. You can get a tent that folds up with the poles in place. You release it and it pops up, ready for stakes. You can get tents with clear plastic windows in the fly, tents with retractable flies (if only this were true of the insect variety), tents with little hammocks that hold gear overhead . . .

And there are caveats on all these. The single-walled tent? It works well enough to be sold by all major Canadian suppliers, but expect more interior condensation than with the tent-and-fly combination, which is tried and true. The mosquito-netting tent? Wind-driven rain will spray in under the fly, as will snow in fall or spring. The tent that pops up on its own? Heavy. The tent with the window in the fly? Delightful for now, but how long will it be before the plastic loses its flexibility and cracks? The overhead gear hammock? Great for ensuring that your gear stays damp. Etc.

What size tent do you need, and what should it weigh? These two things go together, of course. Generally speaking, a single person of average build will be comfortable in a tent that's at least 210 centimetres long, 130 centimetres wide and 100 centimetres high. Two people can fit into a tent this size, but it will be tight, and there will be little room for gear. Such a tent weighs about 2.5 kilograms.

For two people to sleep really comfortably, with some room for gear, they'll need a floor size of about 175 centimetres by 230 centimetres, with at least a metre of headroom available while both are sitting up. The weight will be about 3.0 kilograms.

You can save nearly half a kilogram by going with a non-freestanding, staked-out tent that's narrower and lower. However, these designs are more trouble to set up, they're generally smaller inside, and ventilation isn't as good. To me, the extra roominess, set-up convenience and better airflow are worth the extra weight.

If you're sleeping alone you could go with a really tiny tent. Such minimal shelter might measure less than a metre wide and only 70 centimetres high. You'll be cramped, but the weight might be only 1.5 kilograms or even less and you'll be warmer on a cool night.

So there's your range in size and weight for one-person and two-person tents, which are the most commonly used types. The cost? For a decently made tent, you can expect to pay from $200 to over $500. Discount-store cheapies are to be avoided, of course.

Larger tents have some real advantages for groups of three to six. For example, each person sharing a 6-kilogram, four-person model carries one part of the tent (one person carries the main tent, one person carries the fly and one person carries the poles) so the weight *per person* averages only 2 kilograms. The fourth person doesn't get off scot-free; he or she carries the stove and fuel.

The larger the tent, the more headroom. I have one in which a short person can stand up. There may be enough floor space to bring all the packs inside. A big tent makes a jolly kip in bad weather, with everyone sitting around in the warmth generated by all those bodies, supplemented by a candle lantern hanging in the centre and illuminating the card games. (Don't use a cooking stove because of the fumes.) The main disadvantages are that individual privacy is reduced, and in any group of four there always seems to be someone who snores. If the tent fails somehow or is lost, you have no backup.

Taking care of your tent

Should you fold your tent or stuff it? Neither approach is particularly terrific. If you fold a tent in the same places all the time, permanent creases result. These become points of weakness and spots for eventual loss of waterproof coatings. If you stuff your tent into its sack, you have to do so carefully to avoid shoving a finger through the mosquito netting or nicking the waterproof coating with a ragged thumbnail.

My choice is to stuff. But I don't pack my tent into the sack it came in. These sacks are always too small, perhaps to convince you to buy the tent because it looks so petite in its bag. Set the original stuff sack aside—you can use it for something smaller—and buy a bigger sack. You'll appreciate this the first time you have to pack your tent on a morning when the fabric is wet and cold. You'll be able to stuff it easily, while the other campers will be howling about their cold fingers and their blankety-blank impossible-to-stuff tents. A larger stuff sack takes no more room in your pack; the tent squashes down.

Don't worry about packing up a wet tent. Go right ahead. It won't mildew unless you leave it soggy in its sack for several days. Between camps, just shake most of the water off the fly and pack it. Get someone to help you shake the fly vertically rather than horizontally, so the water falls away from the fly instead of back onto it. Then, as soon as you get to your next camp, by which time the weather will have turned warm and sunny—right?—you can set your tent up to dry. However, in the absurdly unlikely situation that you'll have to camp in the rain, your tent is conveniently *already wet!*

When you return home from any trip, you should take your tent out of its stuff sack, shake it out and dry it, preferably on a clothesline outdoors. Tents get dirty, especially their floors. Brush any dirt off the tent floor and turn the tent inside out.

To clean your tent, lay it out on the grass or on a floor that can be wetted safely. Apply a mild water/detergent mix to any soiled, stained spots. Let them soak for a few minutes, then gently wipe them clean with a washcloth. Rinse. Turn the tent right side out and do the other side. Hang it up for 24 hours to dry thoroughly before you pack it away. You might want to wash the fly, too. Don't dry-clean your tent—the solvents used might damage waterproof coatings—and never put it in a washing machine, front-loading or top-loading, from which it may emerge in pieces. The machine may be damaged, too.

Tent seams need to be sealed, and they should be resealed occasionally. If the seams haven't been factory-sealed with waterproof tape, you should seal them manually as soon as you buy the tent, while the fabric is still very clean. You can buy liquid seam sealer sold especially for this purpose. It's flexible when dry. The seams to seal are all the ones on the fly, plus any on the tent floor. If these seams have been taped, check to see whether the tape is coming off anywhere. If so, stick it back down with seam sealer.

Tent fabrics are wonderfully thin and strong these days. They don't puncture or tear easily. But if you do get a hole in your tent—perhaps your pocket-knife winds up accidentally slashing the fabric, which happens surprisingly often—then do like any sensible Canadian would. Stick a small piece of duct tape on the gap. Put a matching piece on the inside. Do you have to sew that up properly when you get home? Maybe not. Duct tape is great stuff and sticks for a long time.

Tent zippers may be tough, but eventually they fail. The main door-opening zipper works fine at first, but one day it won't close properly. The track behind it gaps open. You tug the zipper backward, hard, and you get it working again. But soon you have to hold the two edges together as you ease the zipper-pull along, and then that doesn't work, either. So much for the "self-repairing" promise of most of the zippers in use today.

Replacing the pull usually gives a failing zipper a little more life, because wear on the pull is part of the problem, but getting the old pull off and the new one on is a job best done by the store the tent came from. Anyway, even with a new pull, a worn zipper is soon going to become troublesome again. You might as well take the tent to a seamster who can replace the zippers completely. It doesn't cost much. Tip: always replace a worn-out zipper with a heavier one.

Lubrication can extend the life of a zipper. Rub the teeth with a candle rich in beeswax. In the field, lip balm or soap will work. YKK, which makes a lot of the zippers used in tents and garments, recommends a spray lubricant called FastenerMate.

Tarps

For as little as $35 and 800 additional grams in your pack you can bring a 2-metre by 3-metre rectangle of coated tent-fly material that can be strung between two trees, no poles required. These aren't hardware-store plastic tarps. These are real backpacker's tarps, available from specialty outdoor-equipment stores. Silicone-coated versions are a lot lighter—under 500 grams—but are nearly twice the price. A backpacker's tarp may be all you need in mild, bug-free weather without much rain or wind. Such a tarp is made of tent-fly material (or in the case of the Siltarp, even lighter stuff) that will repel a light shower and keep the dew off your sleeping bag. Total weight for shelter: half a kilogram. Total cost: $50–$100. Inviting! But wait, for an even better deal you could go with a large "space blanket" of reflective plastic, weighted down at the edges with rocks—total layout 10 bucks.

However, conditions pleasant enough for tarp-camping are so rare in our country, especially in the mountains and along the coasts, that relying on a tarp for shelter is risky indeed. I've tried it a few times and haven't been very lucky. You'd be better to give this a go while on a snowbird trip to the southern Arizona desert in January.

Still, I always carry a light backpacker's tarp in addition to my tent, even when I'm alone and hauling everything myself. That's because a tarp makes all the difference in the rain. Would you rather be cooped up in a little backpacking tent, trying to cook under the front vestibule, or sitting under an airy tarp with your friends, making supper in relative comfort?

For groups, I pack a large version, 3 metres by 4 metres, which costs $55 and weighs 1.2 kilograms. The weight includes the weight of cords

A tarp slung over a picnic table makes all the difference in rainy weather

tied to the corners, plus the weight of the line used to sling the tarp between trees.

To prepare your tarp, permanently tie about 4 metres of 3 mm braided cord onto each corner and onto the centres of the long sides. For slinging the tarp, you'll need about 12 metres of the same cord to tie between two trees. I carry my slinging cord in two 6-metre hanks. It tangles less that way, and oftentimes one length alone will reach. (See page 213 for knots to use.)

Here's another reason to carry a tarp: you can always pull it out of your pack quickly and wrap up in it if the rain and the wind get to be too much. Three or four people huddling under a tarp together makes for an amusing kip as the storm blows through.

Bivouac bags and hammocks

You may also want to consider the ultimate in lightweight camping: a bivouac bag or a hammock.

A waterproof, bug-proof **bivouac bag** provides greater protection when tarp-camping, but it adds weight and cost. You might as well just use a light tent. Bivouac bags are really for mountaineers intending to spend a night out with the absolute minimum of comfort.

What about using a **hammock** instead of sleeping on the ground at all? A hammock is very light—albeit only for solo sleeping—and it solves the problem of finding a flat spot when the ground is sloping or hopelessly uneven. MEC sells a couple of hammock models. They come complete with mosquito netting and a fly for rain protection. At $200 and less than a kilo in your pack, such a hammock is the equivalent of a tent and a sleeping pad.

Well, not really. Even though the bed of a hammock is off the ground, the fabric is pulled very tight and the sleeping surface is surprisingly hard. You also still need an insulating pad between your body and the chilly night air.

There are other problems with hammocks, too. Sufficiently rigid end support is essential, or your hammock will let you down badly. You have to find two trees the right distance apart, and given the weight of the average sleeper they have to be sizable ones. Wrapping ropes tightly around the trunks is hard on them. Sometimes boulders or lashed-together logs can be substituted. Even when your hammock has been strung tight as a bow string, you may find yourself having to get up at midnight to reef on the ropes again when cord-stretch and fabric-stretch have you bottoming out on the rocks.

The mosquito netting will keep the bugs out, but weather protection is poor in the hammock models I have looked at. The tree branches overhead help, but the fly doesn't extend far enough off the ends or the sides, so a breezy shower will still get in.

Entering or exiting a hammock is done from the side or underneath, which is trickier than crawling into a tent. In the rain you may not be able to manage it without dumping some water from the fly onto yourself. Getting into your sleeping bag while swinging to and fro—be sure your hammock has anti-sway lines on the sides— is a truly gymnastic feat. And did you ever try undressing in one of these things? There's also little room in a hammock for anything else but you. Your pack can go underneath, though, near one end or the other.

Perhaps the biggest drawback for hammocks is the unavoidable curve in them. They're comfortable

Bivouac bag

Mummy bag on top of a rectangular bag to show difference in width

mainly (some people would say only) when you're sleeping on your back. Yet many people sleep on their sides. After a night or two your body adjusts, but the bottom line with hammocks is that they're an acquired taste. Try before you buy.

Sleeping bag

On warm evenings at low elevations in southern Canada the overnight lows are seldom below 10°C. You can get by with a blanket safety-pinned down one side, cheap and very light. But for use in the Rockies, or on the coasts or up north or anywhere that's seen a cold front go through that afternoon, you're going to want a sleeping bag that will keep you warm to 5°C, and in some areas down to freezing. For higher elevations and early or late in the season, revise that figure downward to –5°C.

A **mummy-shaped bag** gives you the best warmth per kilogram, and it packs small. Some people feel confined in a mummy bag, though, and for them, a **rectangular bag** is more comfortable. A rectangular bag also has the advantage of unzipping on two sides to form a thick, comfy blanket, nice for couples using a pair of rectangulars zipped together. Also, you and your companions can spread out a rectangular bag on the floor of a large tent and sit on it.

Your next choice is between **down fill** and **synthetic fill.** This depends on how much money you want to spend and where you plan to do your trekking. Goose down is the lightest, most compressible fill available, and it's warm as toast. If treated well, it will retain its loft almost indefinitely. When the fabric in your goose-down sleeping bag has worn out, you can put that down into a new bag. Duck down is almost as good for a lot less money. But either kind of down loses loft and warmth when it gets damp. After three rainy nights in a row, you may be shivering. And a down bag takes a long time to dry out in humid conditions.

In the Rockies, the air is usually dry, and three rainy nights in a row are rare. Go with down if you can afford it for this area. On the West Coast Trail or in other drippy places, synthetic fill is preferred by many. It keeps its loft better when damp, it dries more quickly, and it's cheap. But do be aware that synthetic fill loses its loft steadily. After a few summers you'll notice that the bag is thinner.

Neither down nor synthetic insulation is warm when it's really wet. For this reason you may wish to consider a bag with a **waterproof/breathable outer shell.** It will be heavier, more expensive and more likely to give you condensation under the surface, but if the tent leaks you'll stay dry.

Cheaper sleeping bags are just quilted together, which makes for cold spots at the stitch lines. The better down bags have a **slanted box construction,** meaning that the down is placed in tube-like overlapping compartments between the inner and outer fabric. This allows the down to expand to its maximum, with no cold spots. More fill has been placed in the part of the bag lying over the sleeper than beneath the sleeper, because a sleeping pad provides far better insulation than a layer of down squashed practically flat by the sleeper's weight. Blocks are sewn along the sides of the bag to prevent down from shifting from the upper compartments to the lower compartments—or in some designs the blocks are intentionally omitted to allow the user to redistribute the down above and below. In either case the surface of the bag is smooth. With synthetic insulation, overlapping the quilted layers of batting eliminates cold spots.

A good goose-down mummy bag will have a **down-fill-power** figure of 400–500 cubic centimetres of fill per gram of down (750–850 cubic inches per ounce). Such a bag should give you sufficient insulation for nights down to freezing at well under a kilogram in weight, but at a price of $200 and up. The equivalent in duck down will weigh about 1.3 kilograms and cost only $120. Equivalent-warmth synthetic-fill bags weigh about 2 kilograms but cost as little as $80.

Lightest combination: mummy bag and foam sleeping bag

Here are some things to look for in a good sleeping bag for summer backpacking:

- Sufficient length.If you're near the upper end of the height range for a particular bag, buy the next size up. You don't want your feet pressing against the end: they'll get cold. Get into the sleeping bag, zip it up, pull the hood tight around your face (or if it's a rectangular bag, slip inside until your head's covered) and point your feet. If you can feel the end, the bag's too short. What if the next size up is longer than you need? Try a different model. It might fit you better. Or, if you really like this particular design, buy it anyway. The additional length won't add much weight.

- A beefy zipper that works smoothly and doesn't snag the material beside it. This is very important. Try the zipper over and over. If it's at all cranky, don't buy the bag. The action will get worse, and soon you'll be wrestling with the thing every time you enter or exit the bag.

- A full-length zipper, so you can open the bag wide on hot nights. If you're right-handed, you'll want the zipper on the left side, because it will be easier to open by reaching across. Vice versa for lefties. For couples, identical bags with full-length zippers on opposite sides will allow you to zip your bags together. In addition to the snuggle factor, zip-togethers add a lot of warmth. Try zipping together in the store first, though, to make sure that it works.

- An overlap along the opening side to provide insulation between you and the zipper.

How can you keep your sleeping bag dry? In Canada, with our cool nights that nearly always drop below the dew point, you can't. Unless the air is unusually dry and the night is very warm, by morning the exterior surface of your bag will be damp from perspiration and your own breath. There will be moisture inside, too, concentrated just below the surface.

How can you dry your bag when it gets damp? The quickest way is to drape it over dry shrubbery in direct sunlight. Do this while you're close by, to ensure that the bag doesn't blow away or get soaked by a sudden shower. Another way is just to leave the bag spread out in your tent for a couple of hours in the warmth of the afternoon, a good reason to pitch camp by 3:00 or 4:00 p.m., which is good practice anyway (see page 182). Don't try to dry your sleeping bag by a fire; this almost always results in ember-melted holes in the fabric—and sometimes catastrophe.

Should sleeping bags be stuffed or rolled? It's entirely up to you. Rolling is easier on the lightweight interior baffles, but it's difficult to roll a sleeping bag tightly enough to fit into its sack and very awkward to slip it in. For this reason, all good bags are sturdy enough to be stuffed.

How often should you wash your sleeping bag, and how should you do it? Wash it whenever you feel that it's getting smelly and/or it's beginning to show grime, which appears first around the head end. Most people can get at least 20 nights before it's clearly time to wash the bag. If the fill is goose down or duck down, wash it with special soap formulated for this purpose and follow the instructions on the bottle. *Don't dry-clean a down bag.* This will remove the natural oils on the down filaments, damaging them. If the bag is filled with synthetic insulation, follow the instructions on the tag. You can machine-wash a down bag in a front-loading washing machine (top-loaders are too rough on them), but I wash my down sleeping bag by hand.

First I soak it for several hours in soapy water in the bathtub, starting with warm water, not hot water. It will become cold, but that's okay; the soap will still work. During the soak, I agitate the bag by walking around on it a few times in bare feet. If the bag is really dirty, the water turns grey. I don't pick up the bag and knead it while it's wet and heavy. You need to be careful in handling a wet bag, because the heavy insulation may tear

Ben Gadd

Rinsing a sleeping bag in the bathtub. Okay to roll it to extract water; don't lift it wet and unrolled.

the interior baffles. The same thing applies to handling a bag that has become wet on a trip.

After the soak, it's important to rinse the bag well and to wring it out carefully. Leaving the bag lying in the tub, I drain the soapy water. I squeeze the soapy water out of the bag by rolling it up in the shallow end, squeezing it well with my hands to extract as much water as I can. Then I unroll it until it's again flat in the tub. I refill the tub with warm rinse water and gently pat the bag around in the clean water until it turns grey again. I drain the rinse water, roll up the bag as before to squeeze the water out, and repeat the rinsing until the runoff is clear.

After the last rinse, I wring the bag out well by rolling it tightly. When I've removed as much water as I can, the bag is safe to pick up whole and carry to a dryer. I tumble it slowly on low heat. When it feels nearly dry, I put a couple of clean tennis balls in with it to loosen any down that might still be in clumps. After the bag comes out, fluffy and smelling great, I let it air for a day or two to dry it really thoroughly before storing it.

On a backpacking trip your sleeping bag is unlikely to become as wet as when it's being washed, but you still need to handle it with care. Roll it up on a picnic table or a flat rock surface or on a tarp spread over the ground. Slip the bag into its sack rolled, not stuffed, and dry it well at the first opportunity.

How should you store your sleeping bag between uses? Don't leave it stuffed. This is hard on down and very hard on synthetic fill. The better models of sleeping bags come with two sacks: a small stuff sack to use on the trail and a much larger one to use for storing the bag loosely. Keep the bag in a dry place, such as in a closet on the main floor or, better still, upstairs—not in the basement or garage, where it could be ruined by mildew.

Sleeping pad

A sleeping pad does more than just keep your hips and shoulders off the rocks. Canadian soils are cool year-round, so you need some insulation under your body at night or you'll be shivering, regardless of how much loft your sleeping bag has. The following qualities make for a good sleeping pad:

- The insulating/padding material should compact progressively, getting firmer as weight is put on it but never reaching the same density as hard ground.
- It should insulate well, meaning that circulation of air between the sleeper and the ground is prevented.
- It should not soak up moisture
- It should take up little space in the pack
- It should be light in weight.
- It should be durable.

Two kinds of sleeping pads are popular: (1) thin, non-inflating pads of dense closed-cell plastic foam and (2) thicker, inflating pads of less-dense foam (and also down or synthetic insulation in some models) within an airtight cover.

The non-inflating foam pads are inexpensive and very light in weight—$10 to $40, 200 to 600 grams—but they don't pad the user as well as inflating pads do, they offer less insulation, and they don't pack down as small.

Inflating pads are heavier and far more expensive (600 grams to 1.7 kilograms, $60 to $150), and they're susceptible to puncture. But they're *much* more comfortable. You open the valve of an inflating pad and air rushes in as the foam expands within it. After a few minutes the pad has mostly inflated by itself. You can top it up with a few puffs. When you're ready to pack up, you open the valve and roll the pad up tightly, squeezing the air out, then you close the valve to keep it out.

The older I get the more I appreciate a cushy sleeping pad. These days I use a thick self-inflator, very cushy, that weighs 800 grams. It cost me a hundred bucks and was worth every penny. It's 5 centimetres thick, 51 centimetres wide and 119 centimetres long, the "three-quarter length,"

Foam sleeping pads and inflatable pad

which is fine for summer camping. (When camping on snow, a full-length pad is necessary.) To have something under my feet, I empty my pack—there's not much left in it anyway when it's bedtime—and place it at the end of the tent. Like many internal-frame packs, it has a built-in foam back-pad that works well as a foot-pad.

In my 20s and 30s I could sleep comfortably on a centimetre of closed-cell foam, and for young backpackers the non-inflating pad is still the lightest, cheapest way to go. A bottom-of-the-line cheapie blue-foam pad may get you by. It can also take a lot of abuse. Such pads are great for lounging around outdoors: no worries about getting punctures, dirt and mud wipe off easily, and if the surface gets wet it dries quickly.

It's not a good idea to put an *inflatable* pad down on the ground or up against a boulder you're using for a backrest, because it may get punctured. Use your pack, not your pad, for a backrest.

Lots of backpackers carry their foamies rolled under the top lids of their packs or on the sides. That's fine if you're carrying a non-inflatable, *but be sure to keep an inflatable pad in its sack,* which protects it from getting snagged on broken tree branches and other sharp stuff as you walk. Better yet, fold the pad into a shape that will fit inside your backpack. Not much in there ought to poke a hole in it, but keep it in its sack nonetheless.

Before unrolling an inflatable pad for use, check the floor of your tent for thorns, juniper needles and other pad-pokers.

What happens when your inflatable pad springs a leak? You wake up feeling a bit deflated, so to speak, a bit let down. Here's an instant repair that's worked for me: stick a blister pad over the hole, or a piece of duct tape. Unless it's a large tear, meaning longer than 2 centimetres, this should at least slow down the leak enough to get you through the night. If you're out with a group, you'd be wise to ensure that at least one of you has brought the proper patch kit that comes with each pad.

To locate a slow leak, go down by the creek or the lake. Inflate the pad until it's taut. When you hold the pad underwater you should be able to see where the bubbles are coming from. Mark the hole with a pen and let the fabric dry before applying a patch.

How should you store a sleeping pad between trips? Non-inflatables can be left rolled up. The valve on an inflating pad should be opened, and the pad should be stored self-inflated. This takes up more space in the closet, but it prevents the interior foam insulation from compacting and losing its insulating value.

What if you're using a hammock instead of sleeping on the ground? You'll still need an insulating pad under you, because on a cool night the air under a hammock is just as cold as the ground.

What about sitting pads? A sitting pad is a piece of closed-cell foam about 30 centimetres wide, 50 centimetres long and 1 centimetre thick. It weighs very little. You round the edges and slip it down the inside of your pack, next to your back if the pack is unpadded, thereby securing some protection from angular objects. Or, if the pack is already padded, you carry it slipped down the opposite side, the side away from your back. This helps to protect the exterior of the pack from abrasion. Pack fabric is rather easily damaged when something hard inside the pack contacts something hard outside the pack.

A sitting pad is terrific under your bum in camp, especially in the evening. It's also great under your feet in the tent at night, on top of an empty, flattened pack. If you're using your backpack as a day pack, you might want to carry that sitting pad along for having lunch among the rocks. If someone is injured and lying on the ground, a couple of sitting pads provide comfort and insulation.

Stove and cookset

Rather than build a campfire to cook a meal, most backpackers use a small, lightweight stove. Stoves add weight to your pack, but not a lot: under half a kilogram, complete with enough fuel for a weekend trip. They're quicker, cleaner, safer and less messy than fires—and legal to use when open fires are prohibited.

Perhaps the simplest backpacking stove is a lightweight folding box in which you place a small can of Sterno (jellied alcohol). You pry off the lid of the can and light the fuel. A Sterno stove is a no-brainer piece of equipment, but the can is heavy, heating is slow, and you can't regulate the flame very well.

The Esbit Pocket Stove is similar, but it uses solid-fuel tablets, which are also alcohol-based. Esbit is lighter to pack for a short trip than Sterno because you need carry only the tablets required rather than a full can, but this fuel can be heavy if you need a lot of it. Popular in Europe, Esbit tabs can be difficult to obtain in Canada.

How about a wood-burning backpacking stove? You put twigs in it and light a tiny fire. The F.H. Enterprises Bushbuddy, which is a Canadian design by Franz Handel of Iskut, BC, is one brand (www.trekstov.com). The Zip Ztove Sierra comes complete with a tiny fan (www.zzstove.com). The Kelly Kettle company's venerable Irish Volcano Kettle is a time-tested design that boils water very quickly in its integral water-jacket (www.kellykettle.com).

The weight of the heavier wood-burning stoves is about on par with that of petroleum-burning or alcohol-burning stoves with enough fuel for a weekend's use. So why do so few people use them? There are several reasons: wood-burning stoves are sooty, the twigs must be dry to burn properly, heat regulation is difficult, and they're generally not allowed during fire bans. Wood-burning stoves don't require petroleum and are thus somewhat more environmentally friendly, if you discount the need to burn vegetation, usually gathered from around the campsite.

LPG stove, best for summer backpacking

For many years the more popular backpacking stoves have been liquid-fuelled. In Canada the liquid fuel of choice is **naphtha**, more commonly referred to as "white gas." **Alcohol** is an alternative fuel, and unlike white gas it's a renewable resource. But alcohol stoves such as the Trangia models aren't as easy to regulate. The proper kind of alcohol (denatured alcohol, which is a mix of ethanol and methanol that's also called "methyl" alcohol, and isopropyl alcohol, which is also called "rubbing" alcohol) is not as cheap or readily available in Canada as naphtha. White gas burns considerably hotter than alcohol, so it heats faster, and it's readily available at gas stations, grocery stores, hardware stores, sporting goods stores and many department stores.

Some petroleum-based stoves burn a variety of fuels—kerosene, diesel fuel, regular gasoline, even alcohol—but these models all have their downsides and are really intended for use in countries where white gas is not easy to find. If you're planning to do your camping mainly in Canada, and you want to use liquid fuel, you might as well buy a white-gas stove.

However, you might not want to use liquid fuel. That's because there has been a major improvement in stoves fuelled by **liquid petroleum gas** (LPG). Older versions of LPG stoves burned butane—the same fuel that cigarette lighters use—which was less

How much fuel do you need?

For LPG, in summer you'll probably go through 40–50 grams per person per day (if you're simply making enough hot water to rehydrate freeze-dried food and instant noodles, make tea, that sort of thing, no simmering or frying) and perhaps twice as much per day if you're preparing food for longer periods, making more hot drinks, heating washwater, sponge-bathing in the tent and so on.

For white gas, the minimum figure is about 100 mL per person per day. For alcohol cookers, which use a lot more fuel, bring twice that. Again, double these figures if you're planning to run your stove a lot.

efficient than white gas, especially at cool temperatures. The stoves themselves were simple, quiet and cheap, but the butane cartridges were heavy and expensive compared to naphtha—okay for a weekend trip but not very practical for a week in the wilds. The stoves are still simple and cheap, and the cartridges are still expensive (at time of writing, a 225-gram cartridge of LPG costs $6 at MEC), but the rest has changed. The fuel is now a propane-isobutane mix, which burns even hotter than white gas, so heating is very rapid and fewer cartridges are required. LPG is good down to about –10°C, which is fine for summer use. LPG stoves don't require the priming that liquid-fuelled stoves need. They start instantly, are more reliable and can be regulated precisely.

For all these reasons, I have switched to LPG. My complex and lovely MSR Dragonfly liquid-fuelled stove comes out only for winter trips, when the temperatures are too low for LPG. In summer I use a tiny little MSR stove called, rather fittingly, the Pocket Rocket that packs into my cup and weighs 440 grams, complete with one full cartridge. It boils a litre of water in three minutes, even faster than the Dragonfly, which I always thought of as a portable inferno. Properly rationed, a single LPG canister can last me a week. The equivalent liquid-fuel rig weighs well over a kilogram, plus the spare-parts kit you need for a white-gas stove when it gets cranky.

It's difficult to go wrong with any of the second-generation LPG stoves currently sold for backpacking, and they're only going to get better. They're all easy to use and reliable. The canisters aren't refillable (yet), but the steel in them can be recycled. Just bear in mind the following rules and tips about LPG stoves:

- Don't carry the canister attached to the stove. The canister screws on and off, and it has its own check valve so it won't leak when the stove isn't attached to it. However, if the stove's valve opens while the canister is attached, you'll lose a lot of fuel in a hurry. This can mess up a trip. If LPG is leaking inside your pack, and someone beside you lights a cigarette, a lot more than your trip can be messed up. So disassemble your stove before putting it into your pack.

- A wind-screen will save considerable fuel, but it can cause overheating of the canister. Any gas cools as it expands. As the LPG flows up from the pressurized liquid in the canister and vaporizes, it cools the canister, helping to prevent heat build-up. But in one-piece canister/burner designs, as most LPG stoves are, the hot burner head is close to the canister. Air-cooling is required as well. A tightly fitted wind-screen can allow the canister to overheat and explode. An exploding gas canister is a bomb. It can kill you.

- Be sure that there's plenty of airflow around the canister. Alternatively, consider a two-piece design in which the canister is connected to the burner by a hose. A bit heavier, but safer and more stable, since the stove has its own base, which sits close to the surface on which it's placed.

Once a canister has been used, it's difficult to estimate how much fuel is left. A canister has to be less than half full before it feels significantly lighter in the hand. The Brunton company makes disposable gauges for canisters ($5 for a packet of six, non-reusable stick-on strips), but most people end up bringing fresh canisters along on each trip to be sure they have enough fuel. This means that the partly used canisters accumulate at home. What to do? I use these for car camping, melting wax for boot waterproofing and such, where knowing the amount of LPG left doesn't matter much. To ensure that I don't accidentally carry a half-full canister with me instead of a full one, I mark any partly full canister before putting it away.

Single pot, pot lifter, mug and spoon—all you really need

Okay, you've got your stove and sufficient fuel for a weekend backpacking trip. So far the weight is only about half a kilogram. Good. Then you add a three-pot stainless-steel cookset, some steel utensils, a metal plate, bowl and cup, and now your kitchen weighs, uh, 3.5 kilograms. Urk.

Fortunately, this is what titanium pots and instant food were invented for. If you're willing to forego the pleasures of doing *real* cooking in the backcountry, with fresh vegetables on the cutting board and several pots bubbling away at the same time, then here's all the equipment you need: one pot, one plastic cup and one spoon. The pot is used only for boiling water. The boiling water goes into bags of freeze-dried food, cups of instant soup, cups of instant beans and rice, cups of hot chocolate and tea, that kind of thing. One titanium pot, capacity 1.5 litres, weight 150 grams, will do for two or three people. You never boil soup in it, which means you never have to wash it. You don't need a knife or fork or spatula because all your food is gloppy. (For crunch, I carry some fresh edible-pod peas to eat raw. See page 143.)

Such meals can be eaten from the cup, with no need for a plate or bowl. You can eat freeze-dried meals right from the bag with your 5-gram Lexan spoon. If you like to spice up your food, carry a few restaurant-type envelopes of salt and pepper instead of those cute miniature combination shakers. They're surprisingly heavy.

The total weight of my kitchen, including the stove, a week's worth of fuel, a 1.5-litre titanium pot, a pliers-style pot-lifter—better than the pot's tippy wire bale, which I've removed—and my large plastic mug, which holds the stove and itself nests into the pot, is 900 grams.

Still, there's the problem of *coffee*. You can make it from bags, like tea, but there are folks out there who just gotta have their 'spro in the wilderness. By golly, for $46 they can buy a one-shot espresso-maker at MEC that adds only 218 grams to the load. (See also page 150 for "magic beans.") A 200-gram combination coffee press and insulated mug can be had for only $14.50, and the mug can be used as your usual cup.

Coffee grounds and tea bags should be packed out rather than tossed down the pooper (attracts bears) or burned (see page 280 for reasons not to build campfires). For packing out freeze-dried food pouches, soup wrappers and so on, grocery-store plastic bags will do. They have handles that can be used to advantage (see the picture). Remember to keep your garbage away from bears and other wildlife.

For more on using stoves, cooking meals, cleaning up and so on, refer to pages 185–193.

Water filtration and disinfection

Sad to say, you can't drink the water straight from the creek in Canada's pristine wilderness. Time was, you could. But in the late 1970s we in the Rockies learned that **giardiasis**—popularly known as "beaver fever"—was becoming a problem and that we'd better boil any surface water we used in the backcountry.

A problem indeed. The little *Giardia lamblia* protozoan parasite was rife in the region, inducing epidemics of tummy upsets, cramps and diarrhea in town after town. After a couple of embarrassing outbreaks, first Banff then Jasper changed their water supplies from surface water to wells. Alas, it was too late for me. In 1980 I went into hospital

Ben Gadd

Keep your garbage bag handy during meal prep by hanging it under a table or from a branch one night with pain bad enough to be from appendicitis. The doctors obliged and removed my appendix. Turned out it was just giardiasis.

By the way, it's not fair to blame the beavers. This situation is largely our fault, not theirs. Yes, *Giardia* is spread in the feces of beavers and other water-dwelling mammals, but it's also spread by any mammal that carries it, because the cysts wash into streams and lakes from poop left on land. We backpackers, and especially our dogs, have carried the bug everywhere. Just about the time the mammals of any particular watershed are building up some immunity, we keep refreshing the local *Giardia* gene pool with new organisms from all over the world. Thus, *Giardia* is everywhere. There's no practical field test for it. You're taking a chance if you drink any surface water.

However, you may be able to handle *Giardia*. Your drinking water may have come from a surface source while you were small, exposing you to it in infancy. Your body may have learned to live with it. Perhaps you can drink the water and not suffer. Perhaps. However, other things are coming down the pipe, so to speak, and they'll probably be new to you: *Cryptosporidium*, *Campylobacter*, the nastier strains of *Escherichia coli*, hepatitis A . . . yow! Better not get sloppy. Better not quench your thirst without quashing the beasties in it.

There are several ways in which to ensure safe drinking water in the wild:

- Carry water you know to be safe. This is okay for an afternoon's outing, but you'll want at least 2 litres—more in warm weather—for a full-day hike, and that quantity gets heavy. Filtration or disinfection en route makes better sense, as long as there is water to be found.

- Drink only from springs, and only from those springs that aren't the downstream ends of cave passages that may have carried contaminated surface water from somewhere else. In regions underlain with limestone, this is something to consider carefully.

- Bring your drinking water to a boil, or, if you suspect bacterial contamination or hepatitis A, boil it for at least one minute. Bringing water to a rolling boil will kill most pathogens in it, but the virus that causes hepatitis-A liver disease does require 60 seconds of boiling to ensure deactivation.[2] Boiling for one minute is a tried-and-true method, effective to an elevation of 5,500 metres. Except for the summit area of Mt. Logan in the southwestern Yukon, all of Canada lies below this elevation. However, boiling uses a lot of fuel, imparts a metallic taste and takes time.

- Disinfect the water chemically with chlorine compounds that kill the organisms in it. You mix a few drops of two reagents together to form chlorine dioxide, then wait a half-hour or so before drinking. Sounds simple, but if the treated water is cold, which is the case in most of Canada, it has to sit for up to seven hours before *Cryptosporidium* is killed. The taste is okay, and it's certainly much better than that imparted by those nasty old Halazone.[3] tablets of the past, which didn't kill *Cryptosporidium* anyway. Chemical disinfection is the most expensive water-treatment method over the long haul (up to a dollar a litre), but the cost per kit is low—$15 to $25—and the weight is under 100 grams. The kits have a shelf life, and you're drinking chemically treated water. Still, it makes sense to carry a disinfecting agent with you always, even on short hikes, to use personally if you should unexpectedly run out of drinking water or as backup for whatever method the group is using if that method fails.

- Disinfect the water with organism-killing oxidants that you make from rock salt and water in an electrical device. The MSR MIOX water purifier is the only readily available device that does this. It looks like a small flashlight, uses lithium batteries and weighs a bit over 200 grams in its kit. Developed for military use, it's touted to

---

2 Hepatitis A is common in third-world countries, which is where Canadian travellers usually catch it from drinking contaminated water, but it's seldom acquired here. Hepatitis A is not as serious as hepatitis B or C, but it's nasty enough.
3 Halazone is a chlorine-based mixture of monochloraminobenzoic and dichloraminobenzoic acids, both of which are halogens, while the iodine-based tablets sold by Coghlan's and others are tetraglycine hydroperiodide.

kill any bug you can think of, and quickly. This gadget takes a while to learn to operate correctly, but it's supplied with water-testing strips that helped me to get satisfactory results. Its main drawback is that it's expensive: $154 at time of writing.

- Sterilize the water with ultraviolet light. This is the latest method, and while expensive—about $150 for the device—it's also very simple: you dip a small, battery-operated ultraviolet lamp into a full 1-litre water bottle and stir with it for about 90 seconds, or until the unit indicates that it's finished. All pathogens, including viruses, are killed. The device imparts no taste to the water and it has no moving parts. It's light: only 230 grams, including four AA batteries, good for treating about 15 litres. If you're going to be using it for a week, you should bring an extra set of batteries, adding to the weight. Also, if the water is murky, you have to filter it before sterilizing it, which takes additional time.

- Use a pump filter, which requires no waiting period other than the time spent pumping. A pump filter screens out pathogens and adds nothing new to the water. The faster models produce about a litre a minute, cost under $100 and weigh about 500 grams. As long as the filter removes particles larger than 0.2 microns, protozoan parasites and bacteria are filtered out. Viruses such as hepatitis are much smaller and get missed, but they usually stick to particles that are larger and thus don't make it through the filter anyway. To ensure disinfection, some filters come with chlorine or iodine additives to kill viruses. The lightest, cheapest pump filters are small units that work inside a

Pump filter

water bottle. The filtration process is slowed to sipping speed, and the filter can't be cleaned, meaning that it soon has to be replaced when drinking silty water, but the weight is only 120 grams, including the bottle, and the cost can be as low as $17 if you already have a water bottle into which the filter element fits. Here's a clever way to use this rig. Fill the bottle with safe water from home, carry the filter element separately, then pop it in if you empty the bottle and need to refill it at a stream or lake. (Be sure to disinfect the bottle when you get back.) If you're planning to hike for only a couple of hours, you may not have to resort to the filter at all. But if you need it, you have it.

Which of these methods is best? Pump filtering is currently the most popular method, because it's quick, easy and reliable. Pump filters gradually plug up, though, and they do so fairly quickly if you're filtering from murky water. Well, they should plug up in such conditions. It shows they're working. Fortunately they're easily cleaned. The filtration cartridges in these devices need to be disinfected before long periods of storage, otherwise you risk the growth of mould and bacteria in the cartridge. Disassemble the device and let the cartridge air-dry, or boil it for five minutes (check the manufacturer's directions to see if boiling is okay). Flush the hoses out with clean water and detach them so that air can flow through. Store the parts in a cool, dry place. Alternatively, just shake out any water left inside the pump and pop the whole works in the freezer. This will keep anything from growing in it.

Pretty colours, but plain grey polyethylene may be better for your health

Water bottles, water bags and pee bottles

That old standby, the wide-mouthed Nalgene bottle, continues to be the water container I see in use most often along Canadian trails, sloshing the contents up the imbiber's nose if the bottle is tilted back too quickly. Tough, non-leaking, easy to fill and inexpensive, Nalgene bottles come in two types: polyethylene and polycarbonate (Lexan). Polyethylene is cheaper and lighter, but this kind of plastic tends to hold the taste of whatever has been in contact with it, while Lexan doesn't. And, more importantly, Lexan can be made in cool-looking colours. However, you might not want to use Lexan. Studies have shown that when polycarbonate plastic is washed in harsh detergents it releases bisphenol A (BPA), which has been linked to birth defects, genetic abnormalities and miscarriages in laboratory mice,[4] while polyethylene has not.

A wide-mouthed bottle is easier to fill from a stream than a narrow-mouthed bottle, but given the growing necessity of treating drinking water, the wide-mouthed version is no more useful than the narrow-mouthed version. The narrow neck is easier for most people to drink from, and the smaller cap is more reliable. Some filters attach to wide-mouthed bottles only or require an adapter for small-mouth use.

An alternative to the water bottle is the **water bag.** Sold by several manufacturers as "hydration systems," water bags are becoming more popular. They hold a lot of liquid—good for hikes with no potable water available en route—and they make it instantly available through a hose with a suck-valve at the end. You fill the bag, stow it in your pack, thread the hose over your shoulder and take a sip anytime you like. No need to locate your water bottle, open it, drink from it and put it back.

Filter/bottle combination, two-chemical treatment set, drinking-water tablets

4   The initial study was by Patricia Hunt and colleagues at Case Western University, as reported in *Current Biology*, April 2003.

Popular with runners and mountain-bikers, water bags are used mostly in hot places, which much of Canada is not except during a summer heat wave. But even then, when I'm hiking I like to stop, sit down, pull out my water bottle and drink from it while enjoying the spot and chatting with others in the group. A social tool, the water bottle.

Another social nicety comes in the form of a large, water-hauling bag you can use to carry a lot of water from the creek or the lake to your campsite. Look for a light water-hauling bag made of tent-fly fabric and about the weight of a small stuff sack, not a heavy canvas water bag or its plastic equivalent. My hauler carries 10 litres, a quantity much appreciated by everyone when the water source is some distance away. I hang the bag on a tree or under the campground table (see picture on page 186). Water can then be pump filtered for drinking directly or poured into pots for boiling tea, soup, etc.

> ## Share your water bottle?
>
> I don't. Drinking from someone else's water bottle (other than my wife's) nearly always gives me a sore throat the next day, leading to a nasty cold. Someone with a cold wouldn't knowingly offer a water bottle that must surely be contaminated, but I get sick regardless of whether the owner of the proffered water bottle is sick. I'm not alone in this; others have told me the same thing.
>
> When a group is using a pump filter, it's easy to cross-contaminate water bottles by dipping the same hose into one bottle after another. Either keep the hose out of each bottle—this makes for awkward pumping—or wash off the end of the hose before feeding it in (see page 199 for an easy technique).

I don't recommend using a heavy metal canteen in a canvas jacket. Those were invented for use in the desert, where the jacket could be wetted and would cool the contents by evaporation—not the most useful item for a trip along the West Coast Trail, already cool and wet much of the time. Neither do I recommend those cute leather-clad plastic wineskins. They nearly always spring a leak.

The cheapest water bottle around, and also very light and surprisingly sturdy, is an ordinary plastic juice bottle or pop bottle. Why recycle when you can reuse? Note that you need to clean and rinse the bottles thoroughly and then let them air-dry completely before reusing them. Never use a bottle that's damaged.

Some plastic juice bottles have rather wide openings, which makes them perfect for use as pee bottles. A pee bottle is the most valuable thing in your tent when it's 3:00 a.m. and your bladder is complaining and the rain is pouring down. With practice, women can use pee bottles, too. But they hardly ever have to, owing to the superior capacity of the female bladder.

Personal hygiene and grooming

At the minimum you'll need a **toothbrush**, travel-size reel of **dental floss** (or just a length of the stuff), **pocket comb** or **brush,** lots of **toilet paper** and **feminine hygiene products** if required. You might also consider a small bar of soap in a zip-lock bag. The new **antibacterial hand gels** are popular, but anything touted as antibacterial helps to breed the antibiotic-resistant super-bugs that are becoming such a problem these days, so I don't use them. **Biodegradable liquid soap** made for backpacking is a good alternative. It works well for washing most anything in the backcountry—a greasy pot, your body, your hands—and it comes in small squirt bottles, making it easier to use and store than a wet bar of soap. Whatever you use, remember not to rinse it into the creek or the lake. This pollutes the water. Do your rinsing and dumping of soapy water at least 30 metres away from the nearest water body.

Keeping your bum clean on a backpacking trip is a good idea. It prevents chafing and other troubles. Take a pot of warm water into the tent—you might want to move wettables outside first in case of a spill—to clean your face, underarms and nethers. Even on a cool day, the heat of the water will warm up the tent, and with the door zipped there is no chilling breeze.

Washing your hands after pooping helps to prevent the spread of *Giardia*, salmonella, troublesome forms of *Escherichia coli* and other gastrointestinal ailments. World champion long-haul backpacker Chris Townsend, the first person to walk the full length of the Canadian Rockies in one go,[5] carries **moist towelettes** with him for washing his hands after defecating. So do I. Carrying one or two of these little sealed packets per day won't break your back. Baby wipes are a little bigger, and they come unscented, which my wife appreciates.

Body odour in the outdoors is not the issue that it is in the television ads we are so happy to escape for a few days. On the trail everyone smells

---

5   Chris Townsend's books about his long, long backpacks are good reading. Look for *High Summer*, about his trek from one end of the Canadian Rockies to the other, and *Walking the Yukon: A Solo Trek through the Land of Beyond*. Chris is also the author of several how-to books on backpacking, including *The Advanced Backpacker: A Handbook for Year-Round, Long-Distance Hiking*.

the same—of hard-earned, happy sweat, worn with pride—and hardly anyone notices. Of course, after several hot days you and your companions may be wrinkling your noses as you follow each other along, at which time a wash is a good idea.

Plastic trowel

But deodorant? Mouthwash? Douche? Razor? Aftershave? Depilatory? Acne cover-up? Perfume? Lipstick? Eye shadow? Nah. I don't even bring toothpaste. It just attracts bears. If you brush with plainwater after every meal and floss briefly after supper, your breath should be as sweet as alpine wildflowers. Just don't overdo the garlic. Speaking of toothbrushes, the kind that comes in a case takes quite a while to dry out. Unless it's washed out with soap and rinsed well, a wet toothbrush shoved into a case becomes smelly from bacteria incubating between uses. I bring a regular toothbrush, no case, carried loose in the head-flap on my pack. It dries quickly in there and doesn't fester. (Yup, I cut the handle shorter to save weight.)

If your skin tends to split around your lips and nails, beeswax lip balm instantly seals off all those exposed, bleating nerve endings. Naturally contained bee-antibiotics promote healing. Burt's lip balm works great and is the only cosmetic-like substance I carry.

Don't forget the toilet paper! One full roll lasts most people a week. Carry it in a plastic sealable bag, and bring another one for packing used paper to the next point of disposal, meaning the next biffy. Used tampons and condoms can go in the bag, too. Don't burn toilet paper, and don't bury it, either. Animals dig it up. I carry it to the next campsite biffy along the trail, or all the way back to town if necessary. Even a week's accumulation of used toilet paper weighs very little. It doesn't smell, provided that you carry it in a sealable bag, and it squashes into a small wad. Used menstrual pads and tampons are more of a hassle, and they're thought to attract bears. You could bury these items, but bears have been known to dig them up. So it's probably better to carry them, too.

You may wish to pack a lightweight plastic trowel for digging poopholes, also known as cat-holes. Outdoor shops sell such things designed expressly for backpacking, with a ruler etched into them to help you get the proper depth of hole. Digging with a trowel is easier than using your boot-heel, although the boot-heel, unlike the trowel, won't break. (See page 203 for more on backcountry excretion.)

Towel

After an outdoor bath, a towel is a creature comfort for drying off on a day that's none too warm. But it's extra weight. I'll be dry in 5 minutes on a sunny day, in 10 minutes on a cloudy day, no towel required. (But sometimes patting down with my bandana is nice. It dries quickly, too.) How about bringing a towel for drying your dishes? Nope. A basic rule of backcountry sanitation is to let things air-dry. A towel used on one cup typically winds up used on another, thus spreading germs.

Handkerchief/bandana

For sure you'll want a handkerchief, or its larger relative the bandana, in your pocket or somewhere else that's easy to reach. Unless your nose runs a lot, your hanky will be used mainly for wiping sweat from your eyes, or for cleaning sunglasses. You can tie a bandana around your forehead to catch the sweat before it gets into your eyes, or tie it around your neck for a jaunty look.

A handkerchief can be whipped out and applied to a bleeding wound requiring pressure. My hanky has been used for this several times over the years.

You might want to make your bandana a red one, or some other bright colour, just the thing to wave around when trying to attract someone's attention—the bigger the better. ("See us? We're way up here!")

Smaller stuff

Now we're into the bits and pieces: the hardware, the little bottles of stuff, the incidentals. In this section I describe the small items I take into the woods—or avoid taking into the woods, with the reason why not.

Tip: When buying pocket-knives and such it actually makes sense to consider their colour. Bright colours make it easier to find something small in your pack or tent. If your expensive GPS unit gets left beside the trail and you have to go back to look for it, you'll be glad that it was orange or yellow, not grey or black. You can also make dark-coloured items brighter by applying coloured tape. Even better is to use light cord to attach easily lost items to your body or your pack.

Headlamp

Hardly needed during the short, bright nights of June and July, a light is still one of the Canadian 20 essentials (see page 350) and deserves a place in your pack. A headlamp is preferable to a flashlight, because it frees up your hands while you're reading or working on some night-time repair job in the tent. The new LED-type headlamps are modern miracles, bright and incredibly light in weight. They run a very long time on small batteries, which is just as well because the silver-oxide batteries you find in some of these units are expensive, and they need to be recycled as toxic waste. Some models have a clever retractable band to fit on your head, wrist or whatever as required. I don't recommend large flashlights, fluorescent camp lanterns and Coleman lanterns—yes, people actually do pack the things—which are all overkill.

If you're sharing a large tent with several others, a **candle lantern** is a nice low-tech item to hang in the centre, especially late in the season when the nights are getting longer and darker and colder. Made of aluminum and very lightweight aside from the candles, one of these lanterns can keep your card games going long into the evening. But not when other folks are camped nearby. Lights out at 11:00, please.

Incandescent-bulb headlamp   LED headlamp—much lighter

Lighter

Forget those waterproof matches. Too often they turn out to be strike-proof as well. I bring two butane lighters with me, one of which is in my pocket all the time, mostly to have handy for lighting stoves but also because you never know when a fire might be required. Everyone else's lighters might be back at camp. The other lighter I carry in my first-aid kit as a spare, kept dry.

Can't get to sleep?

My wife was sitting beside the bed of our four-year-old grandson one evening. He told her, "I'm going to think about trains now," and he fell asleep.

This *might* work for you, but if not, here's an alternative that works for me. Think about the trail you followed to camp, or about one of your favourite hikes. Let your mind go back to the trailhead. Ah, yes; the group picture there. Then the first bit of the trail, the part where you walked up that little hill above the parking lot, then down the other side to the bridge over the creek. That was where you saw the mink. And then around the corner and into the woods, where the owl looked down at you—that was neat—and past that rock outcrop with all the ferns on it, then the beginning of that long uphill grade, with the first switchback, and the second switchback, and the third one, and . . . zzzzzz.

Earplugs, sleeping pills

Maybe you don't snore, but in case your tent-mate does, or the people on the next tent pad, earplugs will help. These flyweight foam wonders can be found at most drugstores and all safety-supply stores. Squash an earplug into a thin cylinder and wiggle it in, turning it as you go. When it's fully inserted, hold it in with your finger until it expands. You can hear the snoring fade away. Ahhhh . . .

That will certainly help you get to sleep. However, for many people the first night of the trip can be a tosser-and-turner, what with the difference in venue—a sleeping bag in a tent is just not the same as your usual bed at home—and perhaps the difference in altitude if you've come from near sea level a day or two before to a treeline camp in the mountains. Moving from a low elevation to a much higher elevation causes some degree of insomnia for most people. The problem goes away in a few days, but in the meantime one solution is to take an over-the-counter sleeping pill such as Nytol, or some other brand that uses the antihistamine diphenhydramine hydrochloride (trade name Benadryl) as the active ingredient. Antihistamines have the side effect of making the user drowsy, and this one is very effective. It can give you a good night's rest when you wouldn't otherwise get one. I wouldn't take it for more than a couple of nights, though. After using it for four or five nights in a row, the following night can be sleepless because you *didn't* take it. Further, the compound seems to contribute to dryness of the eyes in middle-aged people.

Eyeglasses, contact lenses

My eyesight is weak, and my glasses look like the bottoms of Coke bottles. They fog up horribly on cool, misty days. I've tried glycerine-based stuff rubbed onto the lenses, but it doesn't work very well, and it attracts dirt. A better solution is to wear contact lenses. For those of us old enough to need bifocals, we can carry a pair of slim, stored-in-a-tube reading glasses to wear over the contacts as required. Or we can use bifocal contacts.

But then there's the problem of having to remove and insert lenses every day. The outdoor environment is grubby, and it's difficult to get those lenses in without inserting a payload of grit at the same time. Using extended-wear contacts solves the problem. You wear them all the time, day after day, night after night. There's no fumbling for your glasses when some beast bumps into your tent at midnight. There's no need to carry a bottle of lens-storage solution or other contact accessories, aside from a spare set of lenses in case you lose one or have terminal problems with the ones you're wearing. (Plus a pair of glasses in case you scratch your cornea or otherwise have to remove the contacts.) Be sure to insert extended-wear contacts several hours ahead, to make sure they're going to be comfortable for the duration.

Sunglasses

Ultraviolet light causes cataracts, so sunglasses are essential in these days of reduced ozone-layer protection from UV. Look for sunglasses that block both the UV-A and UV-B wavelengths; these will carry a designation of "UV400." Don't buy them too dark, though, or you'll be stumbling over roots along shady sections of trail.

I like my lenses to be brownish-yellow rather than green or grey. They warm up my view of the world on a dismal day and stop the transmission of blue light. (Removing the blue wavelengths provides slightly crisper vision.) Polarizing lenses cut glare, but they can cross-polarize with the LCD screen of a digital camera, making it look black. Frames advertised as being unbreakable might actually be so, eliminating the requirement for a heavy case; you need carry only a soft bag—fleece

Very cool sunglasses

Mountaineer's sunglasses—less cool, but your nose won't get burned

works great—to prevent scratching of the lenses while they're stowed in your pack.

Sunglasses are definitely a fashion item. Frame sizes change from year to year, but large, close-fitting lenses offer the best protection. Lots of outdoor folk put a neck-strap on their shades, so they can take them off briefly for social squinting, so buy a bag or case big enough for the strap, too.

Tip: Sunglasses get scratched and lost on outings, so you might want to leave your pricey $70 jobs in the car and take a less-expensive pair. Just be sure they have that "uv400" rating.

Sunscreen

Ultraviolet light not only blinds you, it also causes skin cancer. Long pants and long-sleeved shirts protect against uv, but they can become uncomfortable on a hot day, in which case most of us switch to shorts and a tee-shirt and slather ourselves with sunscreen rated with a high spf (sun protection factor) number. You should always wear a hat that shades your face and neck. Even so, you may want to put sunscreen on these places, too, because they can still burn from light reflected upward on bright days. Most tee-shirts allow too much uv through the weave, so you may want to put on sunscreen under your tee-shirt. For more on all this, go to www.dermatology.ca.

When choosing sunscreen, find a brand with minimal odour, such as Neutrogena's Sensitive Skin or Terrapin's Fragrance Free. Some brands are heavily scented, making a group of daubed-up hikers smell like a department-store perfume counter. And where do you put the most sunscreen? On your sniffer, of course, where the scent will always over-power the fragrance of the natural world you're trying to enjoy.

For this reason I use little or no sunscreen on my face, preferring to sunburn my nose until it tans out. My dermatologist tells me archly that since I'm over 60 I no longer have to worry about sun protection. Given the 10-to-30-year lag between bad sunburn and the cancer it in-duces, I'll probably be dead before my peeling nose exacts its revenge on me for my negligence. The precancerous lesions the guy blasts off my face with liquid nitrogen every couple of years probably started when I was a kid, ruining my skin at the swimming pool, before any of us really understood the potential for damage.

Now we know better. So here's some heartfelt advice to parents: please protect your children properly when you take 'em outdoors with you. Sunglasses, big hats and plenty of—yuck—sunscreen.

Insect repellent

In the east it's deer ticks (Lyme disease) and blood-sucking blackflies. In the west it's wood ticks (Rocky Mountain spotted fever, tick paralysis). Everywhere it's mosquitoes (West Nile virus). This is Canada, and we have bugs. How should we deal with them on the trail?

Operating under the principle that the fewer chemicals on my skin the better, when I'm in buggy places I wear tightly woven long pants and a long-sleeved shirt. During tick season I check for the little darlings every evening. (See pages 131 and 307 for more on ticks.) Biting insects aren't a serious problem where I live in the Rockies, but elsewhere you may want a head-net and gloves.

There are times, though, even in the Rockies, when you just have to use a little insect repellent. DEET, short for N,N-diethyl-m-toluamide, actually works. Despite the claims for other substances, recent third-party tests have shown that DEET is far more effective than anything else touted for such use, including citronella and some cosmetics. Biting insects find you by homing in on the carbon dioxide in your breath. DEET works by plugging a bug's CO_2 receptor with the wrong molecule. If a mosquito can't track CO_2, it can't find you. Any repellent containing at least 30 percent DEET will do the job for several hours. A greater concentration of DEET doesn't significantly improve its effectiveness, and it's a heavy-duty organic solvent at higher concentrations, so it's best not to buy the really strong stuff. Studies have shown little danger in using DEET—the danger of contracting a bug-borne illness is much greater—but I'm still suspicious of it and use as little as possible. (See www.pmra-arla.gc.ca/english/pdf/pnotes/deet-e.pdf for a discussion of safe use of insect repellents.)

The best way to apply repellent for maximum effect at minimal dosage is to use a small pump-spray bottle. Given that I'm already in long pants and a long-sleeved shirt, thus not exposing much skin to the bugs, I spray my neck, the underside of my hat-brim and the backs of my hands. My wife has worked out a good application technique. She rubs her face and ears with the backs of her hands, thereby keeping DEET off her palms, where it will get wiped on everything and where you don't need it anyway. Clever! When DEET was new on the scene, hikers quickly discovered that it dissolved the plastic of their cameras, binoculars and sunglasses. Manufacturers of these items have reformulated their synthetics to resist DEET, but gear more than 20 years old may be vulnerable. Again, use the minimum and keep it off your hands.

Pocket-knife, multi-tool

Note that it's "pocket-knife," not "hunting knife," "Bowie knife" or "machete." You're unlikely to get any more use from a 15 cm blade than you will from a 5 cm blade. A sheath-knife worn on your belt quickly identifies you as a greenhorn—although I know of a long-haul hiker in darkest, bushiest British Columbia who routinely carries an axe in his hand, ready to deal with whatever Green Hell awaits.

My favourite Swiss Army knife is less than 8 centimetres long when closed. That's small enough to be comfortable in my pocket, yet large enough to be useful. It does a whole lot more for me than any large single-blade knife could do, except to poke a hole in a grizzly bear, which is not something I want to be doing anyway.

This small knife may be all you need

In addition to your basic blade for slicing sausage and cheese, spreading peanut butter and cutting cord, you'll want a small pair of scissors for trimming moleskin, cutting tape and such, a fingernail-filing blade and a screwdriver blade. Most Swiss Army knives also come with tweezers for pulling splinters. On some models there's even a plastic toothpick.

You may need more tools than this. I often do, since a guide is expected to fix things when they break. Multi-blade knives can be found with everything on them but a drill press. However, those knives are big and clunky, and they lie in your pocket like a lump of steel. You could buy a special case in which to carry your Swiss Army machine shop on your belt, thereby saving a hole in your pocket, but maybe a pocket-knife-style tool chest is not really right in the first place. That's because the basic design of the pocket-knife is such that really reefing on any blade can break the knife.

Larger knife, but not a really big knife

Multi-tools are the better option. Essentially a pair of needle-nose pliers with other tools and a good knife blade folded into the handles, the Leatherman was the original tool of this breed. It's way tougher than a pocket-knife. The pliers are also wire cutters, a combination that can be used to make backcountry repairs to most anything made of metal. In your average multi-tool—there are now several brands and dozens of models—you'll find beefy and tiny flathead screwdrivers, a Phillips screwdriver, a saw, file, can opener, bottle opener, corkscrew, wire stripper for those backcountry soldering jobs . . .

Okay, there's no need to overdo it. These gadgets get pretty heavy when they're loaded with hardware you're unlikely to use. A do-everything, all-steel multi-tool weighs

Multi -tool, plus one party member to carry it

300 grams or more. By using titanium and aluminum alloy in the handles, newer models trim the weight by up to 75 grams. (And increase the price accordingly.) However, if the entire gadget is made smaller, with only essential blades, a useful multi-tool can come in at 60 grams. This is what I carry. It has pliers/cutters, a file and a couple of sizes of screwdrivers. Between this multi-tool-on-a-diet and my little pocket-knife, I have everything I need.

Regardless of what you carry, keep its cutting blades sharp. I live in a part of the country in which quartzite pebbles are readily available, and they work okay as whetstones, but why not just put "Sharpen knife" on your list of routine to-dos before heading out into the wilds?

Tape, cord, wire

Two kinds of tape are useful for repairs in the backcountry: duct tape, which is wide and very sticky but not particularly strong, and filament tape, also called "strapping tape" or "fibreglass tape," which is narrow, not particularly sticky and very strong. I carry some of each, rolled around a piece of cardboard or, as suggested by hiking friend Ed Dominguez, wrapped around a water bottle. Duct tape is great for patching torn fabric; filament tape and duct tape together can repair a broken tent pole or walking pole, using a stick for a splint.

Cord doesn't stick at all, of course, but it's quite strong. If you bring 10 metres of light camping cord, you can use it to tie an extra line on your tent in strong wind, replace a frayed guy line or hang out wet clothing to dry.

Wire is the ultimate repair stuff for metal parts that break, e.g., a pack frame. First, duct-tape the broken joint together to hold it in position—ideally with an internal stick connecting the two parts, or an external splint—then wire the parts together as tightly as you can and top the repair with more duct tape.

Map, GPS receiver, altimeter/barometer, compass, clinometer

GPS (Global Positioning System) units have become very light—under 100 grams—and even the most basic, least-expensive model, sometimes selling for under $100, will nearly always pinpoint your location within 10–15 metres. For this you'll also need a decent topographic map of the area, such as a 1:50,000 NTS (National Topographic System) federal topo map or the commercial equivalent. (See page 210.)

More money will buy you a basic digital map built into your GPS and even better accuracy. For yet more money you

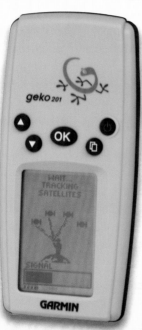

A small, basic GPS receiver will do the job

can have a device capable of holding detailed digital topographic maps, complete with contour lines, that are nearly as good as those paper 1:50,000s. The set included on Garmin's TopoCanada CD—about $150— covers the whole country. You download the maps you want onto a memory card in the GPS unit. The greater the capacity of the card, the more maps it will hold; my half-gig card easily provides coverage of the entire Canadian Rockies and adjacent ranges.

But there's no need for all that. You can tell your plain vanilla GPS receiver to remember where your car or your campsite is, so you can get back to it after a day of wandering in complex terrain. You can tell the gadget to remember the actual route you took, complete with all the twists and turns, and it will guide you back the exact way you came. Even if you've never been on a particular hike, say a complex route through trackless forest, you can give your GPS the map coordinates of points along that route, arrange those points in sequence and let the GPS lead you from one point to the next. Wow!

Basic GPS receivers do other cool things. They can tell you how far you've walked and for how long, what your current and average speeds are, how far it is to a particular destination and when you'll reach it if you maintain your current pace, what your elevation above sea level is, what the exact time is ("exact" meaning atomic-clock accuracy), when the sun will set and rise at your present location—handy for knowing how much daylight is left or when it will be light enough for you to see the trail—and more. If you've sprung for digital maps, when you get home you can fire up your computer and upload your route. You can see exactly where you went, and you can save your path for future use. You can share it electronically with friends who would like to do the same hike, or, as I have done, use GPS data in combination with digital base maps and graphics software to draw accurate, good-looking trail maps. You can go the other way, too: trace a route on the computer version of the map, download that route to the GPS unit and follow it on the ground.

If you buy a GPS unit, be sure to try out all the features it offers and practise using them before you head into the woods. Pick up *GPS Made Easy*, an excellent book by Lawrence Letham on getting the most from any GPS unit, with lots of practical examples and far more information than I can provide here. By using digital maps you can leave your paper maps at home. However, a paper map cannot fail as a GPS unit can, and I like to scribble notes all over my maps, so I will probably always carry paper maps with me, too.

You can print your own maps, too. Every federal 1:50,000 topographic map in the country can currently be downloaded free of charge from Natural Resources Canada at http://geogratis.cgdi.gc.ca/. You have to

Sighting compass

know what the map number is, e.g., 82-O/4, the map for Banff. You can find the number by going to http://maps.nrcan.gc.ca/topo_meta data/. Then work your way into the site, from the main NTS number—shown as "082"—to the "O" portion, and then finally to map "04."

You can also get the corresponding 1:50,000 satellite imagery at http://ftp2.cits.rncan.gc.ca/pub/canimage/50k/. All the Geological Survey of Canada geological maps are available through http://apps1 .gdr.nrcan.gc.ca/mirage/. (This site is rather technical and difficult to navigate, so be prepared for that if you plan on exploring it.)

Gem Trek and other Canadian mapping companies have produced their own paper versions of NTS maps for popular hiking areas. Such maps are usually more up-to-date on cultural features such as roads, trails, campsites, huts and so on than the official ones are. They work fine in conjunction with GPS units, and some of them even include position references you can enter into your GPS to help you find important places such as huts and backcountry campgrounds.

GPS receivers provide your elevation above sea level as well as your location. Does this matter on a hike? Not around Winnipeg or in the southern Alberta grasslands. But elevation can be important when you're wondering just how much higher you and your tired, cold family need to climb to cross a particular pass.

For technical reasons, hand-held GPS units aren't as accurate in the vertical plane as they are in the horizontal plane. Early models could give wildly inaccurate elevation readings, and the location readings were not very precise, either.[6] But these days, even basic GPS units for hikers and backpackers provide elevation readings that are routinely accurate to plus or minus 20 metres, and usually much better.

Still, you may wish to carry a separate air pressure–based **altimeter,** or a GPS unit with an air pressure–based altimeter built into it. Such altimeters aren't any more accurate than GPS units—without frequent recalibration they're less accurate—but they're useful anyway, because air pressure–based altimeters are also **barometers,** useful in forecasting the weather, as follows. You go to bed with the clouds stirring around fitfully overhead, and you wonder whether tomorrow will be fair or foul. You note the elevation the altimeter shows at bedtime: 1430 metres, say. The next morning the altimeter tells you that your campsite

---

6   From the time the first GPS satellite went into orbit in 1978 until 2000, the system broadcast intentionally inaccurate information. Spot-on positioning was available only to the military and other specially authorized users, the idea being to keep normal folks and Eastern-bloc spies from locating anything too closely. Never mind that the Eastern bloc had its own GPS satellites and normal folks were getting in trouble precisely because "Selective Availability," as it was called, made their GPS units inaccurate. On May 2, 2000, the US Clinton administration changed that, so now everybody gets accurate broadcasts.

has risen 100 metres in elevation. It hasn't, of course; the air pressure has dropped. Uh-oh. Bad weather on the way. Better not go up the mountain today. Better wait for higher pressure tomorrow.

Most wristwatch-type altimeters can keep track of your ups and downs along the trail, show them graphically, calculate total elevation gain and loss and do other interesting things. So can many GPS units.

Relegated to last place in this section is the compass. It's essentially nothing but a bit of magnetized steel on a swivel, plus a protractor, yet until the advent of GPS it was *the* instrument for navigation in the wild. Properly used, with three known landmarks arrayed in a favourable way, present on your map and visible from your location, a good sighting compass set for the correct magnetic declination can tell you where you are within about 100 metres. When you're hiking through dense woods or across a socked-in icefield with at least one other person to help navigate, and over a distance not exceeding a couple of kilometres, a compass can take you on a straight-line course to arrive within 100 metres of the objective. With luck and dead-reckoning skill, you might even be able to negotiate a corner or two on your route. However, a GPS unit does a much better job of establishing your position and leading you around, with very little knowledge and skill required.

So why carry a compass at all? Well, the batteries in the GPS unit might wear down, or the thing might fail altogether. Both have happened to me. However, a compass is not likely to get you home if your GPS can't. A compass is just not as good an instrument, and it's certainly not as easy to use. Fortunately, these days so many people carry GPS units that if yours goes on the blink, probably someone else in your party will have one that's still working.

But you might want to carry a sighting compass anyway, partly for old times' sake and partly because a sighting compass has a *mirror*. Not only can you primp and shave in the backcountry with that mirror, you could flash someone a signal by using the sun.

If you're going to carry a mirror-equipped compass, it might as well be one with a built-in *clinometer* to measure slope angles, i.e., the steepness of the slope you're about to cross. If it's steeper than 30° and there's no trail, you might not want to venture out there. That slope could be scary—especially if it's snow-covered and you've no ice-axe with which to stop yourself if you slip. In winter the slope might avalanche.

Also, with a sighting compass, or a GPS unit equipped with a sighting function, you can find out if a particular landmark—a peak on the horizon, say, or a fire tower you're trying to reach—is the one you think it is. You point your compass or your GPS-compass combo at the landmark. Assuming that you know your location exactly (your GPS will tell you), you read the angle over to it. You draw a line on the map at the proper angle from your position, or you do the same thing electronically if the GPS unit holds the current digital topo map, and you see if that line crosses that particular landmark. If it does, you have confirmation that the object on the horizon is, indeed, Mt. Invincible or the Green Mountain Fire Tower or whatever.

Camera

Camera choices are so personal that I'm hesitant to recommend anything here, except to offer the obvious: for use in the wilds, pick a lightweight, sturdy, trouble-free camera that you know how to operate well.

The digital revolution has provided backpackers with wonderfully versatile cameras. They're also complex, and several of my clients have been unable to make their cameras work properly on trips because they didn't pack the instruction manual.

Tip: Copy and carry the pages from the manual that explain how to work the self-timer, the flash, etc.

Digital cameras go through a lot of juice. Look for one that uses standard AA-size NiMH (nickel metal hydride) rechargeable batteries instead of a special rechargeable battery pack. The NiMH AAs are less expensive and easier to find, and in a pinch you can substitute regular alkalines, although they don't last very long compared to NiMHs. To conserve power on a backpacking trip, shut off the viewing screen and use the optical viewfinder instead. Carry enough extra memory cards to hold lots of high-resolution photos.

I carry my camera like a piece of rock-climbing equipment, slung round my shoulder on a loop of nylon webbing. As shown in the illustration, the camera is attached to the sling with a short cord. The camera can be raised easily to the eye but can't be lost, and if it's dropped it can't hit the ground.

A handy accessory for your camera is a **tiny tripod** such as the UltraPod, which weighs only 60 grams. It doesn't provide much height because the purpose is just to hold the camera steady while you take a slow-speed exposure in dim light or—a more common use—to support the camera when you trip the self-timer and quickly run over to be in the photo yourself. With its small legs extended, the UltraPod sits securely atop a boulder. It folds cleverly into a shape suitable for strapping to a tree or to a tripod made of walking poles. For this it even has

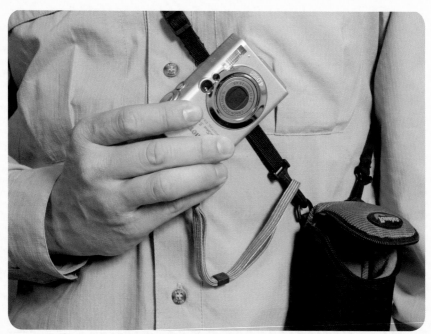

Good way to carry your camera—handy and safe

its own Velcro strap. A newer model, the Gorillapod, weighs more and costs more but has bendable legs that make it easier to place in uneven spots. The legs can be wrapped around a branch, too.

Binoculars

Although seldom really necessary, binoculars add a lot of joy to a back-packing trip. They bring the birds and the beasts up close, allowing you to identify critters and find out whether that shape way over there is actually a bear or just a boulder. They can also add a lot of weight if you tote the classic type, large and heavy, dangling from your neck. As a naturalist I can't go anywhere without my binoculars, which aren't the smallest, lightest ones available but small and light enough. They have these essential qualities:

- A very crisp view, with enough magnification to be useful but not so much that the image is jiggly.
- Minimum focal distance of 3 or 4 metres.
- They work in dim light.
- They stay in alignment well (i.e., the interior prisms aren't easily knocked out of place) and can be realigned if necessary.

At 350 grams my Bausch & Lomb Audubon Custom Compact 7 × 26 binos[7] fill the bill nicely, and at around $300 they're not terribly expensive. Objects appear with sufficient enlargement to give good detail, yet the image is steady.

Binoculars of 10× and up are difficult to hold without excessive jiggle. Further, with high-powered compact binoculars the field of view is quite small. It's easier to pick out whatever it is you want to see when the power is 6, 7 or 8 than it is at 10 or more. Birdwatchers, who must often get a fix on the object of their attention while it's on the wing, recommend powers of 6–8×. A front-lens size of 26 mm (not the same as a 26 mm camera lens, it doesn't indicate wide-angle) has enough light-gathering ability to be useful on dull days and at dawn or dusk, although the lenses are too small to be as good in dim light as 50-mm models, which are much larger and heavier.

I don't recommend binoculars stronger than 8× and binoculars with lenses of 40 mm or greater, especially cheap ones with poor alignment: the view in one eye is slightly shifted relative to the other eye, which causes strain.

To test binoculars in the store—and a store is a surprisingly good place in which to test binoculars—start by asking to see an expensive pair. You may not want to spend that much money, but the high-quality instrument will give you something with which to compare the binoculars you might actually buy.

First check for heft. Binoculars that seem heavy for their size probably contain a lot of metal, and that's good. Light, all-plastic binoculars typically go out of alignment quickly. So check next for alignment. Open or close the binoculars until the distance between the eyepieces matches the distance between your eyes, i.e., until the two circles of view overlap comfortably. Using the centre-wheel focus and the individual focus on one of the eyepieces, get a crisp view of something at the far end of the store. Look at it for a moment, then lower the binoculars from your eyes as you continue to look straight ahead. If your eyes take a moment to adjust, as if you've been looking slightly cross-eyed, the alignment of the binoculars is off. If you can alternately look through the binoculars and lower them without noticing this subtle shift in your vision, then the alignment is good. If you're unsure, try the expensive pair, in which the alignment will probably be very good. Then compare with the ones you're considering.

---

7   "7 × 26" means seven power, with the front lenses 26 mm in diameter.

A small pair of binoculars is a pair you'll actually take with you

Next, focus on something with sharp edges—a lettered sign or poster is perfect—and see how clear and bright the image is. Move the binoculars a little to the left and right as you view the object, so that the image is off-centre, close to the outside limit of the field of view. Is the image fuzzy? Not good. An object that's sharp in the centre should be nearly as sharp when viewed near the edge. Is there a thin line of purple, red, green, or some other unnatural colour along the edge of the image? There should be little or none of this. Compare for sharpness, brightness and colour halo with the expensive pair.

Finally, see how closely you can focus. It's handy to be able to focus on objects within 3 or 4 metres of where you're standing, so you can watch things that aren't distant but usually can't be approached any closer: butterflies, for instance, or the little organisms seen in the water near the shore of a pond.

To get the best use of your binoculars you'll have to practise with them, not so much to become faster at focusing on objects but to become faster at finding them in the field of view. After a while you'll be able to see something with the naked eye, then raise your binoculars and pick that same thing out right away.

Timepiece

Should you take your watch to the wilderness? Hmm. One reason for taking a three-day walk in the woods is to escape the clock-watching world. Free of that, you can live by the natural daily rhythm of sun-up and sundown.

Of course, if you plan to meet someone at the trailhead at a particular time, you'd better bring the means to know when. But what if you're going to be backpacking on familiar trails for a week, with no appointments during or after? Knowing the time won't really matter. You could leave your watch at home.

But then you won't have it should an unforeseen situation require it. Perhaps you'll need to take someone's pulse, or write down the time that something happened.

Ah, but someone else in the group will surely bring a watch.

But if they don't, your GPS will give you the time.

But it's a pain to haul out the GPS all the time, turn it on and wait for it to acquire satellites. So you'll have to leave it running, which wears down the batteries. Oh, my. Suddenly things are getting complicated. That wasn't the idea.

My take is that a wristwatch weighs very little and can go into my pack when I'd rather not have it on my wrist. So mine comes with me to the wilderness. And since it's going, what the heck, you might as well have the model with the built-in altimeter and elevational-profile display, thermometer, GPS unit, compass, heart monitor, five alarms, calculator, international currency converter, radio link to atomic-clock time . . . and a weightlifter's wrist. Not. My watch is a plain Timex job with a chronometer (sometimes it's good to know how long you've been hiking, to estimate how long it will take you to get back) and a loud alarm.

Radio, MP3 player, PDA, Game Boy and other "tentertainment"

A tiny AM/FM "weatheradio" can provide you with forecasts and news reports while you're on the trail. But why do that? The weather will be what the weather will be. Short of a hurricane warning, a radio forecast is unlikely to change your plans a great deal. You can walk in the rain. And you can walk quite happily without knowing what's happening on Wall Street or in Cairo. In fact, sometimes that's the whole point of the exercise.

An MP3 player allows you to hike along with your favourite music in your ears. But again, why would you want that? Aren't the sounds of the trail—birds calling, the river running, the wind through the leaves, the constantly varying sounds of your footsteps, the friendly voices of your companions—preferable to some oft-heard album pounding into your head? And do you really want to annoy others with the electronic swish-swish of your headphones?

I don't bring the world with me on my backpacking trips. One of the reasons I go on these trips is to leave the world—it's tempting to call it the "outside world," but really it's the *inside* world because we are the ones who are outdoors—far behind.

Whatever you do, please, please don't let your kids bring one of those electronic games that goes "bee-boop" for hour after hour in camp, right next to my tent.

Time for a confession. I often take my electronic organizer with me. Not to play solitaire when I'm bored, but because (1) I keep my daily journal in it, from which it can be downloaded to my computer when I get back, and (2) it's full of information that I can't remember but my clients are always asking me about, such as the age of the universe or how old a particular rock layer is or how many grizzly bears live in Jasper National Park.[8]

What do you do on a rainy day in the tent? Well, besides that. When everyone is bored silly, a deck of cards will get you by. My wife and I bring a tiny Scrabble game. Many backpackers carry some **reading matter**—a cheap paperback book or a magazine—which doesn't add a lot of weight to your pack. On a long trip you can trade your reading matter with that of other hikers.

Martin "backpacker" guitar

You could go for **edutainment** on the trail, choosing a natural-history guide instead of a trashy romance. As the author of one of these (the natural-history guide, not the romance), I'm all in favour of that. Impromptu Trivial Pursuit game, anyone?

8   As of 2007, perhaps 80–100.

Keeping a **journal** during a backpacking trip allows you to relive the better and worse moments, and may help you see the lighter side of the darker moments. Many a fine piece of writing has come from notes scribbled into a small notebook during a long trip on foot. And nothing draws upon your memories like a **sketchpad** (with a few coloured pencils, a small watercolour set and a brush or two, very lightweight) full of the art evoked by your adventures in wild places.

Like to sing around the campfire? Musically you'll get the most tune per gram from a small **harmonica.** Can't play any instrument? Can't sing on key? All the more reason to try the harmonica. It's very easy to learn, and singing is impossible while you're playing it. A plastic **recorder** offers the same promise. For guitar players, the Martin company makes a cute little **backpackable guitar.** It costs about $300, is only 90 centimetres long and quite narrow, weighs a little over a kilogram and is sturdy enough to strap onto your pack without a heavy case. Of course, the sound is as small as the guitar. Never mind; around the campfire any guitar is always a hit. There are other packable guitars out there, too.

Whatever your instrument, just remember to put it away at 11:00 p.m., or earlier if you notice that others in the campground are wanting to go to sleep.

Which brings me to **intoxicants**. Marijuana seems to send its devotees off to their tents quietly and early, and a sip of good scotch at moonrise can be a lovely thing, but there's nothing like a bottle of whiskey to turn a pleasant evening into a nightmare for everyone in camp. I can recall more than one wilderness party that went terribly wrong due to alcohol or some illicit substance.

It's easy to see why people use alcohol and other intoxicants in the city. Escape is the goal, if only for a few hours. How much better to escape for days at a time by going to the wilderness! The wilderness is the real world, the natural world in which our species grew up. When I go to the wilderness I'm going home. For that I don't need intoxicants.

Cell phone, satellite phone, two-way radio

Should you take your **cell phone** on a backpacking trip? It weighs very little, and it could save someone's neck if you need to call for help. At other times, you and your loved ones can reassure each other that all is well. But that same call can also bring the world crashing in on you. Do you really want to have to deal with problems at the office when you're in the wilderness? Would you abandon a trip if your spouse became ill? Selfishly, wouldn't it be better not to know? The decision to tote your cell or not can have ethical implications. On that, it's your call, so to speak. Suggestion: have things worked out in advance. "I'll carry the phone with me, and I'll check it for messages from time to time, but please don't call me unless you absolutely have to."

Often the question is academic. Much of the Canadian wild is devoid of cell towers, so there's no signal anyway. I hope it stays that way.

Ah, but this is why **satellite phones** were invented. If you really must be able to call for assistance from anywhere—as many horse outfitters and hunting guides feel they need to do when they're far into the backcountry—then a sat phone will do the job at a weight of only 200 grams. Calls are pricey, though.

When I'm guiding clients on my home turf of Jasper National Park, which is mostly cell tower–free, I carry a small, rather expensive five-watt VHF transceiver. I have permission to contact the warden service in an emergency, and the park has provided me the various frequencies. To date I have never had to use my radio for its intended purpose. But you can carry a two-way radio if you like. No-permit-required FRS **transceivers** (FRS stands for Family Radio Service) are now so small, so light—under 200 grams—and so inexpensive that people carry them on hikes, to stay in touch.

To stay in touch about what? Consider the following scenario:

Click. "Alice, where are you?" Click. "Right over here, honey." Click. "Well, where is 'over here'?" Click. "I don't know." Click. "Well, get out the GPS unit and tell me." Click. "Uh—you've got the GPS unit, Bob." Click. "Oh, that's right. I do." Click. "So now what?" Click. "I don't know!"

Technology can't always help you when *you've* done something stupid to begin with.

Whistle

Click. "Oh, wait, Bob. I can blow my whistle!" Click. "Great idea." Heard faintly from off to the left: "Tweet!" Click. "Heard you, baby!" Click. "Oh, thank heavens." Click. "Headed your way. Blow it again." Click. "Tweet!" Click. "Sounds closer." Click. "TWEET!" "Hi, there, Little Lost Hiker!" "Oh, Bob! Boo hoo hoo . . ." (Or some similar highly sexist happy ending.)

Bring a whistle. Be sure that it's an ear-splitting one, and that it's always on your person, not hanging off your pack. The pack and you may become separated.

If you blow your whistle **three times in a row,** this is the universal distress signal. Whoever is nearby should come over to help you, no two-way radio required. Just don't give three toots in a row for fun, okay? No fair whistling wolf.

Whistle on a cord—something every hiker should carry

First-aid kit

Forty-five years of backpacking have taught me that by far the most common injuries on the trail and in camp are (1) blistered heels and (2) burns from the sun or from cooking. Statistically, then, the only first-aid supplies you really need are blister pads, sunscreen and better sense when using the stove. Throw in a few Band-Aids, since first-aid kits are always supposed to have Band-Aids. And, what the heck, add some bigger bandages, a pair of scissors, a splint, a litter, a medevac helicopter . . .

Okay, it's easy to overdo the first-aid kit. The rest of this section details what I actually carry in my kit. It's stuff that has either served me well or I've been happy not ever to have had to use. I keep it all in a waterproof plastic box of the type used for storing leftovers in the fridge.

- Blister pads. The old standard here is adhesive-backed felt (moleskin) that you cut to size from a fairly large sheet. I still carry some of that because it's great for making small or specially shaped pads, but I get a lot more use from the newer fixed-size blister pads sold by Band-Aid, Spenco or Dr. Scholl's. These do a fine job of covering a hot spot before it becomes a blister, and they offer more relief than moleskin after a blister has formed, because they put a layer of slippery gel between the blister and the boot. I carry a half-dozen of these gel pads, mostly in the larger size, which is good for heel blisters.

- Fabric Band-Aids (e.g., Elastoplast), which stay on better than plastic Band-Aids. I carry a half-dozen regular-size ones, plus a couple of large ones and a few small ones.

- Several butterfly bandages, which are good for closing deep wounds.

- A couple of larger dressings for sizable bleeding scrapes. They need to be held on with tape. For large bleeding wounds requiring pressure and padding, menstrual pads make excellent dressings.

- Small roll of adhesive tape and a section of nylon stocking, which is very good for holding large dressings in place around an arm

Basic First-aid Sequence

1. Is it safe? If not, back off and get help.
2. Ask victim "Are you okay?" Speak loudly. May have to pinch victim's shoulders to get response.
   → Got response? Identify yourself and ask for permission to help. If "no," back off.
   → No response? Call for help (9-1-1), then:
3. Airway clear? Tilt head back and look. (Turn victim onto back if necessary.)
4. Breathing? If not, give two slow breaths. Blockage? Clear it with CPR-type chest compressions.
5. Circulation? Check on neck for pulse.
   → If circulation but no breathing, start rescue breathing: tilt head back, pinch nostrils shut, give adults 1 breath every 5 seconds, children or infants 1 every 3. Check for pulse every few minutes.
   → If no pulse, start CPR: 1-and-2-and-3-and-4-and-5. Three sets, then two slow breaths. Check for pulse after four complete cycles.
6. If breathing is okay, check full body for bleeding and apply pressure if necessary. If possible, elevate any wounds.
7. Once bleeding is controlled, check full body again for broken bones and other injuries. Write down vital signs (pulse, breathing, level of consciousness, dilation of pupils, skin condition).
8. Treat for shock. Put victim in recovery position and cover for warmth. Serious blood loss? Place victim on back, legs elevated.
9. Write down who, what, where, when.
10. Keep checking vital signs until medical help arrives.

or leg. Plus you can use the stocking on your head when robbing convenience stores.

- The classic triangular bandage we're all taught to use in our first-aid classes. I carry one in the kit and others in the bottom of my soft-type binocular case, where they also serve as padding. I can't remember all the different ways of tying a triangular bandage, so I have a little card in my kit, copied from a page in a first-aid manual, that shows a few of them.

- An elastic bandage such as the Tensor for wrapping a sprained ankle or holding a dressing that requires a fair bit of pressure.

- A silvered plastic sheet (space blanket) to cover someone or put underneath someone. Comes folded into a very small package.

- A couple of alcohol pads (swab pads), for cleaning the skin around wounds. Helps tape to stick better. If the wound itself needs cleaning, first-aid books recommend plain water, sterilized if possible, or at least pump-filtered, but okay if not.

- Paramedic's gloves to put on when dealing with blood or other bodily fluids, which these days might carry HIV or hepatitis C. These gloves roll into a little ball and are very light.

- Rescue-breathing mask for performing artificial respiration on someone whose mouth you don't wish to touch with yours. In the heat of the moment I doubt that I would remember to use it, but this mask is very small and very light, and it might be helpful if the rescue breathing takes a long time. So I carry it.

- A neat little tool for removing a tick that has attached itself to you. Called the Pro-Tick Remedy, it's essentially a slim steel lever

Tick remover

that slips between the tick and the skin. You push the lever down, which pulls gently against the tick's head. After a minute or two the tick gets the message and pulls its mouthparts out. This is way better than ripping the tick off your body, leaving the mouthparts imbedded, where they can infect. For more on ticks, see page 307.

- Small roll of calcium-carbonate tablets (e.g. Tums) for stomach upsets.

- Extra butane lighter (Bic-type lighter), kept in the waterproof first-aid box.

- Tiny folding can opener. I hardly ever carry canned food on a trip, but people who do often forget to bring an opener or a knife that has an opener on it, in which case I can help.

- Extra pocket comb and an extra Swiss Army knife, a tiny one that nonetheless has scissors and tweezers, in case I lose my pocket-knife, which has happened a couple of times.

- Earplugs for noisy nights in camp.

- A stick of beeswax lip balm, for cracked skin anywhere.

- Spare contact lenses, if I'm using them. Regardless, I always pack a spare pair of glasses.

- An empty blister-pad box that carries my pill supply: vitamins, some aspirin and ibuprofen (Advil), some prescription Tylenol 3 —for me; can't give it to others—and some over-the-counter sleeping pills.

- A fever thermometer. Not something you're likely to need very often, but I have had occasion to wonder whether someone in my party was just suffering from fatigue or was ill with some kind of pathogen, and a thermometer has been the tool to use in telling the difference.

- Some 3" x 5" lined note cards and a pencil for keeping records about someone who is hurt or sick and may need evacuation.

- My gear seems to need first aid more often than I do. So I carry wire, duct tape, fibreglass tape, heavy elastics, needle and thread (a large needle and some dental floss) and a piece of stick-on ripstop nylon, all for making repairs.

- A $20 bill, my keys, my credit card and bank card, my driver's licence and my health-care card. None of this is likely to be needed in the wilderness, but it may be required en route to or from the trailhead, or at the hospital (we hope not). Why pack your whole wallet or purse when these few items will do? A first-aid kit is a good place in which to keep them safe and dry. Another good spot is in a small plastic bag in the flat zippered pocket under the head-flap of your pack.

There's lots more you can carry, of course. Various ointments, more dressings, a cardboard splint (carry this in your pack, against your back—or use your foam sitting pad if you carry one there). Under the lid of my first-aid kit, so that it's always easy to find, I have a simple **instruction card** (see page 130). It's my own step-by-step list of essential actions, and it's based on standard first-aid practice at time of writing. Feel free to copy it for your own use.

On page 310 you'll find a step-by-step plan for dealing with any emergency. As a guide, this is what I provide to institutional clients who need such information from me for their insurance agencies. It has never been rejected. You might want to copy that list and carry it with you.

Pepper spray, bear bells

Capsaicin spray is routinely used by the Mounties on out-of-control partiers, but for us civilians it's intended only to ward off animal attacks. As a guide I'm expected to carry it. I've never had to use it, but it's there, hanging by my side, just in case. Does that highly visible canister engender client ease and confidence in grizzly country? Perhaps, although it also alerts everyone to the possibility of bear attack. That's actually a good thing (the alert, not the attack): it encourages people to make some noise along the trail in grizzly country and to be cautious about leaving food in the tent.

Beware the temptation to swagger around in the wilds, can of bear-blast on your hip like a loaded pistol, almost daring the ol' bruin to take a run at you. Bruin just might take you up on your challenge, and things might not turn out as planned. It's better to act as if you're unarmed, keeping a careful eye out for bears and making a point of avoiding them, so that both you and they can enjoy the day in peace. (For more on bears, turn to page 296.)

If you're going to carry pepper spray, be sure to carry it where it's instantly reachable. My canister rests in a neoprene sleeve by my right trouser pocket, below my hip-belt. It can be pulled out, aimed and discharged very quickly. The sleeve hangs from a light belt that I wear whenever I'm up and about, not just when I have my pack on. After all, most bear encounters occur in camp, when one's pack is not on one's back. A group in which each member carries pepper spray at all times is extra prepared.

You should also be aware that pepper spray is classed as a weapon and you should handle it accordingly. Capsaicin is not lethal—although the Canadian Police Research Centre reports that at least one death has occurred from police use of it[9]—and its effects are not permanent, but anyone who has been sprayed will tell you that the stuff hurts like hell and takes a long time to wear off. You really don't want it going off accidentally, especially in your tent. Check the safety interlock on the valve. I once spent an afternoon hiking with a group, blissfully unaware that the interlock was dangling by its cord. (The interlock should be secured to the canister with a cord, so that it isn't lost if it pops off.)

You can't take pepper spray on an airplane (except inside one of the floats of a float plane) or in a helicopter. I know of at least one incident in which a can went off in a helicopter, instantly disabling everyone on board, including the pilot. Fortunately the machine was still warming up on the ground.

All pepper-spray canisters gradually lose their pressure over time. Ignore this inevitability at your peril, something I very nearly learned the hard way. While mountain-biking, I had a run-in with a black bear. The bear was convinced that I planned to take over the deer carcass it was scavenging. It approached me threateningly, slapping the ground and growling, but I didn't retreat. After all, I had pepper spray. When the bear was within 10 metres of me, I raised the canister, popped off the safety, took aim and prepared to press the valve. The bear stopped, made indecisive motions, then stepped off the trail and moved away. Hah! I had successfully intimidated a bear. With a flourish I holstered

---

9   On the web you'll find *Comments on the Use of Capsaicin Spray*, Canadian Police Research Centre document TM-01-98, by Jeremy Brown, MD, chief, Occupational Health Services Directorate, Royal Canadian Mounted Police, 1997. There is debate about the effect on asthmatics.

the spray, got back on my bike and continued my ride. A kilometre later I thought, "This pepper spray is outdated. Is it actually still good?" I stopped and let off a shot. It barely reached past my front tire. There was no second shot. Yikes! *Always read and heed the expiry date on pepper spray.* After that date, use that particular canister for practice—far away from anyone or anything that could be irritated by it unintentionally and buy a new one for the trail.

Should you test a new canister of pepper spray? One school of thought says no, that discharging the canister even briefly may speed up the pressure loss. However, the manufacturers I checked with said that a brief test wouldn't cause significant pressure loss within the shelf-life period. A friend always tries a quick toot on a new canister. In one case the canister was completely flat!

Some years ago the manufacturer of a pepper spray commonly sold in Canada—Bear Pause—was fined by the American Environmental Protection Agency for mislabelling the canister's contents and

failing to register the product. Health Canada had issued a recall notice, but that hadn't stopped the store that sold Bear Pause to me from continuing to sell the stuff well after the recall. **Lesson:** Buy only pepper spray that's registered under the Pest Control Products Act (displays a PCP number), or has an EPA registration if made in the US.

As for **bear bells**, few experienced hikers use them. These bells aren't loud enough to alert a bear for any distance, but they're annoying to listen to, jingling away all the

Pepper spray

time. A bear can't hear any better than we humans can. A bear bell isn't audible until the person wearing it is only 10–20 metres away from the bear. A bit too close, eh? If you're going to use a bell loud enough to give the bear adequate warning, you'll have to get one off a locomotive. It's far better to use your voice. When you're in bear habitat, and especially when the trail is brushy or it's paralleling a noisy stream, and particularly when you're heading into the wind—if the wind is coming from behind, you can be smelled by a bear a long way away—you should be making noise frequently. A favourite technique among hikers in grizzly country is to shout "A-yo!" (that's "A" as in "day") every few minutes. I cup my hands and bellow out a loud "HOO-HOO-HOO-HOO-HOO!" ahead of me. It carries farther than "A-yo." If you're giving more than one shout at a time, remember to give two, four or five shouts in a row, but never three, because a three-shout call is the universal distress signal.

In grizzly country, every person in a group should make noise, so that a bear gets some sense of the size of the group. The group should stick together, not be stretched out over 100 metres of trail. There is no confirmed record of a group of six or more ever being attacked by a grizzly bear. (The darkly humorous addition to this is " . . . and returning to report the attack.")

Slimming down your pack

You've bought a very light tent and a very light sleeping bag, saving over a kilogram on the weight of each. You've chosen a light backpack. But you hoist on that pack, stuffed full before a six-day trip, and it weighs 23 kilograms. Whoa! Why did you spend all that additional money on the top-of-the-line tent and bag? Where did all the extra weight come from?

It comes from your food, your clothing and the cumulative weight of small but individually heavy items. Luckily, though, it's not difficult to reduce the mass of all this by a quarter to a third.

You can save a lot of weight on food by (1) going with freeze-dried dinners and (2) taking fewer snacks. Are you coming back from your trips with five uneaten granola bars, half a bag of trail mix, several unused envelopes of drink mix and so on? If so, try going out for a few days with less of all this. You probably won't miss it.

See page 99 for how to save weight on cooking gear. If you like to divvy up your food and gear among a number of coated stuff sacks, which seem individually light but get heavy in quantity, use mesh bags or lightweight plastic bags instead. Or do less divvying-up. Pack loose foods such as bean flakes in zip-lock bags rather than in heavy plastic bottles.

Speaking of bottles, what about all that heavy liquid you're packing in your water bottle or bag? If you know that it's not far to the next stream, there's no need to keep your water supply topped up. Carry just what you need. And the means to make it safe, of course.

Save weight on clothing by choosing lightweight garments and not taking too many of them. Check the weight of your hiking pants, your outdoor shirt and your weatherproofs. Clothing sold for outdoor use is more robust than that intended for everyday wear, and is therefore heavier, but you can buy lightweight apparel that's also strong enough. You might find that time spent searching it out was time well spent.

Jackets and rain pants are heavy when outfitted with extra pockets, zippers and snaps. Go for plainly designed outerwear of lightweight materials. Compare the weights of fleece items to find a jacket that provides the best loft for the least weight. If you're absolutely certain that the nights aren't going to be cold, leave your down jacket at home.

Do you really need a complete change of clothing for a seven-day trip? No. An extra set of underwear, perhaps—although even this is not really required. Wash your undies and tee-shirt on a sunny afternoon in camp and wear only your outer clothing for a couple of hours.

It's difficult to manage without a spare set of socks, and they don't weigh much anyway, but do you really need that pair of heavy-soled Teva-type sandals for wearing around camp? Maybe you could leave them behind. Or substitute a pair of cheap, foam-soled flip-flops, which are very light. A pair of neoprene slippers used for crossing cold rivers can also be used in camp.

I've heard it said that saving 100 grams on your feet is like saving a kilogram on your back. Boots and walking poles vary quite a bit in weight. Try the lighter models, and if they don't hold up for you, go to something heavier. Walking poles made from fibreglass cross-country ski poles are about the lightest ones around, and they're stronger than the lightweight adjustable aluminum jobs.

Then there's your purse, your wallet. Will you actually need all those credit cards, schedules and whatnot in the backcountry? Why carry the actual wallet or purse at all? These things can be surprisingly heavy. So, as I said earlier, I carry my driver's licence, one credit card, my health-care card, bank card and a little folding money, slipped into a zip-lock bag.

Lastly, consider all the bits and pieces you were planning to carry: your pocket-knife, multi-tool, flashlight, GPS unit, compass, guidebook, paperback book, etc., etc. For a particular trip, do you really need all of these? And for those items you can't do without, can you find extra-light versions that will do the job? Instead of packing the whole guidebook, copy out just the pages you need. Instead of reading in your tent in the evening, just lie quietly and listen to the sounds of the night. Instead of packing a first-aid kit suitable for open-heart surgery, take the minimum: blister pads and Band-Aids. Someone else—some anal-retentive type like me—will have packed the full operating room.

The same goes for other doodads. The group really needs to have only one multi-tool, only a couple of GPS units and water-purification devices and bird books. You can get together beforehand and work this out.

Backpacking on the cheap

The foregoing is all for people with means. To be attired and kitted out in the latest and greatest will cost a couple of thousand dollars. Can you still go backpacking if you don't have that kind of money? Of course you can. There are two approaches. One is to borrow everything you need from family and friends. Depending on your luck with that, you might head off with a lot of great stuff on your back. If not, you can still go—you just can't go to all the kinds of places that the gear I've described will let you go. You have to choose places where the weather is moderate, such as the Okanagan Valley or southern areas down east or lower elevations in the Rockies, and you have to go there at times when the bugs aren't particularly interested in you. With this in mind, here's how to spend a few days on the trail at minimal cost:

- Dress as you normally would, no special outdoor clothing required. Just be sure that you have a cap to protect you from sunburn and a pair of long pants for the evening chill.

- It's okay to wear runners. Your pack will be very light, so you'll be more agile than you would be with a heavy pack, making it less likely that you'll need the extra ankle protection that expensive boots provide. Still, watch your step.

- For warmth, bring two or three old sweaters. Wear them in layers, putting one on or taking one off to suit. You may also need a tuque and a pair of gloves.

- Buy one of those inexpensive plastic raincoats to wear if the weather goes bad. This shouldn't cost you more than $5 or $10. Or try the ultimate cheap raincoat: a big plastic garbage bag with holes cut out for your arms and head. While walking in the rain, keep your arms outside the bag or you'll fall hard if you trip.

- For a sleeping bag, safety-pin a couple of blankets together. Fold them double. Want additional warmth? Share those blankets with a very close friend.

- Buy a cheap foam sleeping pad, about $10 at any store selling camping stuff. This is money well spent. Maybe you could sleep on the ground without any padding, but probably you'll want some insulation under you. The soil in this country is cold. It's no fun waking up at 2:00 a.m. and shivering until dawn.

Derek Hammell

- For shelter, buy a tube tent, often called an emergency shelter, for under $10. This is a tubular piece of lightweight plastic about 3 metres long and 2 metres in diameter. You run a length of nylon camping cord through the tent—camping cord is cheap—and sling it between two trees. Crawl in at one end or the other, lay out your foamie and blankets, and there you are. If you can't find a tube tent, or if you want something stronger, buy a piece of heavy plastic at least 3 metres by 5 metres in size and use that as a tarp. Hold the sides down with rocks. There will be no bug netting with either a tube tent or a tarp, of course; you'll have to depend on insect repellent.

- Borrow an old backpack from someone. Lots of people have packs they no longer use. Or search the bargain stores, close-out aisles and used-sporting-goods exchanges. However you acquire your pack, try to find one with as many of the good qualities described on pages 63–71 as possible.

- Instead of an expensive backpacker's stove, make a hobo stove from a paint can. Burn twigs in it to heat your meal and your tea. Use another can as a pot. For placing it on and off the stove while it's hot, bring an old pair of work gloves. Your cookset will quickly become blackened and sooty, so bring a heavy plastic bag in which to pack it.

Hobo stove

- Use a pop bottle for a water bottle. The jury's still out on the advisability of reusing plastic, but make sure you wash, rinse and air-dry bottles thoroughly before reusing them, and never use a damaged bottle. When refilling it on the trail, you need to ensure that the water is safe to drink. Chlorine dioxide treatment is the cheapest for an occasional trip (see page 102), or boil enough water at breakfast and dinner to refill your water bottle.

- For food, bring inexpensive stuff from the grocery store: instant noodles and cheese, bread and jam, summer sausage, instant hot cereal.

- To avoid camping fees, hike in places that don't ask for them.

- Instead of buying maps and trail guides, go to the library and copy the few pages you need.

- Go through the list of "20 essentials" (see page 350) and bring what you can. For sure you'll want a lighter, sunscreen and insect repellent. Bring a few extra plastic bags. Big ones.

- Be prepared to suffer a little if the weather is bad, and be prepared to gloat if you're perfectly comfortable in Camp El Cheapo among folks who have spent a lot of money to have essentially the same experience.

Food and drink

My approach to eating and drinking in the wild is pretty basic. Food is fuel. It needn't be exciting. Rather, it has to be calorific, light in weight and easy to prepare. Drink is what I need to keep the inside of my body wet enough. If I start to dry out in there, I'm not a happy hiker. So I drink, and I make it the wettest stuff there is: plain water.

Food for day-hiking

The weight of your food doesn't matter much when you're out only for the day. So bring whatever you like, including fresh fruit (but not bananas or ripe pears; they squash). My favourite trail lunch is a yummy submarine sandwich eaten in a beautiful place. Good day-hiking snacks are the same as good backpacking snacks: granola bars, dried fruit, jerky, sausage, cheese, crackers and trail mix (nuts, raisins, etc.). You may wish to bring cookies, candy and other high-energy treats.

We should all be eating more nuts and dried fruits anyway—being mindful of allergies, of course—because they're good sources of antioxidants. Antioxidants help to counter the harmful effects of free radicals in our systems, which do bad things to us over time and seem to build up quicker during outdoor pursuits owing to increased physical stress and greater exposure to uv light, especially at higher elevations.

Be sure to eat a good, balanced breakfast of carbohydrates, fats and proteins before your hike. Heading out on an empty stomach is no pleasure, and it can make you crabby with your companions. If you have to drive a couple of hours to reach the trailhead, have a pre-hike snack just before you start walking. Eat a protein-rich supper after your hike. It will help you to sleep well as your body rebuilds worn tissues and grows muscle.

Food for backpacking

Entire books have been written about food and food preparation in the wilderness. If you want to become a backcountry gourmet—words found in the titles of more than one of these volumes—then by all means do so. I know people who delight in whomping up amazing spreads out there, meals as good as or better than they would enjoy at home.

However, you'll find your pack heavier for it. That's because preparing food of the sort you eat at home usually requires numerous ingredients, more cooking time and more implements than does food intended for backpacking. Food for backpacking has to be nutritionally sound, if not as interesting to the palate. If you have allergies or other medical dietary needs, it has to meet those requirements. No one wants to risk gastric upset in the backcountry. The bottom line: plain food is generally best.

If it's important that your meals are right for you in quantity and ingredients, then you'd be wise to bring your own. If you depend on others to supply all the eats for the group, you may regret it. See page 148 for a classic example.

If you're only going to be out overnight, meaning that you'll be eating no more than four meals—lunch, supper, breakfast and another lunch—then perhaps you should do what my wife and I have done for years on such short trips: freeze some spaghetti or some other supper fare, put it in a plastic container, wrap the container in a jacket for insulation, and pack that. On a short trip we have no need for expensive freeze-dried food. It makes sense to bring something cooked ahead of time and easily reheated, convenient and tasty. Never mind that it's also

heavy; the total weight of food in the pack isn't much on such a short jaunt. If we're going to walk for only an hour or two before camping, supper need not even be frozen. That insulating jacket will keep it from spoiling until it's eaten.

Given the usual cool Canadian nights, you can apply a similar philosophy to breakfast. Fresh eggs, fresh mushrooms and cheese will keep overnight in anything but very hot weather. To prevent egg breakage, break them before you go, i.e., carry them in liquid form in a plastic container that seals reliably. You can stir in some spice if you like. Put the container into a plastic bag as backup and wrap the container in a jacket for insulation through the warm afternoon and early evening. Then, when the temperature has dropped into the teens, pull the container out and expose it to the night air (still sealed, of course, and kept safe from animals). The next morning you can be enjoying a yummy omelette while other campers are consuming porridge.

Not that you can't have the porridge, too!

For a multi-day trip, good backpacking food should be light in weight, non-spoiling and easy to prepare. **Freeze-dried meals** certainly meet these criteria. A packet of freeze-dried food with a net weight of 150–200 grams typically provides 1,200–1,600 kilojoules of energy (300–400 kilocalories), enough for supper if supplemented with a cup of soup. (My wife will tell you that in my gut a fair bit of that energy goes into producing gas. This seems to be true to some extent for most people when they eat freeze-dried meals. Packing Beano helps.)

To deal with my craving for fresh vegetables, I pack **edible-pod peas,** the best of which are known as "sugar snap peas." These things have no stringy parts, are wonderfully sweet and stay crispy and fresh-tasting for several days on the trail—up to a week in cool conditions. Wash them to get mould spores off, then pat 'em dry and pack in a zip-lock bag. Close the bag quickly each time you extract some of the peas, so that they stay moist.

Clever sweet and savoury food items for backpacking

- **Asian shredded pork or beef.** Very lightweight stuff. Can be eaten right out of the pouch. Excellent in soup.

- **Japanese instant noodles.** So-so on their own, but great for plumping up a cup of some other kind of instant soup mix. Just add hot water.

- **Hot Jell-O.** It takes a real sweet tooth to slug this back, but hot Jell-O can be the perfect thing on a cold, wet morning. Try the raspberry-flavoured variety.

- **Small oriental crackers.** Made from rice and glazed with something salty, these are flavourful and very light in weight. Look for the mix that includes crescent-shaped red crackers, which are peppery.

- **Crystallized ginger, crystallized pineapple and other sugared fruits.** Great combination of sweet and sour.

- **Romney's Kendal Mint Cake.** The original and best sugar rush in the wilds, this is the English candy that still gets teams of British climbers up Himalayan peaks. Kendal Mint Cake can be hard to find in Canada, but, surprisingly, it can be ordered from REI in the US (www.rei.com).

- **Stuff you dry yourself.** Dried fruit, jerky and the like are expensive in stores, but you can make your own for a lot less. A fruit dryer makes a good group purchase for a hiking club. Recipes and advice are available on the web.

In the wilds I eat a freeze-dried supper every night. In the package is a single item. It rehydrates into what the manufacturers call "casserole" or "rotelle" or "primavera," but basically it's a bag of glop. It's tasty glop, though, and there's plenty of variety available, both in vegetarian and meaty versions. For most brands, preparation is a no-brainer. Boil up some water and pour it right into the package. Stir it around, let it sit for 10 minutes and eat it from the pouch, no bowl required, no washing up afterward. Supplement it with a packet of instant soup and a couple of edible-pod peas while you're waiting for rehydration, and hot chocolate for dessert. When it's over, I'm stuffed.

I've also eaten freeze-dried meals for breakfast—why not?—but these days I prefer a 50/50 mix of instant bean flakes and instant rice, fattened up with a lump of cheddar cheese and spiced up with a dollop of mild salsa, plus some corn chips thrown in for crunch. I learned about beans and rice for breakfast from instructors at the Audubon Expedition Institute of Maine, who feed it to their students. Two cups of this for breakfast (two cups when reconstituted; one cup when dry) and I'm set. It sticks to my ribs way better than a little packet of instant porridge, which burns off in an hour and sees me hitting the snacks pretty hard until lunch. Fartacious combination? I'm afraid it can be, but a tab or two of Beano solves that problem.

The proper kind of bean flakes can be hard to get. Check at health-food stores for a package containing nothing but bean flakes and a bit of salt. Other kinds are doped up with dried spices and aren't as good. For instant rice you can't go wrong with Uncle Ben's, of course—available anywhere.

Few backpackers haul out the stove and make a proper lunch on the trail, although a cup of hot soup eaten under a tarp goes down well on a chilly, soggy day. For me, snacks and lunch are the same thing: stuff you can eat by just putting it straight into your mouth. I like crackers, cheese, dried fruit, granola bars, trail mix, jerky, sausage, cookies and candy. Mostly carbohydrates, in other words, which is what your body needs at midday to keep you plodding on through the afternoon. Be sure to snack at rest stops.

Okay, so what should you carry all this in? The usual thing is to take noodles, rice, etc. out of the boxes they come in and repackage them in plastic bags. Freeze-dries come in their own bags, which should be left sealed until use. The same applies to anything else that might otherwise spoil or seems sensibly packaged in the first place.

To protect food from animals in places where stringing it up isn't possible or doesn't work—above the treeline, for example—you may have to place it in bear-proof containers such as the Ursack Kevlar bags or Backpacker's Cache heavy plastic tubes sold for this purpose at MEC. Be aware that a bear might not be able to bite through a Kevlar bag,

Tastier fare . . .

Eating on the Super-Light-No-Cleanup plan has its advantages, but many backpackers don't mind carrying a few extra grams and washing a pot in order to have a dining experience that complements the beauty of the surroundings. (People who have allergies to common ingredients in packaged foods, or are vegetarian, can take foods to suit.) It usually works better to prepare a pot of main dish for every 2–4 people. Single servings are more difficult to fix as it's more difficult to keep a small quantity from scorching.

For weekend (or even longer) trips, tasty, not-too-heavy-to-carry, one-pot dinners can be combinations of:

1 an instant or quick-cooking starch (instant brown rice, whole-wheat couscous, potato flakes, ramen or rice noodles) *with*

2 a protein: nuts (almonds, cashews, peanuts), nut butter, dried bean flakes, cheese, jerky or even little cans of fish, chicken, turkey *and*

3 dry spices (curry, poultry seasoning, chili, thyme, oregano) which weigh nothing and add flavour, as do dried vegetables or fresh garlic or part of a small onion.

A small package of instant sauce (many flavours to choose from) from the grocery store or a spoonful of dry soup mix are light and tasty additions to the pot. For example, how about instant brown rice, curry powder, cashews and/or canned chicken, dried veggie flakes and maybe a package of cream gravy simmeredwith enough water to produce a good "glop" texture? Yum!

Choosing, preparing and drying food in a home dehydrator is a fun and interesting way to add variety and nutrition to backcountry meals. Jerky (dried meat) is a tasty snack, and can be shredded up and added to a one-pot meal. Dried vegetables, if sliced thinly before drying, can be rehydrated quickly. Some people even dry homemade spaghetti sauce. Home-dried fruit can be made without sugar and added to morning porridge or packaged pudding mix for dessert.

You can make your own breakfast muesli with enough oatmeal, nuts and dried fruit to stick to your ribs until lunch. (Even gluey instant oatmeal packets can be improved in both nutrition and flavour by adding copious quantities of nuts and dried fruit while adding boiling water in your cup.)

—Cia Gadd

Logan bread

3 ½ cups	whole-wheat flour	875 mL
1 tsp	baking powder	5 mL
1 tsp	salt	5 mL
1 tsp	cinnamon (optional)	5 mL
⅓ cup	non-fat dried milk powder	75 mL
⅓ cup	molasses	75 mL
⅓ cup	brown sugar	75 mL
⅓ cup	honey	75 mL
⅓ cup	vegetable oil	75 mL
⅓ cup	sunflower seeds	75 mL
⅓ cup	sesame seeds	75 mL
1 cup	water (more or less, to make a very stiff dough)	250 mL

Grease two standard loaf pans. Preheat oven to 150°C (300°F).

Mix everything together in the order listed. It will probably have to be kneaded a bit by hand, to make sure it's evenly mixed.

Add to the prepared loaf pans and bake for at least 1 hour, or until it feels firm when you push on the top with a finger. Then, lower the heat to 100°C (200°F) and dry the loaf for at least an hour longer. When cool, wrap tightly in two layers of plastic bags. Freeze the other loaf if you aren't taking it with you on this trip.

This makes a sweet, dense, durable loaf that will last at least a week in a pack. It was worth the weight in my pack to see the surprise and delight of the kids we took on 10-day outings when late in the trip I pulled Logan bread out of my pack and handed around slices spread with peanut butter and jelly.

—Cia Gadd

Running on empty in the Andes

While I was in Chile, a transplanted Spaniard named Eduardo offered to take me into a new and remote ice-climbing area for a few days. I organized the hardware and Eduardo organized the food. A friendly, rail-thin guy, he handed me the food bag and said, "I hope you like Chilean food." The bag was about the size of a loaf of bread. I looked at it questioningly, but Eduardo said, "It's very light, only dry foods, but *mucha comida*."

Well, Eduardo was by all reports an experienced alpinist, and I was willing to learn some new tricks. Still, that bag looked awfully light to a 170-pound Canadian in winter-eating mode. At the last minute I bought a dozen packages of candy and some cookies.

After an eight-hour approach, at our first camp Eduardo pulled out a package of dried bits. Soon the tent was filled with great-smelling steam. The only problem was the quantity of food producing the steam: perhaps one cup each of a tasty but watery mixture. Oh well, I thought, maybe this was just the first course. Nope. In fact, Eduardo informed me that normally he and his friends would make one packet last two nights. Eh??? My cookies went down well for both of us as "dessert."

Okay, dinner was a bit weak, but breakfast surely would be a bigger event. In the morning I lit the stove and made tea, then looked over at Eduardo for the monster bag of oatmeal or whatever else we were going to cook. He removed a Pop-Tart-sized packet of well-smashed crackers and a small plastic container of caramel sauce. "It's very good, I hope you like it." Yes, I liked it, but a smear of caramel sauce on a few broken crackers is NOT breakfast. My stomach rumbled, and I finished the remainders of my backup cookie supply. Eduardo then mentioned that I'd just eaten tomorrow's breakfast, too, but he had some extra crackers so it was all right. That afternoon I mumbled something about pizza, and as we returned after a stellar first ascent to enjoy another one-cup dinner, I started openly whining about the food situation.

After three days of this we hiked out. Only crumbs were left in the food bag. I was several pounds lighter and seeing visions of Chilean marmots roasting on a stick. I promised Eduardo that when he came to Canada to go climbing, I would bring elk steak and lots of butter.

—*Will Gadd*

but it will nonetheless be in possession of it until it gives up trying, by which time it may have taken your food supply someplace you cannot find it.

Drink!

It's important to drink plenty of water during the day. (But not in the evening. If you down a lot of liquid before bed, you'll be up in the wee hours, especially if you've been drinking peppermint tea.) People who use sucky-hose water bladders find it easy to stay properly hydrated on the trail. For those of us who prefer a water bottle, it's important to make the effort to haul the thing out when we stop to rest and eat.

If it's noon and you haven't peed—or felt the need to pee—since breakfast, you're dehydrated. Even slight dehydration affects your balance and coordination, and moderate dehydration adds a headache. Don't wait for the top of the pass to stop for a drink. If you're at all thirsty, knock back some water now. Better yet, make a point of drinking before you become noticeably thirsty. Thirst indicates that you're already somewhat dehydrated.

Should you be using **athletic drinks?** Many hikers do, buying a good-sized bottle and using that as the day's water bottle. Some backpackers carry envelopes of Gatorade or similar to mix along the route, hoping to keep their electrolyte levels balanced and so on. Many experienced backpackers, though, will tell you that plain water is the most thirst-quenching thing there is, short of a cold beer at trail's end.

Since plain water is none too appetizing with the first meal of the day, you might find yourself substituting tea, coffee, hot chocolate or sugary drink mixes in the morning. These all taste good, but they don't provide enough H_2O to make up for the overnight drought, especially if you've taken my advice and not had much to drink after supper. So here's some more advice: if you haven't opted for plain water at breakfast, then make a point of downing about half a litre of water just before you hit the trail. Otherwise you'll be starting out dehydrated—not a good start to your day.

Caffeine, nicotine

It's not difficult to have your morning and evening hot cuppa on a backpacking trip—coffee and tea come in convenient single-use bags—but what about those mid-morning, noon and afternoon coffee breaks? On the trail you're unlikely to get them. And if you're caffeine-dependent you'll miss them, perhaps to the point of irritability and headaches. The solution? **Chocolate-covered coffee beans.** A friend of ours gave these the perfect name: "magic beans." You eat a couple whenever the craving hits. Chew them up well for maximum effect. I always carry a stash of magic beans to offer to clients who are lagging and clearly need a fix. ("The first one's free, kid, but after that it's street prices, okay?")

Be aware, though, that it's all too easy to overdo the magic beans. If you pop them like candy you'll get terribly wired, which feels great for a while, then you'll crash on the last couple of kilometres to camp and be fussing along in the rain. Another drawback to using caffeine in the backcountry is that you probably won't sleep as well.

Tobacco tends to be less of an issue for hikers and backpackers, most of whom are healthy types who don't smoke and don't care for the odour of cigarettes. If you're a smoker and want to come along on a group hike, the polite thing is to start off in clothes that don't smell of stale smoke, then wear a nicotine patch, chew nicotine gum, use a nicotine inhaler or nibble nicotine candy instead of lighting up along the trail. This is easier and more acceptable than trying to grab a hurried smoke at every rest stop. No matter how hard you try to stay downwind, the most militant anti-smoker in the group will catch a whiff and begin a slow burn. I don't recommend chewing tobacco or snuff, as they're terribly cancer-causing in the mouth and oesophagus.

People trying to kick their nicotine addictions sometimes go cold turkey on backpacking trips, and this can work, but more often than not it ruins an otherwise pleasurable experience. My advice: until you're certifiably non-smoking, coddle your vice outdoors with Nicorettes or whatever and enjoy yourself. You'll also be a more pleasant companion. Then, when you get home, break the habit before your next trip.

Slimming down

As mentioned earlier, backpacking is an enjoyable weight-loss activity. There's no need to diet with this pastime: you can enjoy those carbohydrates and trim your middle anyway—although you might not notice much weight loss at the end of an early-season trip. You build muscle when you hike, especially when you're carrying a heavy pack, and muscle weighs more than fat by volume. However, fat shrinkage quickly overtakes muscle-tissue gain over the course of a summer, and you'll probably find the kilograms melting into many kilo*metres* of footprints.

If you're hiking vigorously and often, yet not noticing much weight loss, perhaps your food intake is too great, especially your intake of sweet or fatty stuff. A long walk can generate strong hunger, and the trick is not to overeat afterward. I get terribly hungry after exercise, yet I once lost 18 kilograms in three months (too much too fast, actually) simply by eating less, exercising more and resisting the urge to hit the cookie jar when I came back from mountain-biking. This was without much regard to what I ate. The first week was hard, but after that my appetite came under control and the rest was easy. Other people have reported the same thing. They have been mostly men, who generally seem to lose weight more easily than women do.

Part 3
Going backpacking

I love to go a-wandering
Along the mountain track
And as I go, I think I know
This pack will break my back
    —How that song should REALLY be sung

Hiking in the Selkirks, Glacier National Park, BC
with Mt. Sir Donald in the background

Choosing a route and companions

You've got all the gear. You've walked all over Winnipeg getting fit. Next stop the Rockies!

Uh—what's the sequence? How do you plan this thing? Where should you go? How much food should you take? Who should you ask to go with you? What the heck are you getting yourself into, anyway? A pleasurable experience, we hope. Here's how to go about it.

If you're new at this game, you'd do well to choose a short and popular route. Try a three- or four-night trail with enough challenge for you to learn the ropes but nothing that's likely to get you into trouble. The trail should be popular with hikers, well maintained and easy to follow. Rivers should be bridged and there should be established campgrounds.

This seems like a lot to ask, but you can find it all in the national parks of the Rockies. Check the guidebooks, call the information number for one of the mountain parks or ask experienced backpackers for help in choosing a route that offers a bit of everything you wish to experience: walking in lush subalpine forests, crossing a pass above the treeline, hopping across creeks on boulders (the larger river crossings are bridged) and camping at various elevations in sites maintained and regulated by Parks Canada. You may also encounter the typical Canadian Rockies negatives: bugs, horses and people who are taking up space in the backcountry campsites without having made reservations or paid fees.

Suppose, then, that you're a first-time backpacker and you're going to do a three-day trip on one of the trade routes. Good choice. Now then, who's going with you? You say you're going alone? Well, yes, it is a well-travelled trail, which means that there will be other hikers to help you if you have a serious mishap. Stay on the trail, though. Don't be tempted to go off bushwhacking alone in some side valley that gets visited by three people all summer.

Better yet, don't go solo at all. There's a saying among outdoors people: approach new activities and new places cautiously. This is absolutely true, not so much because you might get hurt flinging yourself into the wilds alone and unprepared—people have certainly got themselves killed this way—but because you'll have a much better time if you go with people who've already been there and know what they're doing. You'll learn a lot, and in an easy, pleasant way. Not to push my own vocation, but this is what guides are for.

However, even better than a hired guide, and available cost-free, is an experienced friend who is also a good backpacking companion.

Hikers near Mt. Assiniboine, BC Rockies

As a pair, or a threesome or a group of four to six, you'll almost certainly have a great time together. Here are some criteria for being good trail buddies:

- You know each other well. You've gone adventuring together before.

- You look out for each other, keeping an eye on the group and the circumstances it finds itself in. You think, "That log over the creek looks slippery, and Chuck's about to step on it," and you yell, "Hey, Chuck! How's that log look?"

- None of you are overly bossy or demanding of the others, but neither are any of you shy in stating your views. You're each willing to hear what the others think, and you act on each other's good suggestions.

- You're willing to give each other a chance to lead the party. You share the job of finding the route, setting the pace and so on. And when you're following whoever is out front, you allow yourself to be led.

- You can be honest with one another. You feel no need to exaggerate your experience or your physical abilities or to invent things to disguise a lack of knowledge or fitness.

- You pay attention to others when they speak, and you think before *you* speak. (Heard a great one recently, from Texas: "Before you spit out them words, son, *taste* 'em first.") You don't try to dominate every conversation or one-up what everyone else has to say.

- You wait for your turn to use the stove. You help with the cooking and the cleaning up.

- You're all reasonably physically fit. You don't attempt a trip if you're not up to it in one way or another, which could cause problems for everyone else. You also recognize that each of you has particular strengths and limitations. You keep these in mind through the day, as the terrain varies and the situation changes.

- You all have decent gear, in good repair.

- You all have enough food, so no one is bumming from the others.

- Your boots fit well and don't give you blisters, which could incapacitate you and perhaps wreck the trip for everyone if the blisters become severe.

- You stick together on the trail, and you tell each other when one of you needs to stop for something or has to step into the woods for a moment. No one just disappears, leaving the others wondering where that person went and whether she or he is okay.

- Each of you has particular talents that the others can make use of. One person is really good at reading maps, for instance, while another can always seem to fix things that break.

- None of you snores. (Well, not too loudly.) Or if one of you snores, *all* of you snore!

Finally, here's some hard-nosed advice: be wary about including people you don't know very well on your trips. An acquaintance may be eager to go with you and may seem well qualified, but this impression may change for the worse a few days into the backcountry, when incompetence or personality conflict or both are turning your dream hike into a nightmare. In my job I often have to deal with people I don't know, people who meet one another for the first time and then spend a week together in the wilds. Usually this works out well. Most party members turn out to have the good attributes described above and are excellent company. Sometimes, though, one or two in the group have a way of irritating the rest, taking the fun out of things. (And let's look first at ourselves, eh? If everyone on your last outing began treating you like chopped liver, there may be a reason. Find out what it was.)

Not that troublesome folk can't learn to be otherwise. On occasion I have taken someone aside quietly and suggested that they change their behaviour. With most people this advice is received well—who wants to be known as a backcountry boor?—and harmony ensues. But if not, the rest of the group may have to lay down the law.

None of my outings has ever melted down completely, with everyone abandoning ship partway through, although you do hear of such things. For that very reason, if you're unsure of someone but you'd like to give them a try, make that first trip with them a *short* one.

High-tech trip planning

Advice about a specific route in a particular area used to be much more difficult to find than it is now. Time was, you'd have to get on the phone and chase down sources—not cheap if you were living in Toronto and headed for Banff! If you lived far from the region of interest, it was difficult even to know where to start.

Today, though, we have far more guidebooks, more shops with knowledgeable staff, more clubs, and—especially—we have the Internet. Search the name of the trail you're thinking of walking, and/or the area of interest, and many times a good description of the very hike you're interested in will pop up, complete with photos. If you're lucky, there will be a GPS file you can download, with a track and waypoints. Of course, like any other information on the net, consider the source of it. Better that it comes from a national park's website, say, than www .duanesbigfootden.ca.

Want to take a look at the terrain before you hike it? Try Google Earth (http://earth.google.com). The visual detail is good, and it keeps getting better.

Chrissy Davey

Story of a
backpacking trip

Story of a backpacking trip

As a way of seeing the hands-on (feet-on?) part of backpacking, let's follow a hypothetical party of five as they hike the quasi-fictional Lillian Lakes Loop in Jasper National Park. These folks are all from Edmonton's fully fictional Capital Mountain Club.

Jacquie and Reg have done the trip three times before. It's their favourite backpack, and they know it well. They prefer the Lillian Lakes in mid-August, after the most crowded part of the summer is over. There are fewer hikers, fewer horse parties and fewer mosquitoes.

Pat and Art are likewise very experienced, mostly from trips in the Appalachian Mountains of eastern Canada. Art has also done some mountaineering in Europe. They met Jacquie and Reg through the Capital Mountain Club, which they joined soon after arriving in Alberta from Ottawa a year ago. Joining the club has been a wise move. Going on club trips has saved them a lot of time and trouble in learning about the Rockies, and they're delighted to have become friends with backpackers as experienced and competent as Jacquie and Reg.

The fifth person is Shannon. The youngest, she has hiked with the others on several day trips, but she hasn't done any real backpacking yet. This will be her first multi-day experience.

What follows is necessarily instructive and rather contrived. For this, please forgive me. I hope it serves its purpose, which is to give practical examples of points made earlier in the book and to introduce some tips and tricks that might prove useful to you as you make your way through the wilderness. Plus I have included some genuine Canadian backpacker lingo. Walk the walk and talk the talk!

Planning and gathering supplies

Several days before the group set off, Jacquie and Reg invite the other three club members over after work to make plans. They're taking three tents: one for each couple and one for Shannon. Pat called Parks Canada in Jasper that afternoon to see about booking campsite space. The evenings of August 8, 9, 10 and 11 will work, with tent pads available at the Rutledge River backcountry campground on Thursday night, at Lillian Lakes campground on both Friday and Saturday nights, which will give them Saturday in which to hike in the area without having to carry all their gear to another campground. There's space for them at Caribou Creek campground on Sunday, then they can finish their trip by crossing Redstone Pass and heading down Redstone Creek on Monday. Five days altogether. The first day will be a short one because they'll have to drive for several hours to get to the trailhead. The last day will be their longest—18 kilometres—but by then they'll be fit, their packs will be light, and the final 12 kilometres of the hike will be downhill.

It turns out that everyone can free up all five days, so Jacquie calls the parks service again and secures the sites, paying everyone's overnight fees on her credit card. The others reimburse her immediately.

Reg asks about stoves, fuel and cookers. Art says that he and Pat always cook together, because of his allergies, so they'll be bringing a stove and pot of their own, as well as their own food. Reg and Jacquie ask Shannon if she'd like to share their stove and cooker. She agrees with some relief since she doesn't own this equipment.

"If we carry the stove and pot," says Jacquie, "would you mind carrying the fuel canisters? They weigh about the same."

Shannon nods. "I won't need to cook much," she says. "All my food is going to be instant." Jacquie and Reg are glad to hear this. They can boil water for Shannon's supper in just a few minutes, pour it for her, then get started on their own meal. No problem with waiting for Shannon's noodles to go round and round in their pot. No clean-up after her, either.

So far so good. If either stove breaks, the group will still have one to use. In this event cooking will be crowded but manageable.

"How about a tarp?" Art asks.

"Got one," says Reg. "That big one we used last time that makes shelter for a whole table."

"Great," says Art. "I'll carry it the first day."

"You're on."

"Who's going to carry water filters?"

"We ought to have two."

"I'll carry one."

"I'll carry the other."

"Check." It's Jacquie, who's been marking off items on a checklist she's made up, adapted from one she saw in a book about backpacking in Canada. "That ought to be enough, eh?"

"I can take my filter, too . . ." Shannon sounds doubtful. Her pack is going to be pretty heavy as it is, since she has to carry her own tent. The filter will add another half-kilogram.

Reg realizes this. "No need. We've had both Art's and mine completely apart out there, and we got them working again just fine."

"Plus I always bring some chemical treatment stuff, just in case," Pat adds.

Jacquie looks at her list again. "I'll bring my water bag, like usual." What Jacquie is offering weighs next to nothing, but it will make getting water much easier for everyone. "Next item is bear spray."

"I'm taking mine."

"Me, too."

"Me three."

"Sounds like we're going to have plenty."

"Too much? We really only need one, don't we?"

"Well, what happens if it's in the tent when we need it?"

"Good point. Might as well have two."

"Three. I want mine when I'm on the potty."

"Oh, okay. Three it is. It's probably safer that way anyhow. Is anyone bringing a GPS?"

"I've got this new one!"

"Reg, you hardly know how to use the thing."

"No, but Art's a pro. Right, Art?"

"You bet. What kind is it?"

"Garmin."

"Perfect. That's what I use."

"Okay. Reg and I have the maps." Jacquie's pen is busy. "Last item. Who's driving?"

Shannon is waving her arm around. "Me! Me!"

"Your new Outback? Hey, I vote for you! We can all squeeze in there."

Pat looks doubtful. "Don't we need two cars?"

"You're right," says Jacquie. "We start at Rutledge Hostel and come out at the Redstone Creek lot."

"It seems a shame to drive two cars all the way out from the city just for that."

Art has an idea. "Hmmm . . . it's all downhill from Redstone to Highway 93, isn't it?"

"Yeah, pretty much."

"We could leave my bike at Redstone, and I could ride it back to the car."

Jacquie considers this. "Well, yes—but then you've got a few clicks to do over to the Rutledge Road turnoff, plus all the way back up to the trailhead by the hostel. That's quite a ways. It's pretty steep. I don't know."

"I haven't got a bike rack anyway," says Shannon. "But I was thinking of buying one."

Art is still pushing his idea. "Well, if you do, I'm willing to bike over to the turnoff and hitch-hike up to the parking lot. There's lots of slow traffic on that road."

"Actually, I've done that before," says Reg. "And I didn't have any problem getting picked up. There were plenty of cars, even late in the day."

Jacquie looks around the table. "So do we want to try this?"

Jacquie

Pat

Shannon

Art

Reg

"Why not?"

"It could be miserable for us all if it's raining. Art would be out in it, and we'd all be waiting and waiting."

"True—"

Art is still hopeful. "But you'll have the tarp, right?"

Pat is sold. "Okay. I say let him give it a go. We could save gas, be better for the environment."

Jacquie agrees. "Okay with me, as long as I'm not the one with the thumb out."

They've now established the dates and the route, as well as the equipment to share and who will be supplying and carrying it. They've even worked out transportation and made their campsite reservations. The next stage is to provision themselves, pack up and go.

Provisioning and packing food

Since Shannon is new at this, she accompanies Jacquie on the trip to buy food and fuel for their threesome. At MEC they pick out freeze-dried suppers, each in a pouch from which it can be eaten directly. Jacquie tells Shannon that they're all pretty good, but the ones with cream sauces or tomato sauces have the edge on the others. "One thing I've learned, though, is that the package says it feeds two, but it really only feeds one." They select enough suppers for each of the three of them for four nights—12 pouches of food altogether—and then Jacquie tosses in one extra.

"Is this in case we're stuck out there another night?" Shannon asks.

"That's possible, but it's more likely somebody will dump one on the ground. Reg usually manages to spill at least one meal on just about every trip."

They pick up some of their snacks at the outdoor-equipment shop, specialty items that are often difficult to find at ordinary grocery stores—snack bars for athletes and organically grown, fairly traded chocolate, for example.

"How many of these energy bars should I bring?"

"I eat three a day. One in mid-morning—we always have a good long break at about ten—then one at lunch and one in the afternoon." Jacquie is throwing bars into her basket. "The carrot cake ones are really good."

"Actually, I'm just remembering that I can't stand any of them."

"No? Well, how about these?"

Shortly after that they're looking at LPG fuel cartridges for the stove they're going to share.

"Just two canisters?"

"We could bring three. We'll only need two if we're careful, but if we have three we can make lots of tea and not have to worry about it. And I've never really foregotten the time I took off for the day and left the valve on the stove just a teeny bit open. It wasted most of the can. Someone else in the campground smelled it and turned it off, but it was too late by then."

"Was it all over the ground?"

"No, it comes out as a gas. Good thing, eh?"

They leave the shop and head to the grocery store. They buy instant Japanese noodles, tea bags, a box of hot chocolate, single-serving packets of Swiss instant soup, a box of instant rice, candy bars—"Two real candy bars for me. Per day," says Jacquie—bags of shelled sunflower seeds, mixed nuts and Smarties; a little tub of soft cream cheese and another of peanut butter; two bags of ginger snaps, a bag of corn chips, a bottle of mild salsa, a box of Norwegian flatbread crackers and enough turkey jerky to add some protein for lunch. Jacquie notices Shannon bagging up three oranges and three apples. "Uh, there's a lot of water in that fruit," she says.

"So?"

"So why carry it? See those dried apple slices and dried apricots over there? They'll be just as good on the trail, and they weigh a whole lot less."

"Well . . ." Shannon looks at the lovely Galas in her basket. "Just one apple, for a treat?"

"Oh, I think you could manage that. You know, if you like fresh stuff, we should get some sugar snap peas. They're great raw. And they stay crisp for days. I don't know how, but they do."

They stop at a health-food store for bean flakes, then head over to Shannon's place to repackage the food and apportion it.

They throw all the nuts, sunflower seeds and Smarties into a bowl and mix them together. "Mmmm, I love gorp," Jacquie says.

"Gorp?"

"Good Old Raisins and Peanuts," Jacquie replies. She laughs. "Even without any raisins in it. Reg can't stand them."

They mix the bean flakes 50/50 with the instant rice, then measure out one cup per day for each person into three sturdy zip-lock bags, the kind that stand up by themselves for easier scooping. The cookies and crackers are repacked, too, as are the corn chips.

Shannon looks at the bags. "Isn't all this fragile stuff going to get crushed?"

"Yes, it will. Gradually. But gingersnaps and flatbread last pretty well. Here, let me do those corn chips." She grabs a bag and starts crunching it in her hands.

"Hey!"

Jacquie laughs. "These are supposed to get smunched. They go into the beans and rice. So I might as well make the bag smaller to begin with." She opens the jar of salsa and pours most of it into a plastic bottle.

They divide the jerky, crackers and cookies three ways, putting each person's share into more zip-locks. These bags, along with the cream cheese and the peanut butter, which stay in their lightweight plastic tubs, go into three mesh bags, one for each person. The mesh bags will be their snack/lunch bags.

Jacquie and Shannon have now sorted everything into three piles of food. Rather than packing their meals together, so that one person carries all the suppers, say, and another carries all the breakfasts, the piles are separated. That way each person can eat as planned if one of the threesome has to drop out of the trip partway along. If that were to happen, reapportioning the food would be complicated and probably wouldn't work out very well. It's better for each person to look after his or her own food.

To each pile, Jacquie adds a couple of wadded-up plastic grocery bags to use for garbage sacks, plus a medium-sized plastic garbage bag. Then she finishes the job of packing the food by putting the provisions for each person into a medium-sized stuff sack. Each sack has a sturdy drawcord for hauling the sack up on the food-storage poles Parks Canada provides at campsites. She explains that the garbage bag will be used to keep the food sack dry while it's hung up.

Shannon lifts her sack to gauge the weight. "Hey, this is pretty light! Have we really got enough food for five days?"

"More than enough. I always seem to have snacks left for in the car on the way home."

Loading a pack

Shannon and Jacquie stop by the university outdoor-equipment depot to rent equipment for Shannon. Jacquie helps her select a comfortable women's backpacking pack, a one-person tent and a summer-weight down sleeping bag. Then they head over to Reg and Jacquie's house. Reg is home, and the two more experienced backpackers show Shannon how to pack up. Their preference, which many people share, is to pack in the following order. Shannon follows their lead.

1. Jacquie's pack is an older model, and there isn't much padding against her back to keep lumpy objects from poking her, so she slides a piece of closed-cell-foam sleeping-pad material into her pack, on the side that will rest on her back. This pad is cut to match the width and length of that part of her pack. When the pack is unloaded, she can pull the pad out and use it as a sitting pad in camp. Shannon's pack is newer, and fully padded. She likes the idea of a sitting pad anyway, so Jacquie locates the old foamie from which she cut her sitting pad and gives it to Shannon, who trims it to size. At Reg's suggestion, she slides the pad down the side away from her back, where it will protect the pack's fabric from abrasion.

2. Then Jacquie unfolds an ordinary plastic garbage bag and slips it down into her pack, which, like Reg's and Shannon's, is the one-big-compartment type. She folds the top of the bag over the pack as if the pack were a garbage can. This bag will line the pack and provide a barrier against rain. It will keep the contents dry if she should slip while crossing a creek and fall briefly onto her back in the water.

3. Jacquie now unfolds another plastic garbage bag, a smaller one, into her sleeping bag's stuff sack. This will keep the bag effectively twice-removed from any moisture. The plastic bag shouldn't tear because it's inside the stuff sack. After stuffing the sleeping bag, Jacquie kneels on the sack to flatten it. Then she twists the end of the plastic bag, closes it tightly with a twist tie, folds it into the sack and pulls the drawstring shut.

4. Jacquie's sleeping bag, now in its stuff sack, is placed flat in the bottom of the pack. It's the last thing that needs to be removed at camp, so it's the first item to go into the pack. It's a relatively lightweight item—good for the weight-distribution rule about light things at the bottom and heavy things at the top—and it fits nicely there.

5. Her down jacket is next, stuffed like the sleeping bag into a sack lined with a plastic bag. The stuff sack is larger than required, so the jacket is not tightly packed into it. "This way, it's comfortable to use as a pillow," Jacquie explains to Shannon. "Check this out." She has sown a piece of soft fleece over one side of the stuff sack. "Oooo, nice!" says Shannon. Jacquie adds, "These days you can buy them already made like this."

6. The inflatable sleeping pad is folded, so it will fit flat inside the pack and thereby be protected from punctures by broken branches and sharp rocks along the trail. If nothing sharp-edged is placed next to the pad in the pack, there's no need for a sack for the pad.

7. Another stuff sack is lined with a small plastic garbage bag. In the bag go extra underwear and socks, long underwear—whatever clothing won't be needed until bedtime.

8. The tent, minus the poles, is denser than the items under it and goes into Jacquie's pack next. The poles, even when folded, are longer than the pack is wide and won't fit on top of the previous layer. Reg carries them in their sack on the outside of his pack, slipped down one side behind the side-straps. The end of the pole sack slips into one of the low pockets sewn onto the pack to prevent anything stowed this way from sliding out.

9. The stove and pot also go into Reg's pack. Their weight, plus that of the tent poles, roughly equals the weight of the tent body in Jacquie's pack. These items are all dense, so they're carried high in the pack. The tiny LPG stove fits into Reg's mug, which fits into the pot along with his spoon, a pot-lifter and a featherweight scrubber. All of this goes into a small drawstring bag. The bag is placed on the opposite side of the pack bag from where the poles will be carried, to counterbalance them. Reg's first-aid kit also goes into this layer. If he had to pack a light rope for pulling food up into a tree for the night—and for this trip he doesn't, because there are bear poles with steel cables at each campground they'll be using—then this would be a good place to pack it, too. The three fuel canisters are set to one side for Shannon.

10. At this point Jacquie folds inward the top of the plastic garbage bag lining her pack. She overlaps the edges, forming a seal. The items below, which she wants to keep dry, are now well protected. The items that will go above aren't moisture-sensitive, and anyway she wants to be able to get at them quickly.

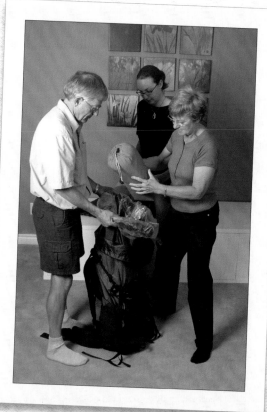

11. Rain pants and rain jacket go in next. Atop these, Reg places his tarp and water filter. The filter is usually put away wet, so having it on top of the waterproof rain gear won't hurt anything. At this point there isn't a whole lot of room left in the pack.

12. The food bag and water bottle are the top items and the heaviest. The bag holds all Jacquie's food, including such bear attractants as toothpaste, so that there will be no doubt when it comes time to raise her food overnight that nothing of interest to a bear remains in the pack. She snugs up the drawstring at the top of the pack. It doesn't close completely; her food bag sticks out a little. Jacquie pulls the pack's extension sleeve up; it reaches higher yet and covers the food bag and the bottle. She tightens this drawstring, too. "Thank heavens for that sleeve," she remarks. "For a trip this long, I never seem to get everything to fit inside. At least my food bag gets smaller as the days go by."

13. Only small items remain to be loaded. After some discussion Reg and Jacquie decide that wading shoes are a must for this trip. The shoes are tucked into the lower pack pockets, held in place by the lowest strap, where they're easy to withdraw for wading streams. The maps and Reg's new GPS receiver go into the big head-flap compartment where they'll be easy to reach, while the flat pocket under the head-flap holds a small paperback book and a zip-lock bag containing driver's licence, credit card, bank card, health-care card, cash and keys. Her sunglasses, sunscreen, insect repellent, maps, headlamp and incidentals go into the head-flap compartment on top of the maps, held in a mesh bag so they don't individually drop out when the zipper on the head-flap is opened.

14. The pack is now fully loaded. Jacquie straps the head-flap down, then adds two finishing touches: she puts a couple of spare twist-ties through a slot in the webbing "ladder" atop the head-flap— "I'm always losing these," she says—and she clips a small carabiner there too.

"What's that for?" Shannon asks.

"It's for hooking my walking poles onto my pack. Otherwise I'll leave 'em sitting at some snack break, I know."

"I'm even worse about that," Reg says, clicking a carabiner onto his own pack. "I lose everything I set down. Poles, water bottle, everything. It's got to be physically attached or it's gone. Here, have one."

Shannon accepts the proffered carabiner. "Is that everything?" She's been keeping up with the packing, impressed with how well everything has fit into her rented pack.

"Not quite." Jacquie puts her pack on the floor, harness side down. She uses a knee to push in on the lower part as she pulls the lower side-straps tight. She does the same for the next set of straps, which compress the middle zone of the pack. She doesn't pull the top straps much, because they would compress her food bag, with its breakable cookies and crackers, but she does pull the extension sleeve's drawstring tighter over the load. She tightens the head-flap straps, stands up and looks at the pack. It's now noticeably thinner than it was before.

"Does that really do anything?" Shannon asks.

"It does, actually. I know it looks stupid to squash your pack like that, but it puts the load closer to your back. That makes a difference in how much it pulls on you." Jacquie holds Shannon's pack up for her to slip the shoulder-straps on. "Here, you haven't compressed yours yet. Try it on."

"This is heavy!"

"Walk around the room with it for a minute." Shannon does as instructed. "Okay, now work the side-straps like I did." Shannon takes the pack off and gives it a good squashing. She puts it on again.

"You know, it *does* feel different . . ."

"Yeah. And after 10 kilometres it's a pretty big difference."

"Oh! We forgot something!"

"What?" Jacquie has been through this packing-up sequence many times and is genuinely puzzled.

"Toilet paper," says Shannon. Jacquie and Reg laugh. They've lost count of the times they've foregotten the toilet paper. Jacquie gives them each a roll. Shannon looks at hers. "Is that going to be enough?"

Reg flattens his roll and fits it into yet another zip-lock bag, then adds a final bag, folded inside, for carrying used paper to the next camp. He slips this combination into the head-flap pocket, which is now bulging. "That depends, on, uh, how full of you-know-what you are," he replies.

Getting There

Early on August 8 Shannon picks up Jacquie and Reg, then Pat and Art. Each is ready to go at the appointed time, with backpack, walking poles (all with rubber tips, for less clacking on the trail) and boots, plus a small bag with some clean clothing to leave in the car for the trip home. Their boots have been freshly treated with wax waterproofing and their packs are ready to carry. Shannon and Art quickly get Art's bike up on Shannon's new rack, which she tried out a few days ago to make sure that it worked. By 7:00 a.m. the five friends are on the highway heading west from Edmonton.

At 10:30 they reach the entrance to Jasper National Park. The person in the kiosk sees Shannon's annual pass hanging from the mirror and waves them through. They stop in Jasper to pick up their camping permit and buy some sandwiches for lunch, then they shuttle Art's bike to the Redstone Creek trailhead, where they plan to come out in four days. Art rolls his bike into the trees, to hide it well away from the trailhead. He asks Reg to come with him.

"How come?" asks Reg.

"In case I forget where I left it."

"Good idea. I'll get Jacquie, too." They stash the bike and drive up Rutledge Road to the trailhead near the youth hostel, reaching their jumping-off point by noon.

Their plan is to have lunch before starting the day's hike, so that they start well fuelled. Lacking a picnic table, they sit on their packs and eat their sandwiches. They put on unscented sunscreen and trade their street shoes for their boots. Reg takes a little longer than the others and they notice him pulling his socks off.

"Blister pads already?" Art asks.

"No. I just read recently that it helps if you wear your inner pair of socks inside out."

"Really?"

"Well, I'm going to find out." Reg finishes rearranging his socks, then tucks his shirt into his pants carefully, to avoid wrinkles under the hip-belt and around the back-pad. He slips on his small binoculars, carried on a bandolier of flat nylon webbing across his chest instead of around his neck. That way the weight is off his neck, the binoculars will ride comfortably rather than banging against him when he leans forward, and he won't have to take them off every time he needs to remove his pack.

In one smooth motion he picks up the large backpack, bending his knees to avoid back strain, swings it over one shoulder and quickly sticks his arm through the other strap. He raises his shoulders to raise the load—**hinches** is the backpacking term for this motion—as he tightens his hip-belt.

"This pack feels way too heavy."

"I weighed mine on the bathroom scale at home. Nineteen kilos exactly." Art puts on his pack in a more stylish way. He lays it on the ground in front of him, harness up, top pointed toward his feet. Then he stoops down, knees well bent, grabs it and flips it over his head, quickly sticking his arms through the pack as it settles, right side up, onto his back. Shannon whoops with delight. She tries this trick and manages it on the second go.

Jacquie is stretching out her leg muscles the way runners do, reaching back to grab an ankle and pulling a leg up behind her. She pulls out a small camera that she carries in a case on her hip-belt to take the customary trailhead photo. An elderly fellow who has been watching the group's preparations offers to take the snap. The five line up in front of the trailhead sign, poles on hands, smiling for the photo. Back comes the camera. It's digital, so they can view the image right away. It looks as good as they feel. Jacquie thanks the photographer, who is from Europe and wants to know a little about where they're going. Always an ambassador for her favourite pursuit, Jacquie takes the time to explain. They're not in a hurry. Their first camp is only 7 kilometres away, and they have all afternoon to get there.

The day has become cloudy and a little chilly. Nonetheless, they start slowly to prevent Pat's asthma from acting up. After 20 minutes, past the time when stopping too soon causes stuffiness for her, she halts briefly to adjust her pack—the sway-straps on top need tightening—and she helps Shannon make a similar adjustment to hers. They all remove a layer, having overdressed a little at the start. They're sweating but it's better than starting underdressed and forcing cold muscles into action too quickly.

On the trail

A half-hour hour goes by as the group follows the trail along the Rutledge River. Shannon stops to check an incipient blister on one of her heels. While she's doing that, Reg takes the opportunity to step into the woods for a pee. Shannon pulls off a boot, removes her socks and lets the skin dry for a bit before carefully smoothing the gel-type blister pad into place over the hot spot before it becomes a problem. Jacquie refills her water bottle. In other words, when one person stops, some or all of the others take the opportunity to attend to their needs, too. This way there are fewer interruptions and less waiting.

After several kilometres, though, everyone needs a longer break. The sun has come back out, inviting them to relax and enjoy it for a while, and they've reached a perfect spot along the river. The packs come off. The water bottles and the food bags come out. The food is at the top of their packs and easy to get to.

A couple of other hikers have caught up to them. Young and male, they look to be in their early 20s. Their packs are huge, and their gear and clothing look new. One of them stops to talk.

"How long did it take you to get here?" he asks.

Reg replies. "Uh—I don't know. Two hours, maybe?"

The hiker glances at a large, complicated-looking instrument on his wrist. "It only took us 63 minutes," he replies jauntily. "We've been doing 5.3 kilometres per hour."

"Ah, youth," says Pat under her breath.

"Where are you headed tonight?" the other one asks

"Rutledge."

"Rutledge? Is that all? We're going to make Lillian. Right, Jason?"

"At least, dude. I'm actually going for Caribou."

Pat frowns. "But you're booked into Lillian, aren't you?"

"Uh, well, actually we're not booked into anywhere. This was kind of a spur-of-the-moment thing."

"So you don't have a permit."

"Oh, uh, yeah, we got one o' those. Well, gotta go. Bye!" The two walk quickly up the trail.

"I hate that," says Pat. "They'll be taking up someone else's tent pad tonight."

Art shakes his head. "Sounds like they'll be rolling in so late there won't be any room for them anyway."

"Great. They'll be guerrilla-camping. Crapping in the woods, probably making a new fire ring."

"Can we report them?" Shannon asks.

"Who to?" Jacquie replies. "We haven't seen a warden here in three trips."

Reg is philosophical. "Ah, well. Let's not get our bowels in an uproar."

"Right," Art replies. "Onward, is it?"

"Yo, 'dude'!"

They all laugh, put on their packs and continue along the path.

Handling a rain shower

A few minutes later Reg feels a droplet hit his face. He looks up the valley. Sure enough, a fuzzy curtain of light rain is headed their way.

"What do you think, Jack? Rain gear?"

Jacquie considers. "Well, it doesn't look like much . . ."

"Right. No need for the full kit." Reg pulls his rain jacket from his pack. "I'll just slip this on over my shirt."

Shannon has been copying Reg. She's puzzled to see Jacquie pulling out her fleece. "Won't that just get wet?"

"Yes, but I'd rather have a nice, thick layer of that on me than icky old Gore-Tex over a tee-shirt. It makes me sweaty and cold at the same time. Fleece is nice and comfortable. Especially at the tail end of a shower, you know? When the air is always cooler? And it dries out really quickly."

Shannon can't decide what to do. She looks over toward Pat and Art. They're each holding a small umbrella!

Shannon laughs. So do they. "You guys," she says. "Okay, so who's right about this?"

"Oh, just pick one," says Pat. "It's not like we're walking into a typhoon."

Shannon puts on her rain jacket and the party moves on, enjoying the growing fragrance of wetted subalpine fir needles. Art and Pat have each attached their umbrella to their pack—"So that's what that

little extra strap is for!" says Shannon—and can thus keep their hands free for their walking poles. The umbrellas cover their packs as well as their heads and upper bodies. There isn't enough wind to push rain under the umbrella or turn it inside out.

Reg's and Shannon's jackets are soon wet, but the moisture is beading up on the silicone-treated breathable fabric, allowing their perspiration to escape. Jacquie's fleece is covered with droplets, but it's still obviously puffy and warm, not packing down.

Twenty minutes later the rain has stopped. Everyone stops to readjust. Reg places his wet jacket under the head-flap of his pack rather than folding it inside, so that it will dry. Shannon does the same. Art and Pat put away their umbrellas. The sun is shining again, but the temperature has dropped several degrees and the air is chilly. Out come the fleece jackets—except for Jacquie's. She already has hers on. She winks at Shannon, who grins back at her.

Setting up camp

Despite the late start, they're the first ones to arrive at the Rutledge back-country campground. The weather is threatening again, with thunder rumbling in the distance, so shelter is the first order of business.

"I'll pop up the tarp," says Reg as he pulls it from his pack. He has carried it near the top, ready to pitch in a hurry.

"I'll help you," says Shannon, who wants to see how this is done.

"Hey, thanks. Just pull it out of its stuff sack, okay? Oh—I need the cord first." Shannon hands Reg a length of camping cord tucked into the sack after the tarp went in. He looks at the situation—two picnic tables at right angles to each other—and decides which one will work best with the tarp. He walks over to a tree growing near the end of one of the tables, reaches as high as he can and loops the end of the cord around it three times to ease the tension on the trunk and not injure the tree. He ties a simple knot that looks like a bow knot with only one bow.

"What kind of a knot is that?" Shannon asks. The wind is rising, and the tarp billows in her hands.

"Pop knot," Reg replies. "It's really easy to untie, even when it's iced up. You just pull the end and it pops."

"Will it stay tied in this wind?"

"No problem."

"How do you tie it?"

"I'll show you later. Here's the rain."

Indeed, the first drops are hitting. But Reg has pitched his tarp many a time and has the cord slung between the trees in under a minute. The two of them throw the tarp over it and go to work securing the ties on the corners and the sides. They don't need stakes; there are other trees, shrubs and rocks available. By the time the rain is really coming down, everyone is sitting at the table under the tarp, their packs with them, their fleece jackets, gloves and tuques on to keep them warm and comfortable. Pat gets her stove out.

"Tea?"

"Oh, yes!" says Shannon.

"Well, go get us some water then. Here's a pot." Shannon runs down to the river. A strong gust of wind hurls rain under the tarp and threatens to blow it down, but the tarp has been pitched tightly. It doesn't catch the wind and balloon out. It just flattens briefly and snaps back. Lightning flashes, and the boom that follows makes Art, who has been watching the top of Aster Mountain disappear among black clouds, tell everyone that he's glad not to be up there right how. In the Alps he experienced electrical storms on the heights, and he knows just how terrifying and dangerous they *(continued on page 184)*

Typical camping sequence

1. Arrive at camp early enough to beat the crowd.
2. Select a tent site and set up your tent.
3. If it's going to be some time until supper, stash all your food and other animal-attracting items (toothpaste, soap) where wildlife can't get it; for example, up on the camp bear pole.
4. Unpack your sleeping bag and pad. Spread the bag out in the tent to let it air before bedtime. Be sure there's nothing edible (or otherwise animal-attracting) in the tent. Zip up the bug netting.
5. Pitch your tarp to provide shelter for cooking and eating. Do this even in good weather. It might rain overnight, and the tarp will keep the spot dry.
6. Fill a water bag and hang it up on a broken branch or dangle it from a table (see photo on page 186).
7. Set up a pump filter with its intake hose in the bag, so that you use the bag, not the creek or the lake, as your water source. Pump only water you intend to drink cold. Water to be boiled can be poured directly from the bag into the pot.
8. Get the stove going and begin heating water for supper. Heat only as much as you need for a cup of instant soup, a freeze-dried meal, a hot drink and a little water for rinsing your cup.
9. Retrieve your food bag and assemble your supper while the water's heating. Pour the soup mix into your cup (no need for a bowl).
10. Add boiling water to the soup mix. Pour plenty of boiling water directly into the pouch holding the freeze-dried meal. Turn the stove off to save fuel.
11. Drink the soup while the meal is rehydrating in its bag. When the soup is gone, swish a little hot water around in the cup and drink that, too.
12. Eat the meal directly from the bag, trimming the bag down as you near the bottom to reach into the corners without smearing food on your fingers.
13. Your cup is now clean enough for tea or hot chocolate. When finished, swish some more water in the cup and drink it. The cup is now ready for tomorrow's breakfast. Lick the spoon clean, perhaps using a little water to rinse it.

14. The pot has been used only for boiling water. Unless the area is frequented by animals that might steal your cup, spoon or pot, just leave these items on the table or on the ground overnight. If you're concerned about them, stash them.
15. Store all edibles out of reach of animals for the night.
16. There's no need for a fire. If the evening is becoming chilly, just put on a warm jacket, gloves and a tuque. Spend the time after supper chatting with your companions, going for a stroll or perhaps just sitting quietly by yourself a little way from camp, enjoying your time in the wild.
17. Retire to your tent by 10:00 p.m., which is quiet time in the campground. Place your headlamp, toilet paper and other might-need incidentals within easy reach. Good night.
    (For breaking-camp activities, see page 197 of the story.)

can be. Five minutes later the water has reached boiling temperature, killing any microscopic *Giardia* parasites or other pathogens that might have been in it. Pat pours water from the pot into all the mugs, being careful not to scald anyone. She uses a pliers-like gripper on the pot rather than its bail, because she has better control that way. "Put your cup down, Reg. Then I'll fill it for you."

The campers finish their hot drinks as the afternoon storm moves off down the valley. The sun returns, now low in the west. Pat is fiddling with her camera. "I'm going into photo mode," she says. "I'll be down along the river." She takes good pictures, and they often wind up in the club newsletter.

"Okay," says Jacquie. "Thanks for letting us know where you're going. Got your pepper spray?"

"Yup. See you in 20 minutes."

Art and Reg head over to the tent pads, which are located about 30 metres from the tables. Parks Canada knows that bears come around at night to check for spilled food, so they've separated the cooking area from the tenting area.

The two men have brought their packs, and those of their wives, over to the tent pads. Reg and Jacquie's tent is several years old; Reg has set it up many times and works quickly. Art and Pat's tent is new, but Art has practised its set-up sequence at home and finishes nearly as quickly as Reg does.

"Good thing I tried this puppy out already," he says, wiggling a stake into the tent pad. "One pole was missing when I got it home from the store."

Art and Reg then extract the couples' self-inflating sleeping pads from the four packs. They slide each pair of pads into a tent, opening the inflating valves and orienting them toward the head end. They make double beds by joining two pads side by side with bands of nylon fabric (Therm-a-Rest sells these).

All that remains in each pack is rain gear, a down jacket, a bag of clothing and a sleeping bag in its stuff sack. The down sleeping bags are pulled from their stuff sacks, fluffed up a little and zipped together. By bedtime the down will be fully expanded, light and warm. The down jackets are left in their over-large stuff sacks to function as pillows. Already they're beginning to plump up. The pads are as inflated as they can get by themselves. Art tests his for firmness. He blows a little more air in and tests Pat's. She likes hers a little softer, with just enough air in it to keep her hip from touching the ground. Art judges that Pat's pad is about right and closes the valve. The packs are then emptied completely. The head-flaps are removed, and a pack is placed at the foot of each three-quarter-length pad to lengthen it. When all is arranged inside each tent, the mosquito netting is zipped. The fly and the main door remain open so that air will move through and freshen everything.

Shannon has been watching carefully. Soon she has her own small tent set up, the pad inflating, her own sleeping bag expanding.

Using a water bag, cooking and eating

"It's five o'clock," Pat calls from the table. "Does anyone want to eat? We could do supper now, so we won't have to hang all the food up and then get it back down an hour from now."

"Sure!" This makes sense to Art, who is always hungry. He finds Pat's water bag, takes it down to the river and fills it. Made of tent-fly fabric sewn into the shape of a bowling-ball cover, with webbing loops for handles, the water bag fills quickly as Art holds it against the current. It holds so much water that Art has to struggle to get it back to camp. Reg sees this and runs to help him. They hang the bag from the table, cleverly slipping one of the handles up through a gap in the split-log surface and using a stick to hold it. Art drops the inlet hose of his pump filter into the bag and sets the pump on the table for anyone to use. It's for drinking water only. Water to be boiled needn't be pump-filtered, because boiling will sterilize it. Water to be boiled can be poured directly from the bag into the pot. At the other end of the table Pat has used a stick through one handle of a grocery bag to hang it in the same manner, ready to receive empty food wrappers, tea bags or other garbage.

Both stoves are soon hard at work. They're LPG stoves and hiss quietly rather than roaring loudly as some white-gas stoves do. As the water comes to a boil, the campers empty envelopes of instant soup and packages of Japanese noodles into their mugs. This uses up the hot water supply, but there's more water right at the table. The pots quickly come to a boil again, since some hot water remained in each before it was refilled, to protect the metal from overheating. Now it's time to open the freeze-dried meals.

"Whatcha got?" Art asks the group.

"Chicken and rice pilaf."

"Shrimp alfredo."

"Spaghetti."

"Vegetarian chili."

"*Vegetarian chili?!*" Jacquie exclaims. "That's got textured soy protein in it! You're going to be pooting in the tent all night, Reg!"

"Don't panic. I've brought my good friend Beano, baby."

"Good thing. Or you'd be sleeping outdoors."

Shannon holds up her hand. "Hey, speaking of gassing yourself—"
The others giggle.

"No, really. What if the weather's really bad? Is it okay to cook in the tent?"

"Not with Reg in it," Jacquie offers. "Might ignite, uh—"

"No, seriously."

Art responds. "I never do. Carbon monoxide's nasty stuff. You can't smell it. A couple of skiers died from it in a snow cave a while back. They probably had poor ventilation in there, but even with really good ventilation I wouldn't take the chance."

"So where do you cook in the rain if you haven't got a tarp?"

"Stoves work fine in the rain. You just park it outside the door and make sure the fumes aren't coming back into the tent. Shelter it with your body while you're starting it, then get a pot on it to keep the rain out. It's pretty straightforward."

The water is boiling, and Reg pours some of it into his pouch of chili. It has a zip-lock top, which provides a good seal as Reg kneads the bag from the outside, mixing the contents. He has added more water than the instructions indicate, because he knows that more is always required to avoid clumping in the corners of the pouch.

"Ouch, that sucker's hot." He reaches for a glove.

Everyone slurps soup and chats while their freeze-dries rehydrate. Then they dig in. After a while, Pat turns to Shannon. "Here's a strick." Pat has her pocket-knife in hand, scissors blade out. "You know how you get food all over your spoon and on your hand when you're digging it out from the bottom of the bag?"

"You mean like I've been doing for the last couple of minutes?"

"Okay, you don't have to. Just cut the bag down. Here, I'll do yours." Pat uses the scissors to trim Shannon's pouch down to just above the level of the food. Now it's easy for Shannon to reach all the way to the bottom with her spoon.

"Cool! Thanks!"

"You're welcome."

"Pat, could you do mine, too, please?"

"And mine?"

"Geez . . ."

Cleaning up

Everything has been eaten, so there's no garbage. The messy stuff was consumed directly from the bags it was reconstituted in, and the pots

held only hot water, so there's little in need of washing except the mugs, which had soup in them, and the spoons. Art pours a little boiled water into his mug to rinse it out. He swishes the water around and drinks it. Shannon notices this and smiles. "Good to the last drop, eh?"

"Well, it's better than tossing it into the woods and spreading noodles around. And it gives me a bit more liquid. Pat, would you please hand me the hot chocolate?" He opens the zip-lock bag of Cadbury's and spoons some into his mug.

"Why not just use those single-serving thingies?" Shannon asks.

"More weight, more garbage. It's not a big deal to open this bag and get some. And I can get more if I want." He gives himself an extra dollop.

"Hey!" says Pat.

They turn to finishing the clean-up. Empty wrappers and any spilled food go into the garbage bag at the end of the table. The cups have little in them but drops of hot chocolate and tea. The spoons, well-licked by their owners, are likewise pretty clean. Pat rinses her spoon and mug with a little boiled water. Reg doesn't bother, just leaving his spoon in the cup.

Shannon frowns. "Won't animals take your cup if it's not washed?"

"It's never happened to me," he replies.

"Maybe not in the Rockies," says Pat, "but you don't have any raccoons here. In Ontario they run off with everything."

"I guess you can't be sloppy down east. Shouldn't really be sloppy anywhere, I suppose." Reg rinses out his spoon and mug, then packs them away in his food bag. "Better safe than sorry." He pulls his toothbrush out of the pack head-flap, which has been sitting beside him on the bench. Jacquie has brought a small tube of toothpaste in her food bag. They go over to the toilet and brush their teeth, spitting into the pit. When they're finished Jacquie puts the toothpaste back in the bag, along with their bottles of sunscreen, soap and insect repellent. Even her lip balm goes into the food bag.

"Why did you do that?" asks Shannon.

"Bears," says Jacquie. "You'd be amazed what bears go after. I saw one eat an old smelly runner once. It just tore it up and swallowed the pieces. My rule is, if it smells, stow it up on the bear pole."

"But what about Pat throwing the rinse water from her cup out into the bushes? Won't bears find that?"

"Well, they could. But a bear doesn't care about one grain of rice stuck to a leaf. They go for the big stuff—a whole food bag, that kind of thing. And we make sure that by the time we rinse out our cups there's seldom even a grain of rice in there."

Reg has come over to listen in. He adds something else. "The bears know this is a campground, Shannon. They're always coming around to check it out. I bet we find bear tracks along the trail tomorrow morning. It's not like we're way back in the wilderness, camping somewhere people hardly ever go. Back there we'd be trying not to leave any traces at all."

(For more on Leave No Trace, see page 270.)

Protecting food from bears and other animals

It's time to hang the food up for the night. Well away from the tents and the tables, the Parks Canada trail crew has erected a bear pole for the campground: a log nailed horizontally between two trees, about 5 metres up. Four looped wire cables dangle from pulleys at the top. At opposite ends of each loop, a dog-leash-type snap link is fixed to it. The lower snap link is clipped through an eyebolt screwed into the tree at waist height, to keep the cables from swinging around and tangling in the wind.

Art grabs his food sack, removes a new plastic garbage bag from it and pulls the drawcord tight. A toggle on the cord holds it shut. He pokes a small hole in one corner of the bag, then slips the bag over the food sack and feeds the drawcord out through the hole. The sack now has a rain jacket. The skinny drawcord and the slick plastic will also help to deter tree squirrels that may try to raid the bag. A squirrel might climb the bear pole, but it will find the drawstring rather thin and difficult to grip while trying to climb down onto the food bag, which the plastic bag will make very slippery.

Carrying the sack, Art walks over to the bear pole, unsnaps one of the cables and clips it to the drawcord. "Anyone want to hang with me, as it were?" he calls over to those still sitting at the table.

"Be right there," says Pat, preparing her own food sack and bringing it over. It has a loop of webbing sewn onto the bottom of the sack. Her bag will be hanging upside down, so she makes sure that the drawcord on the top end is pulled tight against the toggle to shut the bag closely. In case the toggle slips, she ties a pop knot against it. Then she pokes the loop through a hole in the plastic bag and attaches the loop to the snap link.

Ben Gadd

"Did you bring your gloves?" Art asks. The two sacks are fairly heavy together, and pulling them up on the wire cable will be tough on the hands. Pat pulls her gloves out of the pocket of her jacket. They have leather palms, perfect for this job. She and Art pull on the cable loop, and the bags rise to the top. At this point the other snap link is in position to be clipped to the eyebolt at waist-level, thereby keeping the bags up there. Done.

Shannon has walked over to watch. "Are bears too dumb to climb up there and get those bags?"

"Maybe around here," says Pat, "but where we used to live the bears are way smart. We have to use metal lockers."

"They're getting to be like that down in Banff," says Reg. He clips his food bag and Jacquie's onto another cable. "But instead of lockers, they've got these cool metal poles. Bears can't get up. Or squirrels. And actually the squirrels are more of a problem around there than the bears."

Art is helping Shannon rig up her food sack. "I remember a campsite in Jasper that had a bear pole just like this one, except they also had big plastic pails for your food. Because of the squirrels."

Shannon asks, "What do you do when there isn't a bear pole?"

"Carry some rope and sling your stuff over a tree branch," says Reg.

"That's not always so easy," adds Jacquie. "And it's really hard on the branch, pulling the rope over it like that. It takes the bark off and kills it. We always try to find a dead branch. Or we'll fix up the rope between two trees and pull the bags up in the middle."

"How much rope does that take?"

Reg replies. "Oh, you need about 15 metres. It doesn't have to be very thick rope, but thicker than camping cord. And a pulley. It's lots easier if you've got a pulley, plus you don't hurt the branch. I use a really light aluminum one, the kind that climbers use to get themselves out of crevasses."

"Crevasses?"

"Holes in glaciers."

"Oh."

"But carrying the rope and the pulley isn't the bad part. It's when there are no picnic tables and you have to carry one of those . . ."

"Very funny. So how do you get the rope over the branch in the first place?"

"I tie a little rock on the end and throw it." He looks over to Jacquie.

"Well, actually, Jacquie throws it. I'm hopeless at that."

She looks back at him sharply. "And you never tie the end high enough up the tree."

"High enough . . . ?"

"The end of the rope. So the bag stays up there." Jacquie looks over to Shannon. "You have to tie it at least head high, so some bear doesn't come along and untie it."

Shannon is shocked. "Really?!"

"Well, not really *untie* it. But bears are way smart. We had one chew through the rope once to get the food bag down."

Pat is thinking about something else. "Did anyone bring the garbage bag over?"

"Not me."

"Not me."

"Oh, nuts . . ."

Shannon offers to lower her food bag, get the garbage bag from the table and stow it in the food bag. She knows that you can't leave garbage out all night.

Going to bed

Everyone is tired from the drive and the hike. They tidy up the table, leaving nothing on it but the two stoves, packed away in their pots, plus the water bag and the filter. Pat, Art and Shannon head down to the river to watch the last of the sunset, which is lighting the Rutledge Glacier at the head of the valley, turning it pink. Later, as nightfall comes and the temperature drops, it's time for bed.

Jacquie goes to the tent first, while Reg is at the biffy. Before unzipping the mosquito netting, she loosens her boots so she can slip them off quickly. She unzips the netting and reaches in to close the valves on their self-inflating pads and checks to see that Reg has remembered to place their empty packs at the ends to provide insulation under their lower legs and feet.

She quickly turns around to sit in the entrance facing outward, kicks her boots off, pulls her legs in and zips the netting up before more than one or two mosquitoes have had time to fly into the tent. Then she unzips just a lower corner of the netting and arranges her boots off to one side of the door, outside the tent but under the fly where they won't get wet if it rains. She and Reg will keep the main door of the tent open all night, with the rain fly tied back somewhat for ventilation—mosquito netting zipped, of course—to provide good

ventilation and avoid condensation under the fly from the moisture in their breath.

Jacquie empties her pockets of small items and places them in one of the tent's interior pockets, where they'll be easy to find in the morning. She lays out her rain jacket and rain pants alongside her, between the sleeping bag and the tent wall. Then she removes her clothes, arranging them atop the rain gear. She spreads her fleece jacket over the down-jacket stuff sack and tucks the corners under it, completing her comfy pillow. As always before bed on these trips, she uses a small packaged towelette to wash herself. Unscented and thus not attractive to bears, it can go back in the zip-lock bag with the unopened envelopes of the other towelettes, one for each day plus a couple of extras. The used one will be put down the outhouse tomorrow morning.

Thinking that the night will be chilly, Jacquie pulls on long underwear from her clothes bag. Her socks, which aren't wet or dirty but are, well, a little smelly from being in her boots all day, are tossed into a far corner of the tent. When Reg gets back she's in their zipped-together sleeping bags, on her side and close to the wall of the tent so that Reg also has room to prepare for bed. The head-flaps from their packs are in the tent with them. These hold their water bottles and all their small items, minus anything that might possibly interest a small animal enough to make it gnaw a hole in the tent. (The bear pole is also a rodent pole.) The camera is in the tent with them, too. Jacquie has tucked her headlamp into the tent pocket.

Reg pulls on his sleeping cap, to keep his bald spot warm. He and Jacquie snuggle up, cozy in the warmth of goose down. At home they would stay up until 11:00 p.m., reading or playing Scrabble, but tonight they're content to close their eyes at 10:00, listening to the sound of the wind in the trees and the river running nearby. No other hikers have come to the campground this evening. Jacquie hears the quiet murmurs of her friends on the other tent pads. Aware of the hour and the mood, everyone is speaking very quietly.

Just as his eyes are closing, Reg hears a branch snap. He raises his head and peers out through the mosquito netting to the opening in the fly. Barely visible in the gloaming, a deer walks into the campground. It beds down for the night only 10 metres from Shannon's tent. A barred owl calls, "Who-cooks-for-you?" Soon everyone is asleep.

Morning in camp

Shannon awakens first. Surprised at how well she has slept on her first night in the wilds, she looks at her watch. It's 7:00 a.m. The sun has already risen over the ridge to the northeast and is warming her tent.

She notes that Jacquie was right about leaving the tent's main door open to avoid condensation. The surface of her sleeping bag is damp around her face and at her feet, which Jacquie told her to expect, but she was warm and comfortable all night. She looks up through the mosquito-netting ceiling of her tent, noting the droplets of condensed moisture on the underside of the fly. One of them falls off and splashes through the netting—her breath revisiting her.

The air temperature feels very chilly, not far above freezing, but the sky is clear, promising a warm and sunny day. Hearing Jacquie and Reg muttering in their tent, Shannon pushes the bag back, gets dressed, pulls on her fleece jacket, gloves and tuque, and unzips the mosquito netting. It's too cool for any mosquitoes or flies to be active yet, so nothing buzzes into her tent. Still, while thinking about insects she can't help but hold each boot upside down and give it a knock before slipping it on as she sits in the door of the tent. "Too many cowboy movies," she mutters. She steps out, zips the netting back up and heads for the toilet.

Sitting there, she notices that a deer is close to Jacquie and Reg's tent, pawing at the moss and licking it. This moss grows everywhere in the campground—everywhere that hasn't been rendered bare by human use—and she, a student of botany at the University of Alberta, recognizes it as some species of feather moss. Then she recalls her bryology professor mentioning that hardly anything eats feather moss.

When she gets back, Reg is coming out of the tent. She asks him about the deer. "Oh, that," he laughs. "I'm so busted. I got up at three last night, kind of, uh, full, and figured that I wouldn't make it to the potty. So I watered that patch the deer is licking—"

Shannon suddenly has a flash of insight. "Salt!" she practically shouts, delighted to have understood. "It's getting the salt in the urine!"

"I guess," Reg says with a laugh. "Hey, you're a backcountry scientist, Shannon."

Art is walking over to the food bags hanging from the bear pole. He puts on his gloves and lowers his and Pat's bags, which he carries over to the table. The tarp has drooped somewhat overnight, so he knocks the dew off it and tightens the lines. Soon he has their stove fired up and a full pot of water on the boil.

"Who wants tea?" he yells.

Everyone moves to the table, food bags in hand. They sit down and extract tea bags, cups and spoons. As the tea steeps, Jacquie and Reg get their stove going, too. Reg pulls out a large zip-lock bag. "Ah, beans and rice," he announces. "The best backpacker's breakfast." He and Jacquie down their tea, which is cooling fast in the chilly morning air, then fill the empty mugs half-full of beans and rice. They add enough boiled water to cover the mix.

Jacquie puts a cube of cheese—she cut the block into cubes at home—into each cup, where it starts to melt. She adds a spoonful of salsa and sprinkles on some corn chips, now thoroughly crushed. The beans and rice have absorbed the water already, and have expanded to fill the cups. Reg sniffs the inviting aroma. "You know, this stuff is so good out here. Why don't we ever eat it at home?"

"Just habit, I guess."

"Speaking of habit, hand me the Beano."

Shannon is having instant oatmeal with brown sugar and walnuts, even quicker and easier than beans and rice. She eats two packets' worth. She glances over to Art, who is dumping a box of raspberry Jell-O into his mug. She can't believe it. "You're actually going to *drink* that?"

"Don't knock it 'til you've tried it," he says. "There's lots of energy in this stuff, and we've got a big hill to do today."

On impulse, she sticks out her hand for Art's cup. He gives it to her. One sip is all it takes. "Hey, that's really good!"

"I used to drink hot Jell-O when I was young," says Reg. "I can't stand it now. It's too sweet."

Shannon gives Art his mug back. "Have you got any extra?"

"Maybe. What've you got to trade?"

"Umm—a praline. I brought some pralines."

"Deal."

The day is warming fast. The tents are already dry on the outside, and the condensation underneath each fly and the minor dampness in the group's sleeping bags will have evaporated within the next half-hour. If this were the first warm, dry day after several cool, rainy ones, the sleeping bags would be quite a bit damper and the group would pull them out of the tents right away to dry them in the sun. However, there's no need for that today.

Breaking camp

"Time to start packing up?" Art is keen to get going. Today will be the hardest hike of the trip, with a lot of elevation gain in the 12 kilometres they're going to walk.

"Fine with me. Just let me finish this cup." Pat is enjoying some after-breakfast tea and makes no move to get up from the table.

Art starts the routine of rounding up their gear and packing it. First he ducks into their tent. Then he pulls his head out and suggests to Pat that they leave their sleeping bags zipped together. He offers to carry them both.

"Sure. I'll carry both the pads."

One of their sleeping bag stuff sacks is intentionally large for this purpose. Art stuffs the sleeping bags in, still zipped together. He opens the valves on their sleeping pads, and, leaving them joined by the straps, folds one atop the other. He rolls them from the foot ends toward the open valves at the head ends. Using his knee, he presses down hard on the pads to squeeze out the air, which whooshes from the pad with each turn of the roll. At the end he presses down on the roll with both knees, expelling as much of the remaining air as he can. Then, with his knees still on the pads, he closes the valves and unrolls the pads, which are quite flat, then folds them into a rectangular shape that will form a layer in Pat's pack.

Art takes his and Pat's items out of the tent, laying them on top of their rain gear in the dewy grass. They work together to take the tent down, shaking the fly between them to get rid of any remaining water droplets on it. Rather than shaking it up and down as if this were a blanket toss, they hold the fly vertically and shake it from side to side. Pat stuffs the fly into the sack. It will be needed last, so it goes in first.

Art pulls the stakes up. He pulls the first one loose with his hand, then uses it to hook the others out. He scrapes off any dirt before putting the stakes in their small carrying bag, which is made of fleece to pad the sharp ends. As a further precaution, Art puts the stakes into the bag with some points facing one way and some points facing the other way. The stake bag goes into the tent's sack along the side and parallel with it. This is all to protect the waterproof coating on the fly, which is easily scratched. Art knows from experience that any scratch will become a leak.

To get the dirt off the outside floor of the tent, Pat simply picks the entire tent off the ground—an advantage of a free-standing tent—and shakes it. She shakes the tent head-end down, with the door open. A few spruce needles and some grit fall out, plus one of her earplugs. Pat sets the tent on its side and they brush off a few resinous twigs and bits of dirt from the outside of the floor. They carefully remove the poles, slip them into their slim sack and set it aside. Then they stuff the main body of the tent into the tent's sack.

Meanwhile Reg and Shannon take down the tarp, shaking the dew off as Pat and Art did with their tent fly.

"How would you like it folded?" asks Shannon.

"No need," replies Reg. "We'll just stuff it. It keeps creases from forming in the same places. If you get creases, the coating eventually flakes away. Or so I'm told."

Part of the morning ritual is to pump-filter water from the group

bag into each container. Shannon uses a bladder-type water reservoir, while the others use polyethylene bottles. Jacquie shows Shannon how to prevent cross-contamination between water bottles. Before pumping water into her own bottle, Jacquie holds the end of the hose up and pumps some water out of it, rubbing the hose as the water dribbles down. This cleans off the part of the hose that has been inside the previous user's bottle.

"But we're none of us sick," says Shannon.

"Not yet," Jacquie replies, with a wink. "Any of us could have something that's contagious before you get the symptoms. Like a cold or the flu. And we don't want to spread that around."

As Art decontaminates the hose and fills his bottle, he says to Shannon, "I just realized that I always start off thirsty because of that sugary Jell-O. Not today." He drinks a half-litre of plain water and refills his bottle. "Anybody else need their water topped up?" he calls. Hearing no reply, he pump-filters the last of the water in the water bag into Pat's bottle. He shakes the bag out, folds it up and packs it, along with the pump, nestled in his rain gear. He used to carry the water bag on the outside of his pack to dry it, but he once tore a hole in a water bag when he flopped his pack down on a rock.

Gradually the packs fill up. Everyone applies sunscreen. Jacquie, the recognized speed-packing champ of the group, is the first one ready to go. But the others aren't far behind her. No one lingers, because they don't want to make the others wait for them.

Right before they leave, each person checks the campsite for litter. Every tiny piece of paper, plastic or foil is picked up, regardless of who might have dropped it. In total, the collected trash from every camp they use will weigh very little, but each bit, if left behind, will offend far beyond its size.

While de-littering, the group checks carefully for any gear that may have been left behind, especially items hanging from trees or spread over shrubs. These tend to be overlooked. Sure enough, Reg has forgotten to take down the line the tarp was slung over.

Soon the packs are on the backs. Art slips his hands through the straps on his walking poles. "All for one and one for all?" he says.

"Yeah!"

Pat is also ready to walk. She stands beside Art. Jacquie and Reg come over. They're forming a circle. Shannon looks puzzled, but she joins in.

"All for one!" shouts Art, who puts the tip of one pole in the centre of the circle. Each of the others does the same with one of their poles.

"And one for all!" everyone shouts together, as they raise their poles up high and bring them down partway to interlock overhead, musketeer-style, clack-clack-clack.

"That was really corny!" Shannon exclaims, laughing. "But I love it!"

Taking a tumble

The group hasn't gone 20 steps before Reg suddenly lurches ahead.

"Honey!" shouts Jacquie. But she can't do anything to help. Reg has tripped over a root, his upper body well forward of his lower body and getting more so as the inertia of the backpack keeps propelling him on. He picks up speed, legs flailing, trying to regain his balance, but he can't.

"Reg!"

He falls. But as he does so, he tucks his head down and to one side. He pulls his arms in and rolls neatly on one shoulder, stopping in a sitting position, laughing. "Well, at least I got that over with early in the hike," he says, brushing pine needles from the arm that was under him on the roll.

Shannon is shocked by the sight of one of the older party members suffering such a spectacular crash, but the others are laughing along with Reg.

"Oh, honey," says Jacquie, "I'm just glad you do this often enough to stay in practice."

Shannon begins to smile. "That was, uh, actually pretty amazing," she says. "It looked like there was some *technique* in how you handled that."

"Absolutely," Reg replies. "But it kind of comes naturally. Just get your head and hands out of the way—a guy I know broke a wrist trying to catch a fall straight-armed—and roll. The pack's heavy, but it protects your neck and your back. It's way more comfortable to fall with this turtle on my back than without it."

"And he ought to know . . ." Jacquie begins.

"Hey, let's not be telling tales."

The others pat the dust off Reg's pack, and soon everyone is moving along again.

Wildlife sighting

The backpackers take their time warming up on the trail. After a while they've removed a layer of clothing and are walking comfortably at a moderate speed.

"Big climb coming up," says Jacquie, who has been acting as the pace-setter this morning. The others look ahead. Sure enough, the trail steepens noticeably.

"Switchbacks?" asks Pat.

"Lots." Jacquie reduces her speed as she hits the grade increase. The pace doesn't change much, just the length of the steps. They're shorter. No one is huffing and puffing; they move steadily along without stopping to rest.

The trail steepens more, then angles rightward across the slope. A small path, though, goes straight up.

"I wonder if those guys yesterday were switchback-cutters, too," Art muses.

"Probably," Pat replies. "I bet they were out to one-up each other

with their"—she flips her poles up and down—"huge biceps."

"Actually, I thought they were kind of cute," says Shannon, "in a dumb sort of way."

A few minutes farther the trail jogs suddenly left. A switchback. "Here's number one!" says Reg.

Half an hour later he announces, "Switchback 14!"

"Have you been keeping count?" Shannon is incredulous.

"Sure. Hey, we all have our obsessions."

"It's actually switchback 15," Art says.

"No way!"

"It is!"

They begin a mock sword fight with their walking poles.

"Okay, boys, time for a rest," says Jacquie. Shannon giggles. They all slump down beside the trail, using their packs as backrests on the steep slope behind them.

"Man, look at that view!"

"I was too busy breathing to look at anything but my feet."

"Hey, is that a caribou over there?" Art has his binoculars fixed on something a kilometre away, in the meadows above the treeline. Pat is reaching for her camera.

Jacquie has her binoculars out, too. "It's not a caribou! It's a grizzly bear!"

"What?!" Shannon looks frightened.

"It is! It is! A big brown one!"

Shannon fingers the can of pepper spray at her side.

Reg notices. "Don't panic. That bear's too busy with what it's doing to bother with us."

"Have you ever been really close to a grizzly?"

"Close? I almost walked on one once! I was trying to decide whether to jump over this brown boulder or step on it, and it got up right under my foot."

"You're kidding!"

"Nope. The bear must have been sleeping. It ran off about 20 metres and looked at me like, 'You weren't *really* going to do that, were you, Reg?' Then it took off."

"Were you scared?"

"Me and the bear both."

Pat has her camera, now sporting a telephoto lens, balanced on a tiny tripod sitting on her pack. Jacquie steps back to take a picture of Pat taking a picture of the bear.

"How come you're not getting a photo of the grizzly?" asks Shannon.

"Oh, Pat will," she replies. "This is just the last-seen-alive photo."

Everyone laughs.

"Snack time?" They all open the tops of their packs and pull out their food bags and water bottles. The snacks are easy to locate in their own sacks within the food bags.

"So is the bear going to come over and join us?" Shannon is still a little worried.

"It hasn't happened yet," Reg replies, tearing the wrapper off a candy bar. "But just in case, I'm going to stuff this down in a hurry. Because of the bear, you understand. Wouldn't want to tempt it, you know. Mmm, yum."

Urinating and defecating in the wild, and sanitation generally

"I'm going to off-load some tea," Pat tells them. "Away from the bear." She is carrying a small roll of toilet paper and an empty zip-lock bag as she walks into the woods. Her pepper spray hangs from a small belt around her waist instead of attached to her pack. That way she always has the spray with her, even when she leaves her pack for a few minutes.

"Me, too," says Art, pulling toilet paper and a similar bag from his own pack. "But mine's going to be a bit more work." He grabs the plastic trowel from Reg's pack pocket and a small item from the head-flap compartment on his own pack. "Wish I could've done this in camp this morning."

He walks 20 metres away behind some trees. He works the trowel around in a 15-centimetre-wide circle and pops up the turf. He digs down an additional 5 centimetres, carefully piling the soil to the side. He squats low, balanced over his boots, depositing his feces neatly into the hole. Rather than throwing used toilet paper into the hole—animals have a way of digging it up and scattering it—he wraps it in clean paper and puts it into the plastic bag. He scrapes the soil back into the hole and puts the plug of turf back into place. Lastly, he opens the tiny packet he has brought with him, removes a moist towelette from it and cleans his hands. The used towelette is made of synthetic material and isn't biodegradable, so Reg doesn't put it into the plastic bag with the used toilet paper. He'll add it to his garbage bag. Later that day, after reaching their next campsite, he'll discard the used toilet paper down the Parks Canada toilet there.

When Art returns to the group, Shannon asks why they have to bury their poop. "The way I understand it is, if there were hardly any of us out here it wouldn't matter where we went or whether we buried it," Jacquie says. "I've read that human poop actually takes longer to break down when it's buried than if it's just left on the ground. At least, way up here where the soil is so cold. But this trail is really popular, so after a while there would be a lot of crap in the woods. And crap carries disease. So it's better to bury it."

"Plus you should always clean your hands afterward," Art adds. "It doesn't make sense to purify your water and then handle your food with hands that might be, you know, poopy, eh?"

"That's one reason I never drink out of anybody else's water bottle," Pat says. "Or let them drink out of mine. You never know where those hands have been . . ."

"What's the other reason?"

Pat looks down. "I always get sick if I drink from somebody else's bottle. I catch cold or I get a sore throat. I mean, your mouth is probably just as germy as your bum, really."

Another group of hikers comes by, headed downhill. The two parties greet one another.

"Hey, Reg!" says one of them. "How are you?"

"Ed! How's your knee?"

"I got it fixed last summer. It's not quite like new, but it's good enough. Man, it's great to be up here again! Hi, Jacquie!"

She smiles and shakes his hand. "Ed, it's so good to see you with a pack on your back. How's Mattie?"

The hikers chat for a while, Ed and Reg make introductions, and Art asks about conditions farther along the trail and at the campsites they intend to use. Then the others go on their way.

"Funny how we keep running into the same people in the mountains," Pat muses.

"Absolutely," says Reg. "It's downright spooky how often that happens."

Shannon is thinking. "There must be some reason. I know somebody over in the sociology department who could run some stats on that . . ."

"Be my guest," says Art. "All I know is, I'm glad *some* people don't come up here." Everyone laughs.

Crossing a stream

The five friends put on their packs and begin to walk again. They've been resting for some time, so they start slowly to re-warm their muscles.

An hour later they round a corner and hear the sound of running water. Soon they're standing on the banks of a stream. Just as Ed had said, there's no bridge. A line of stepping stones goes across, but it looks like a long step between two boulders out in the middle.

"Huh," says Art. "The bridge is washed out."

"That's two of them on this route," Reg notes. "The other one is at Caribou Creek. But this one was here last time, wasn't it, Jacquie?"

"Definitely. Look—I can see part of it over there." She points to some planks partly buried in gravel downstream. "That must've been one heck of a flood."

Shannon looks worried. "How are we going to get across?"

Pat is already unlacing her boots. "I don't think I can jump that middle bit." She takes off her socks, shoves them well down into her boots and ties the boots together. She pulls a pair of neoprene slippers from the low side pockets of her pack and slips them on. She undoes the head-flap on her pack and hangs the boots over the pack with one boot on each side. The boots sit high on the pack, resting snugly against it so they won't dangle and flop around. Pat closes the head-flap. The boots are secured.

She puts on her pack but leaves the waist belt and hip-belt unbuckled, in case she falls down and has to get out of the pack quickly. Using her

poles for balance, she starts across the stream, making her way from one rock to the next. "Art, this one's really slippery!" she calls out, pointing back with her pole to a wet rock. Rather than trying to jump across the gap in the middle, she steps down into the water and wades.

"You mean this one right—?" Art steps on the same stone and slips off it, splashing into water over the top of his boot. "Yow!" He leaps nimbly for the next stone, immersing his foot for only a moment. When he reaches the gap in the stepping stones, he places his walking poles ahead of him in the middle of the gap and uses them as miniature vaulting poles to lengthen his leap.

Pat has reached the other side and is taking off her wading shoes. "Do you want to stop and change your socks, dear?" she asks.

"Naw. Day like today, nice and warm, this boot will be dry in no time. Socks and all."

Reg and Jacquie have opted to wade. "Hey, Shannon!" Jacquie calls after they have crossed. "Would you like to borrow my slippers?"

"Sure!" She hasn't brought wading shoes.

Jacquie tosses them across. Shannon thanks her, happy not to have to wade the icy stream in bare feet.

Using a GPS receiver and a map

Later in the day they stop for lunch, picking an open spot along a creek at treeline. They have a fine view of the Wall, a huge cliff 1,000 metres high and 10 kilometres long, its vertical rock dark and foreboding, its many summits gleaming with snow.

"You ever think about climbing straight up that cliff, Art?" Reg has his binoculars to his eyes.

"No way," says Art. "The Wall is out of my league."

"But you've climbed the Matterhorn."

"Yeah, but it wasn't nearly as steep as that."

Reg takes a pump filter down to the creek and starts refilling his water bottle. "Anybody else?" he shouts back to the group. Immediately he finds that he has four more bottles to refill. He's happy to do his share. Art did the filtering for all five of them that morning after breakfast.

As the group sits beside the trail, eating and chatting, a breeze keeps the mosquitoes away most of the time. There's no need for the chemical odour of insect repellent. Suddenly Shannon says, "Ouch!" and slaps her arm, leaving a little smear of blood. Pat gives her a sly look. "If you do that and the wardens catch you, you get two tickets."

"What? Two tickets?"

"Yeah. One for feeding wildlife and the other for killing it."

Shannon chuckles. "How far to camp?" she asks.

"Mmmmm . . . about 4 kilometres, maybe?" Jacquie doesn't sound very sure.

Reg pulls out his new GPS receiver. "Ta-*dah!*" He hands it to Art. "Okay, so show me how to work this thing."

The unit is a very basic model, small and light. Art turns it on. In less than a minute the screen indicates that they're receiving signals from seven satellites, five of them quite strong, and that their position error is only 6 metres. He looks at a couple of lines of numbers on the screen. "Who's got the map?"

Jacquie unzips the head-flap pocket on her pack and pulls out a zip-lock bag holding the Lillian Lakes federal topographic map, scale 1 to 50,000. She hands it to Art.

"Okay. We're at 163392, which is, is" —he is tracing two imaginary lines on the map, noting where they meet—"right here. Hey, we're on this trail!"

"Well, imagine that," says Pat.

"Hey, it works, doesn't it? I mean, if it told us we were way over here or something . . ." Art pokes at a different point on the map.

"Then I wouldn't believe it."

Art is insistent. "As they say in aviation, always believe your instruments."

"Providing you can read them correctly."

Art looks a little stricken. So does Pat. "Oh, I'm so sorry, dear," she says. "I didn't mean that."

"No, you're right. It's easy to make a mistake. Let me check it again." He retraces the lines. "No, I was right. And so was Jacquie. If this dot is the campground, we've got less than 2 kilometres to go."

"Yeah, that's the campground," says Reg. "Show me how you did that." Shannon moves over to watch.

Art begins. "Okay, you see how you've got these two lines of numbers in the GPS? These big numbers?"

"Yup."

"Those are the UTM coordinates. One is the number of metres east, and the other is the number of metres *north*."

"North of what?" asks Shannon.

"North from the edge of the UTM zone. But never mind that. I'm giving you the five-minute course. Just what you really need to know, okay? You see this blue grid that's printed over everything on the map?"

"It's actually kind of purple," says Jacquie.

"Whatever. Each square in the grid is one square kilometre."

"I didn't know that," says Shannon.

"Oh, I did," says Reg. "Back in the bad old days of compasses, I used to be in orienteering contests."

"He'd win sometimes, too," says Jacquie. "He's very good with a compass."

Art smiles. "After today I'll bet he never looks at one again. Except for shaving in the mirror." He turns to Shannon. "Okay, read me the middle three digits in the top line."

"One-six-three. Why the middle ones? There are seven digits there."

"Those are the only ones you need." He points out the numbers on map. "See these two-digit numbers?"

"I thought you needed *three* digits."

"You do, but start by finding the two-digit number that matches the first two digits you just gave me."

"Uh . . . here?"

"Right. Keep your finger on that number. This is the 'easting' co-ordinate, as they say. You read it left to right from the west edge of the map. Now we need the other number, the lower line on the GPS. Read me the middle three digits of that, please."

"Three-nine-two."

"Okay, now find the first two digits of that number on the map. You read these the other direction, from the bottom of the map to the top."

"Right here?" Now she has both index fingers in use.

"That's it. So you see how each number is on one of the blue lines on the map? What you do is follow the vertical blue line and the horizontal blue line until they meet. That's the square we're in."

Shannon does as instructed. Her fingers follow the two lines. They meet. "This square here?"

"Yup. The numbers get you to the *southwest corner* of that square."

"So the last digit . . . ?"

"That's for inside the square. The square is a full kilometre across, but you want to know where you are closer than that, so the last digit divides the square up. You just eyeball it to the nearest tenth. It gets you to within 100 metres of your exact location."

"Like right about here?"

"Perfect."

Reg is familiar with UTM coordinates, but he takes another look at the GPS unit, to make sure he understands which numbers to use, and checks them against the map. "That was amazing. Way easier than a compass."

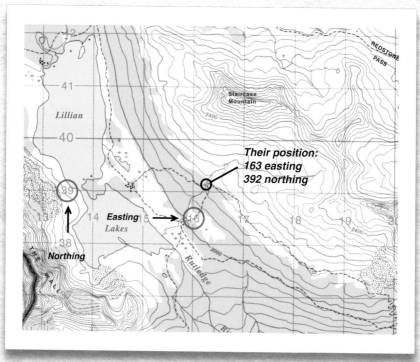

"Yes, but it requires a billion dollars' worth of satellites to do it," says Pat.

"And 100 bucks for the GPS," says Reg.

"Three hundred bucks for this one," says Art, slyly pulling out another GPS receiver. It looks exactly like the one Reg has, but it's a different colour.

"Hey, where'd you get that?" Reg asks.

"I borrowed it from work," Art replies. "We just got a bunch of these new ones."

"So what's so great about that one? How come it cost so much more?"

"Watch." Art turns the unit on. It quickly locates the satellites. "For one thing, it's faster." He presses a button on the side of the GPS. "But here's the really cool thing." He holds it up so that everyone can see the screen.

"Hey, it's in colour!" says Shannon. Then her eyes widen. "And there's the map!" She squints at the screen. "And there's where we are! Wow!"

Art is beaming. "Exactly. I downloaded all the maps for the Rockies into it. You can put in any maps you want. Pretty cool, eh?"

"I'm upstaged," Reg says admiringly.

"But your receiver is just about as accurate as this one," Art replies, "and this one doesn't really teach you much about maps."

"Well," says Reg, turning his unit off and putting it away in the head-flap of his pack, "what I know from my cheapie GPS is that I'm going to be at Lillian Lakes campground in less than an hour, and then I'll have the rest of the afternoon to goof off."

Shannon is still intrigued by the newer GPS. "If I carry this in my hand, can I see where we're going?"

"Sure," Art replies. "It'll even show your track on the screen." He offers it to her.

She takes it from him. "Hey, this will keep the kid occupied until we get to camp," she says, smirking.

"Slip on the wrist loop, okay? So you don't drop it? And hold it like this." He shows her how to hold the GPS in front of her. "You want to keep it a little away from your body, so the signals don't get blocked. Oh, and watch your step. These things are so distracting . . ."

By this time everybody is starting to move.

"I love the way we hike," says Pat. "Take your time, don't walk terribly far, get to camp early. That's the life."

"Hey, why hurry? This place is so beautiful," says Reg.

"If we'd been hurrying, we might not have seen that bear," points out Jacquie.

"If we'd been hurrying, we wouldn't have seen much of anything except the next few metres of trail. And a good set of blisters at the end of the day."

"Do we camp right on the water?" Shannon asks.

"No," Reg replies. "Parks Canada doesn't want people camped right beside the lake. The animals need to get down to it. But we won't be far from it."

"What kind of animals?"

"Well, grizzlies. And caribou every time we've been here."

"Grizzlies go right by the campground?!"

"I saw one right *in* the campground once."

"That's pretty scary . . ."

"No, no. It's what we came for. You know when the last time was that somebody got attacked by a bear at Lillian?"

"Uh, no."

"Never."

"Oh."

"So relax."

Shannon grins. "This is going to be fantastic!"

"Hey, what did we tell you?"

Knot-tying

The Lillian Lakes backcountry campground is idyllic: four tent pads overlooking one of two lovely lakes side by side, each lake about the size of a city block, separated from one another by a meadow filled with wildflowers. Here at the upper edge of the forest the trees are short. Small subalpine firs and Engelmann spruces grow in dense patches between colourful clearings. The valley is wide and so are the views, revealing mountains in every direction. The spectacular Wall is close at hand—occasionally a rock can be heard falling down the enormous cliffs—while across the lakes, gentler slopes reach up from the alpine tundra to castle-like summits.

"There's a mountain goat up on that ledge," says Art, scanning the Wall. "No, wait. Three of them. Four, five . . ."

Shannon and Reg are over by the tables, figuring out how to sling the tarp between the small trees in the campsite. "This one's big enough, but I don't know about that one," says Shannon.

"It's too small," says Reg. "We'll use my poles."

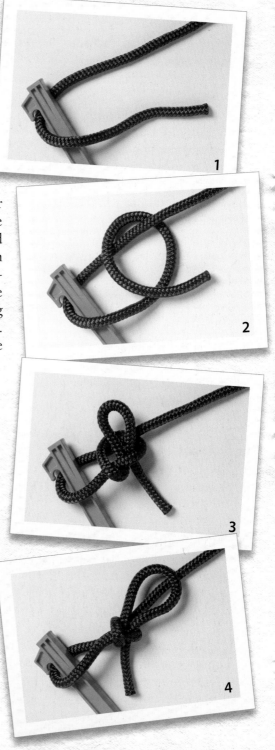

"Oh, right! Your walking poles! You can use them to hold up the tarp!"

"Not as good as a tree, but not bad." He loosens the adjustment to extend both of his poles all the way. Shannon ties the line as high as she can to the larger of the two trees, taking care to wrap the end around the trunk several times to avoid damaging it. Then Reg positions the poles in an inverted "V" at the other end of the table. He wraps the line around both handles several times to lash them together.

"I always do it this way," he says, pointing out how the cord is wrapped around the poles horizontally, not vertically. "It lets me take the poles out without having to undo one end of the line."

It takes a while to arrange the tarp over the poles and tie it out properly. As they work, Reg shows Shannon how to tie a pop knot.

"You start by wrapping the end around, like this. Then you tuck a loop through like this. Okay, then you pull the loop tight like so." He pulls. The knot falls apart.

"Oh, you mean like this?" Shannon's knot tightens nicely as she pulls.

"Uh, yeah. Like that. Just like that."

"And when you want to untie it . . ."

"Just pull the end. You'll find that it almost always releases quite easily."

Shannon tries it. It works. "This is really a handy knot," she says. "Thanks!"

"Oh, my pleasure," says Reg, retying his knot correctly.

"What other knots do I need to know for backpacking?"

"Well, that pop knot seems to work for just about everything," he says. "The only other one I ever use is the overhand loop." He takes one of the side-ties on the tarp and quickly ties this simple knot.

"Oh, everybody knows that one," Shannon says.

"Well, most of them don't know how to tie it this way," he replies, threading the end of a tarp line through one of the other grommets and tying it on in a way that looks impossible.

"How did you do that?"

"It's good, eh? It solves the problem of tying an overhand when you can't just grab a hank of rope. It's perfect for tying things on with, much better than a clove hitch or whatever they call it." He unties the knot and shows her step by step. Taking the end of the line, he ties an overhand knot about 20 centimetres from the end. But he doesn't tighten it; he leaves it quite loose. He pokes the end of the line through the grommet, then he feeds it through the overhand knot, carefully following the shape, until he has the loop version of the knot tied in this unusual way.

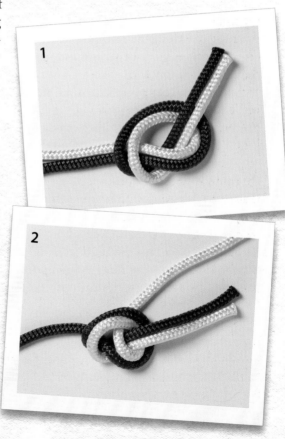

Shannon has been following along with a tarp-tie of her own. "That was really cool," she says.

The others have walked over to watch. Pat says, "Art, show her how to tie two cords together. That new way."

Art takes two tarp-tie ends. "You're gonna love this," he says. "It's great for tent cord." He holds the ends together in one hand with about 20 centimetres sticking out, then ties a simple overhand knot in them.

"And that will actually hold?" Shannon asks.

"Yup. And it unties really easily. But it's only for small cord. If you have climbing rope you need to use a double overhand knot or a fisherman's knot or a water knot. Something safer."

"Right. They showed us that at the climbing wall."

"And you know that yellow polypro rope? Or that really cheap white polypro cord you can buy? That stuff comes apart no matter what knot you try. What you need is real nylon cord, the kind that's braided. It stays tied."

Shannon has successfully produced the cord-joining knot. She pulls hard on each end. The knot doesn't budge. She finds that it does, indeed, untie easily.

"Where can I get this kind of cord?"

"Oh, MEC or some other outdoor-supplies store where they sell stuff that actually works."

Soon the tarp is rigged and taut. Reg's walking poles are holding up one end, the soft hand-grips against the fabric. To pad the support point even more, Reg has placed a glove between the grips and the tarp.

"What happens when you need those poles for hiking?"

"I just unwind the wraps and pull them out. Then the tarp collapses. I tighten it up so it doesn't catch the wind. It works great, actually. Protects whatever's on the table while we're away."

"No food under the tarp, though, right?"

"Absolutely. No dirty pots, either."

It's time to set up the tents. It's mid-afternoon, and the sun is still high in the sky, so the tents, which are still damp, will have plenty of time to dry. The group follows the same preparation routine as they did the day before.

They have tea and a snack, then hang their food bags from the bear pole. An hour has gone by. "That's that," says Pat. "Does anyone fancy a walk around the lakes? Take some photos?"

"I'll go with you," says Jacquie.

"Me, too," says Shannon.

"I'm taking a nap," says Reg.

Art yawns. "Yeah, that's what I need, too. I've gotta crash for a while."

Outdoor photography

Pat has taken out her rather large single-lens-reflex digital camera. Jacquie still has her small camera with her, but she says that she's along just to enjoy, not to take pictures. Shannon has brought a cheap recyclable snapshot-taker.

The closest lake is only a short walk away, and they reach it very quickly. "The light isn't too bad right now," Pat says. "Earlier in the summer we'd have to wait until later, but we've already got some good shadows. That midday harshness is gone." She looks around through the viewfinder, holding the SLR to her eyes as professionals do, left hand cradling the body and lens, right hand on the shutter. She takes a wide-angle shot of the Wall, with the lake off to the right.

"What kind of lens is that?" Shannon asks.

"Twenty-eight to two-hundred macro zoom," Pat replies. "It's a good lens for backpacking. I like it better than having to carry separate ones for wide, normal, telephoto and macro. Would one of you like to pose for me? Kind of over there?" She points.

"Oh, here we go," says Jacquie.

"No, no. Not too much posing, I promise. Just a few, okay? For the newsletter?"

Shannon obliges her. As she walks in the indicated direction, she calls back, "Pat, I'd like to get better at taking pictures. Can you give me any tips?"

"Sure. Like right now, for example, I'm going to get you with the cliffs in the background." She takes the shot, lines it up again and takes another. "You're the foreground. It makes a better picture if you have something in the foreground. Like a tree, or a person, or a boulder—a tent looks good in a picture like this." She swings around, using the telephoto. "This one's going to be really good. Look."

Shannon comes back and takes the camera. Pat shows her how to hold it, cradling the lens with her left hand, her right hand on the controls. Shannon's eyebrows go up as she looks through the viewfinder. "That *does* look really good! The way the tents are in the sunlight and the cliffs are in the shade."

"Hey, that's the photographer's eye, Shannon. You've got it. Go ahead and take a shot. Take a couple."

"But I hate to waste your memory space . . ."

"No worries. The memory card in there is huge. Plus I've got extras. Before we switched to digital, every time you pressed the shutter it cost you money. So people didn't take all that many pictures. But now you can fire away all you like. And that's really good. That's what the pros do. When everything's right they'll get 20 or 30 shots—that used to be a whole roll of film—in a couple of minutes. Do you know what really separates a pro from an amateur? The pros take a lot more pictures."

"Hmmm. All I brought was this one little disposable camera. Twenty-four shots."

"Not a problem. You still have enough to record the trip. Don't go for great art. Just use those 24 to tell the story of the hike."

Shannon holds her snapshot camera up and winds the film. "So I should, like, take a photo of all of us here taking photos?"

"Right. That's the shot that will mean the most in 20 years, not the one of the Wall and no people. You want a good image of you and your friends doing something with the Wall in the background."

Shannon steps back a few paces and gets a photo of Pat taking another picture and Jacquie looking on, grinning and waving for the camera.

"Here's another thing," Pat says when Shannon rejoins them. "For something really tall, like the Wall? Or a big tree? Or a building? Try turning the camera this way." She tilts her camera 90 degrees, so it's on its side. "Try it with yours. Look at the same view with the camera horizontal, then vertical."

Shannon compares the two views. Even through the viewfinder of her $10 convenience-store purchase, the vertical image has more power. "I see what you mean. That tilted shot—"

"Vertical format. It's also called portrait format, because it's used a lot in photos of people's heads. The other is landscape format." Pat chuckles. "Landscape format isn't always the best for landscape photography."

"Last time we were out you showed me some stuff about taking pictures of wildflowers," Jacquie says. "Shannon might like to hear about that."

"Okay. Just let me finish this series on the camp and that valley behind it."

"Hermit Valley," says Jacquie.

"It looks incredibly beautiful. I wouldn't mind being a hermit there. Can we go there tomorrow?"

"That's the plan."

Pat takes several more photos, then she glances around for some flowers to photograph. "Uh, how about those over there? I don't know what they are . . ."

"White dryas," Shannon says. "*Dryas octopetala*. Or is it *integrifolia?*" She walks over and bends down to look more closely.

Jacquie stoops beside her. "You know the Latin names of wild-flowers?"

"Some," Shannon replies. "I took Rockies field botany last summer. Great course!"

"Hey, we're lucky you're along. So what are these others? The yellow ones."

"Umm . . . some kind of *Potentilla*. Maybe nivea. I couldn't tell you the species for sure. But that's definitely the genus."

"I'm impressed," says Pat. She gets down on her hands and knees beside the flowers, then stretches out on her stomach. She raises herself up on her elbows to steady the camera, bracing the lens with her left hand and working the camera with her right as she composes the shot. "Get down low, right on the ground if you have to. You want to be shooting across to the flowers, not looking down on them."

"That's the way I used to take flower pictures," Jacquie offers. "I just pointed the camera straight down. The pictures looked awful. You couldn't tell which way was up!"

"Right. So shoot low. The ideal thing is to find your flowers growing on a steep slope, so you don't have to grovel like this."

"I'll bet that camera really goes through the batteries, too, eh?"

"Actually, no, it doesn't if I don't use the LCD all the time to look at what I've taken. That's what uses up the juice. But even if I did, I'll bet I could do this whole trip and shoot hundreds of pictures and never even need to get out my extra battery."

"But you do carry an extra."

"Yes, and they're special ones, and they're expensive. A lot of the smaller cameras take plain old double-A cells, though."

"I should be writing all this down," Shannon says. She pulls a slim notebook from her pocket.

"Okay, so here's something about focusing on wildflowers. You can go wide-angle and try to get a whole lot of them in the image, and that can look really nice, but usually the better shots are the ones that have only one or two, maybe three—just a few." Pat is working the zoom lens on the SLR, trying different combinations of magnification and focus. "And the other thing is your depth of field. If I set it for a large aperture, I can focus on exactly the flowers I want in the photo. All the others are blurry in the background. That sounds bad, but it looks good compared to a shot with the flowers in focus farther away. Everything looks too busy. And a large aperture gives you higher speed, so when the wind blows the flowers around, the picture's still sharp. Otherwise they'd be blurry." She trips the shutter several times, changing the aperture and the speed each time to get different combinations. "Do you want to try?"

Shannon takes the camera, lies down as Pat did and receives more coaching. Apertures, shutter speeds, focus, composition. "Pat, this is great. I'm going to get a decent camera as soon as I can."

"You should. You'd be really good at this."

The rest of the day goes well. An afternoon thundershower wakes the men and chases the women back to camp, where they sit under their tarp as the rain pelts down and lightning rakes the Wall above them. Shannon takes a photo of the group, snug in their fleece jackets and tuques, happily sipping from their mugs under that wonderful rectangle of waterproof fabric. She smiles, thinking of how her photo will help her remember their tea party in the midst of a storm.

Sitting quietly

After supper, Pat announces that she's going to go do what she calls a "Seton-watch."

"Have fun," Jacquie says.

"What's a 'Seton-watch'?" Shannon asks.

"I learned it at a youth camp a long time ago," Pat replies. "Did you ever hear of Ernest Thompson Seton?"

"He wrote kids' books, didn't he?"

"He also learned how to sit quietly in the woods. Really quietly, without moving at all. He was the guy who discovered that if you do that, amazing things happen."

"Like what?"

"The animals forget that you're there. Birds land right in front of you—or right on you. I had an owl land right beside me on a branch. It just sat there, closer to me than you are, looking at me. I couldn't believe it."

"Were you scared?"

"Well, yes, a bit. But our camp counsellor told us not to worry. No one gets attacked or anything. Another time a little weasel sat on my foot. It was just incredible."

"So how do you do this?"

"You go a little way off from camp and find a comfortable spot. You plunk yourself down there—I always bring my sitting pad, and I try to find a rock or a tree to rest my back against—and you wait. You don't move at all. No looking around, no fidgeting, no nothing. You just sit really, really still. You just breathe and blink, that's all. If it's buggy I'll put on repellent so I don't have to slap."

"And then what happens?"

"You never know. That's the beauty of it. You never know."

"Can I come with you?"

"Sure, but it works better if we don't sit together. Is that okay?"

"Absolutely. I'd just like someone fairly close the first time I try this."

Pat smiles. "Are you worried about bears?"

"Well, actually, yes."

"So bring your pepper spray. Come on."

Pat walks over to the tents to take her sitting pad out of her pack. Shannon does the same. They walk down to the lake together.

An hour later, as dusk arrives, the two return to camp, chattering away happily. Shannon can't wait to tell everyone that a mother ptarmigan and five chicks came peeping by her Seton-watching spot. They stayed near her, picking at bugs and seeds. One of the chicks climbed up into her lap. It settled there—she hardly dared even to blink—and went to sleep.

Day-hiking from a backcountry camp

The morning comes in clear and cold. There is frost on the meadow, and a little clear water left in a pot on the table has a thin skin of ice on it. This is not unusual for mid-August mornings in the high country of the Canadian Rockies, and the rising sun soon warms the air.

Warm in their down sleeping bags, knit caps pulled over their ears, our five backpackers are still sleeping soundly when the sun rises over Staircase Mountain. The warmth wakens Art. He gets up, retrieves the food bags and sets them on the table. He tightens the tarp by releasing the pop knots, shortening the lines and retying the knots. Pat arrives and starts their stove. Soon everyone is up and having breakfast together.

"Did you hear those other people arrive last night?" Art asks.

"What other people?" Shannon looks puzzled. The other tent pads are vacant.

"They've already left. There were four of them, I think. Two tents, anyway. They must've rolled in around midnight."

"I didn't hear a thing."

"Neither did we," says Jacquie.

"It was nice of them not to wake us up," says Art.

"I thought they might have been speaking German," says Pat.

Jacquie nods. "Aha. That explains it. Europeans are the most polite campers you'll ever meet."

"Why's that?" Shannon asks.

"They need to be, considering how crowded their campgrounds are. Everybody just has to get along."

"But why would they leave so early?"

"They're probably planning to do the whole loop in two days."

Art laughs. "Yeah, and half of it at night! What's the point?"

"Oh, maybe that's all the time they have. Or, you know, some people do things just to say they've done them."

"I used to be like that," says Jacquie. "But I've learned my lesson."

"What was that?" asks Shannon.

"I wrecked my knee overdoing it. I've had to slow down, and you know what? It's all for the best. I get way more out of a trip that way."

"So—what'll we do today?" Reg asks.

"We've got the whole day to hike around," Jacquie replies. "And it's going to be a beauty."

Reg is pulling out the map. "How about we hike over to the Hermit Valley?"

"Excellent idea." Pat is pouring some hot water into cocoa mix in her cup. "Refill, anybody?"

"Thanks," says Jacquie, moving her cup over toward the pot. "Oh, Reg, we've got to show Pat and Art the Hermit. That or Staircase Meadows."

"Well, how about we do Hermit today, then nip up to Staircase on our way over to Caribou tomorrow?"

"Fine by me," Art says. "How many kilometres are we looking at?"

"Well, let's see." Reg is looking at the UTM grid on the map, estimating the distance by counting how many squares their proposed route crosses. "All the way to Hermit Lake and back . . . about 12 k."

"I'm good to go," says Shannon. "I slept really well last night."

Jacquie frowns. "Twelve, is it? Hmmm. I didn't realize it was that far. My knee's kind of sore." She rubs the joint. "Maybe I'll just hang around here and have a rest day."

"You sure?" Reg knows that Jacquie's left knee has to be coddled occasionally, and that it won't be happy in the cold morning air. "You could wear your longies at first to keep it warm."

"Yeah, I could try that," Jacquie replies, brightening. "I'd hate to miss Hermit Valley."

The backpackers-about-to-become-day-hikers finish their breakfast, clean up, take their lunch bags from their food sacks and hang the food up for the day. They fill their water bottles, pump-filtering it because *Giardia* can lurk anywhere, even in this pristine-looking place. Then

they go to work on their packs.

Jacquie and Reg have already decided that Reg will be the packhorse and Jacquie, with her sore knee, will be the dude. Her rain gear, gloves and tuque go into Reg's pack, along with their lunch, their water bottles and the big camera.

Art is pulling on his pack's side-straps. The pack is growing thinner and smaller-looking. "Ta-dah!" he says. "Yesterday a backpack, today a day pack."

Jacquie undoes a zipper on the head-flap from her pack. A webbing waist belt lies within. She pulls the ends out, adjusts the length and clips them together.

"Instant bum pack," she says.

"Hey, that was cool!" Shannon says. "I wonder if my rental pack has that." She's looking around the head-flap for something similar. "Nope. I guess not."

"That pack must be an older model," Pat says. "They all seem to come with a bum-pack head-flap these days. But if not, it's easy to sew some webbing on. I did that with one of my other packs. As long as the head-flap comes off, you can fix it up that way."

Jacquie looks at Shannon's pack. "You could still turn this thing into a day pack if you pull in your side-straps like Art did. That would make it a lot smaller."

Pat agrees. "Yeah, you should do that, Shannon. It saves having to carry two packs for a trip like this—although you do see people doing that. It doesn't make sense to me, carting along a flimsy little day pack without any padding or a waist belt that actually works. Just so you look right."

"Hey, it's not how good you are," Reg begins.

"It's how good you look!" Jacquie finishes.

Advice about bears

At this moment a park warden walks up to their table. "Mornin'," she says, removing her hat. "How's everything?"

"Great," says Reg. "Can't beat the weather, eh?"

"That's for sure," says the warden. "Looks like you're getting set for some hiking today?"

"We thought we'd do the Hermit."

"Good choice. I'll be heading over that way myself. But that's partly why I came by. We've had a report of a grizzly bear in the area."

"Oh," says Shannon.

The warden looks toward her and smiles. "It's a bear we know well," she reassures her. "She's a really good bear. Hasn't caused anyone any trouble. She's medium brown, with tan along the legs and on her back. We call her Caramel. If you see her, just give her plenty of room. She doesn't have any cubs this year."

"Um, how much room?" Shannon asks.

"Oh, half a kilometre is good," says the warden. "At least a hundred metres, minimum."

"What if she's like, right there on the trail?"

"Well, she certainly could be."

"And?"

"Like I say, Caramel hasn't charged anyone. Yet."

"So—what do we do? I mean, if she's really close like that?"

"First thing is to bunch up, so she can see there are several of you. Stand close together. Then show her that you're not looking for trouble. Normally you'd be making noise, right?" She looks around. Reg and Jacquie are nodding. "Well, if you see a bear pretty close to you, then it's better not to yell and wave your arms and stuff. To a bear, those are signs of aggression, and that could be upsetting for her. You want to speak normally, so she can hear that you're just regular humans. Don't stare at her. That's also aggressive behaviour. Just give her some time to catch your scent—she

may move around to the other side of you to get downwind—and she'll probably go back to whatever she was doing. Or she'll leave. Then you walk away from her, all of you, sticking together. You go your way and she goes hers. If you see hikers coming toward her, be sure to warn them. Okay?" The warden glances around the group. "I see that three of you have pepper spray."

Shannon touches the canister on her hip.

"Just keep in mind that it's no guarantee of safety. Too many people figure that they don't have to keep their eyes open if they've got bear spray. But believe me, you do."

"Is there a story there?" asks Reg.

"You bet," the warden replies. "An outfitter I know had a client who took after a bear with his can of spray. Figured he was Clint Eastwood or something, firing away. He wound up in hospital."

"The bear wasn't scared off?" Shannon is looking worried.

"Oh, yeah, the bear was plenty scared. It was running before the guy began chasing him. But hey, when you're a grizzly bear and someone picks a fight with you, you fight back."

"So the idea is not to pick a fight?"

"Exactly. The bears treat us like some kind of heavy-duty predator, just like they are. And big predators avoid each other. In a fight, all those teeth and claws, you're probably both going to get hurt. And if a wild creature gets hurt—"

Shannon finishes her sentence. "Then it's probably going to die."

"You got it. So think like a bear thinks. And it's thinking, 'I don't want any trouble.' So you act the same way. You see the bear, the bear sees you, and you both head off in opposite directions. End of story. But the bear I'm talking about will probably ignore you altogether. Caramel's really a good bear." The warden smiles. "Enjoy your hike!"

She starts to walks away, then turns back to them. "And do make plenty of noise as you're walking, okay? Let her know you're coming."

"Thanks for the reminder," says Jacquie. "We haven't been doing that enough."

"See you around," says the warden. She leaves the campground. Looking past her, Jacquie sees her horse tied along the main trail.

"She didn't ask for our permits," Pat says.

"I guess we just looked like the responsible type," Reg offers.

"And we didn't tell her about those two guys," Shannon says.

"Aw, who cares, really?" Jacquie shrugs her shoulders.

Setting a GPS waypoint and using an altimeter as a weather instrument

Reg has his GPS unit out. "Should we do one of these 'waypoint' things for the campground?"

"Sure," says Art. He shows Reg which button to press to get the unit to store its present location, and how to name it "Camp" in the device.

Art does the same with his own GPS. He draws a small teepee-like symbol on the map and writes down the UTM coordinates next to it. "Maybe I'll just keep my unit running. It'll record the route and tell us how far we've walked. When I get home I can upload the track into my computer. Presto, I've mapped the trail." He straps the GPS receiver onto the top of his pack, where it will be exposed to the sky.

Reg is looking at his GPS unit. "Hey look, it's telling us our elevation!"

"Didn't you know they did that?"

"No. But I guess we don't need an altimeter now, eh?"

"Well, not exactly. Altimeters can be more accurate than a GPS for doing elevations—"

"Really? Even though GPS is so good for locations? Like within a few metres?"

"I know, but it's different now. GPS accuracy for altitude used to be terrible, and it still isn't as good for altitude as it is for location. So I always carry my altimeter, too. It's got that barometer function. Speaking of which . . ." Art reaches into his pack, finds his small-items bag and takes a look at the altimeter. "We lost 30 metres overnight."

"Hey, great! The pressure's risen!"

Pat rolls her eyes. "As if you couldn't tell what the weather's like from just looking around," she says to Jacquie.

"Boys 'n' toys," Jacquie replies. She grabs her walking poles and starts up the trail to Hermit Lake.

Bear encounter

An hour later, Shannon stops short. Reg, immediately behind, almost crashes into her.

"Bear!" she says.

Sure enough, not 30 metres away and right beside the trail ahead of them, a brown bear is digging at something in the meadow. It looks up at them briefly and resumes digging.

"Is that the grizzly?" Shannon is fingering her pepper spray.

"Yeah," says Reg quietly. "It must be. See its claws? With black bears you don't see the claws like that. Grizzlies have really long claws. Man, we're so close I can see the silver tips on the fur."

"I'm really scared, Reg."

"Don't be. See how she isn't paying any attention to us? It's probably that bear the warden was telling us about—Caramel, wasn't it? She's used to being around people, just like the warden said. I mean, all that noise we've been making sure didn't scare her away."

"So what do we do?"

"Get closer together." They bunch up. "And don't keep staring at her." They avert their eyes. "And leave." They move off the trail at a right angle to their route, circling widely around the bear before regaining the trail. The bear lifts its head and stands on its hind legs, front paws hanging down, sniffing the air as it faces in their direction.

"Uh-oh!" Shannon yelps. "Look what it's doing!"

"You've been watching too many movies," Reg says calmly. "It's just trying to get a better look at us. Catch our scent."

Ten minutes later they've reached a promontory with a good view back toward the meadow. The bear is still there.

"Would it be okay to stop now and watch?" Shannon asks.

Reg is slipping his pack off. "Sure. I was just going to suggest that." He sits down on the pack and raises his binoculars. "I could use a break anyway."

For half an hour the group relaxes at a safe distance as the bear digs in the meadow, ripping up roots. It stops and rolls about. Then it lies in the sun, its eyes blinking, and it goes to sleep.

"Awww," says Shannon. "What a great big teddy bear!"

"A teddy bear that can rip your head off," says Pat.

"I know, I know," Shannon replies. "But I'm not as afraid as I used to be."

Silent walking, adjusting poles

By mid-afternoon the hikers are heading home. They've had a fine day exploring the lovely glades and interesting rock formations in the Hermit Valley. They've had spectacular views of cliffs, glaciers and waterfalls. Having jabbered to one another about this all day, they follow Pat's suggestion that they spend 20 minutes walking without speaking, putting some space between each other on the trail (well up the valley from the bear). Each person is free to reflect on the beauty of what they've seen, to listen to the sounds around them without hearing the voices of the others and to enjoy the sense of being alone in the mountains. They enter their own worlds for a while.

When they gather for a rest, Shannon tells Pat, "You know, when you brought up this silent-walking thing I had no idea it would be so *good*."

"Most people hardly ever walk quietly like that. Except when they're really alone, of course."

"On the club trips they're never quiet," Reg adds.

"Well, maybe they should try it," Jacquie offers. "We should bring that up on the next club hike."

"For sure." Shannon is thinking of the golden-crowned sparrow she saw and heard, its whistling song sounding very much like the beginning of the theme from *Peer Gynt*.

They start off again. The trail is descending, and the hikers pick up the pace—all except Jacquie, whose knee complains when she's going downhill. She stops to adjust her poles.

"For stuff like this, where it's downhill but not too steep, I like to make them longer," she says to Shannon. "They reach out pretty far ahead of me that way and hold me back a little. And I take short steps. It's easier on the knees." Reg and Art lengthen their poles, too. Pat, rather than lengthening her sticks, collapses them all the way and slips them under the side-straps on her pack. She prefers to do a moderate downhill grade without any poles at all, enjoying the feeling of her arms swinging by her sides for a change.

They reach a short, very steep section. Jacquie further eases the strain on her knee by shortening her poles considerably and using them as canes under the heels of her hands. In this way, the poles take much of the weight. It slows her down, but the others don't mind lingering at the bottom of the hill for a minute or two as she catches up.

Lightning and an emergency

Closer to camp, they leave the trail and climb up through the thinning forest to the alpine meadows above, where Pat gets striking photos of the lake and their camp from an elevated viewpoint on the crest of a knoll.

As Pat is putting her camera away, Art hears the rumble of thunder. He looks around. Clouds have been building and dissipating cyclically since lunchtime, and a few drops of rain have fallen. However, the sun has always returned. This latest build-up, though, is much thicker and darker. Their position is above the treeline and exposed, perhaps half a kilometre from the shelter of the forest below.

"I don't like the looks of this, Reg."

"Me neither. Let's get the heck down." Reg calls to Jacquie, who is with Shannon, looking at lichens on boulders. "You hear that thunder, Jack?"

"Yeah. Shall we go?"

"Quick like a bunny. Down to the trees."

The hikers put on their packs and start downhill. The next rumble is louder, and this time they all see the flash. Big drops of cold rain are starting to fall. The wind is rising.

"This is getting pretty scary," says Shannon. She starts to run.

Jacquie yells after her, "Whoa, Shannon! Running isn't the best plan! You can trip and—"

Shannon takes an awkward-looking step, cries out and sprawls on the ground.

"Oh, jeez, Reg!" Jacquie runs over to Shannon, who is holding her ankle, grimacing in pain.

FLASH! The thunder cracks immediately after, echoing from the cliffs nearby. The rain has changed to hail, and it's coming at them horizontally.

"Shannon! Did you twist it?"

"Oooo, yes, yes, and it really hurts! Oooo!"

FLASH! BANG!

Reg arrives. "We're not going to make the trees, and this is a really bad spot."

Art looks around. "First off, don't panic."

"Like I did. Oh, ow, ow!"

"Do you see that little hollow over there? Let's get into that. We should leave our poles here. C'mon, Shannon, I'll help you. Reg?"

The two men get Shannon's arms over their shoulders. Tears in her eyes, she hops the 20 metres to a depression in the side of the hill. A sound like the buzzing of a bee swarm is growing louder around them.

Art's commands are clear, cutting through the fear. "Okay, now! Everyone crouch down! Really low, over your feet! But don't lie down! Ground currents!"

The flash comes, brilliantly white. The thunder is simultaneous and deafening. Everyone winces.

"Oh no, oh no, oh no," Shannon is whimpering.

"It's okay, Shannon," Jacquie says softly, "we're still here. It's okay. That was probably the" —FLASH! BANG!—"worst." Rumble, rumble, rumble.

The next bolt is farther away, and the next. Five long minutes later it's over. The rain is slackening. The lightning is hitting peaks across the valley.

"That was incredible," says Pat, shaking her head. "We didn't even

have time to get our jackets on. I'm so cold now." She slips on her fleece, then her rain jacket, gloves and tuque. The others are doing the same, even Shannon, who looks very pale as she tries to pull her rain pants over her injured foot.

Then the sun comes out.

Art turns his face upward toward the sudden warmth. "Oh, man, am I glad to see that!" The wind has dropped, and the landscape sparkles.

"This place is completely bipolar," says Pat. "One moment the weather's trying to kill us, the next it's turning back into Shangri-La. We just don't get this kind of stuff down east."

"Well, what about that storm we had up on Mount Carleton?"

"Yeah, well, that time we had about 10 minutes' warning. This thing was instantaneous!"

"I didn't see it coming at all. Where the heck . . . ?"

Reg has the answer. "That's the one problem with this area. The weather comes from the west, and the Wall blocks the view in that direction."

"How's your ankle, Shannon?" Jacquie has her hand on Shannon's boot.

"I, uh, it hurts less, now. I guess we should have a look . . ." She loosens her laces and gingerly slides the boot off.

"Take the other one off, too, okay? So we can compare them and see if there's much swelling."

Shannon nods and begins taking off the other boot. "You're into first aid, Jacquie?"

"For years and years. I've got my Extended First Aid certificate, and I keep it current."

"Okay, so what do you think?" Shannon has both her boots off and her socks.

"Well, your left ankle is a bit swollen. But, you know, it doesn't look all that bad. How's it feel?"

Shannon carefully moves her ankle. "It hurts, but not nearly as much as it did a while ago. Maybe it's not really sprained. Maybe just kind of strained or something. Maybe I'm not going to be crippled after all."

"It takes a lot to actually sprain an ankle, believe it or not."

"Should I put one of those stretchy things on it?"

"A Tensor bandage? Sure. If it'll fit into your boot." Jacquie locates her first-aid kit, extracts an elastic bandage and wraps up Shannon's ankle. "When we get back to camp you should take it off and soak that ankle in the lake."

"How come?"

"Cold water keeps down the swelling."

Shannon puts her boots back on and gets to her feet. She takes a couple of steps "I can—ooo—I can walk, I think."

"Your poles'll help. I'll get them for you." Jacquie goes to fetch the poles.

"I don't think it's far to go, Shannon," Art says. "Oh, wait. I can tell you exactly." He has his GPS receiver tied to the top of his pack, where it has been recording their route. He notes that the instrument is still working despite the close lightning strikes and locates the waypoint he set at the start of their hike. He tells the unit to navigate to the waypoint he named "Camp." It displays the distance—623 metres—and an arrow pointing the direction. "It's about two-thirds of a kilometre over that way."

"I'm going to live," says Shannon, "and I'm never, *ever*, going to go running off during a storm. That was *so* stupid!"

"It's a natural reaction," says Art. "Don't be so hard on yourself."

"Well, from here on I'm going to follow that rule of yours."

"What rule?"

"'Don't panic.'"

"Ah, that rule. Yes."

Camp etiquette, handling youth groups and protecting the ecosystem

When the group returns to the Lillian Lakes campground, they find that every tent pad has been occupied. In fact, the camp is overflowing. Two large tents are being pitched in the meadow nearby. Kids in their early teens are running about, yelling. The sound of splintering wood reverberates from the forest.

"What the—?!" Reg looks shocked. "Aren't there any adults around here?"

As if by magic, a middle-aged man appears. He looks clearly distressed about what's going on.

"I'm so sorry," he says. "We just weren't prepared."

"Uh, neither were we," Reg replies. "What is this, a bunch of scouts?"

"No, we're all from Marcus Kettling Intermediate School. It's in Deer Grove. We do something like this every year, kind of a pre-term trip. But I think we bit off more than we could chew this time. We were supposed to be here two nights ago. We got off a day late to begin with, then we couldn't make it all the way here on our first day, and now, well, here we are."

Pat turns to Art, glowering. "I'm not looking forward to this. It's like that night we had last year, when all those kids showed up at midnight."

"Are you the only adult?" Art asks.

"No, there are three of us. I'm the teacher, and we have two parent volunteers. I'm Ed." He extends his hand.

"Hi, Ed. I'm Art. This is Pat, and Jacquie and Reg. And that's Shannon, over there by the lake. She's hurt her ankle. Listen, how about we get together with those volunteers and powwow a bit?"

"I'll try to find them," Ed replies, hurrying off.

"Well, maybe they can get organized," Reg offers. "One thing we do know is that they have to be tired. They've already had a night out, who knows where. Surely they'll sleep tonight."

Ed returns. Two other adults are walking across the meadow toward them.

"They're basically really good kids," he says. "We just have to watch one or two of them, you know?" He introduces the parents. "This is Jordan and this is Gina." Everyone says hello. Then Art takes the floor again.

"Has the warden come by?"

"Warden?" Ed looks around. "Will he toss us out?"

"I doubt it," Reg says. "They're easy on people who run into problems like you did."

"Thank goodness. There's no way we could walk any further today."

Pat notes the frenetic activity around her. "Well, these kids certainly seem to have lots of energy left."

"I don't know where they get it. When we arrived, they all spent half an hour lying on their packs, whining," Jordan replies.

"At least they got their tents up," says Gina. "When that storm hit, they all figured they were going to die or something."

"Okay," Pat says, noticing a group of kids coming into camp from the woods, dragging a large dead branch with them. "I think we need to sort out some rules here and maybe go over the campground rules . The first one is no campfires allowed."

"What? We always have a campfire every evening." Jordan is looking annoyed.

"Sorry. Check the sign over there. No fires."

"How come?"

"Well, basically there's not enough wood. And anyway you're supposed to use the stuff lying on the ground, you can't go breaking off branches like those kids just did."

Jordan laughs. "What's wrong with breaking off a dead branch?"

Pat breathes deeply. "At this elevation, every bit of wood counts, even dead branches. There aren't many, and birds need to sit on them."

"That's the silliest thing I ever heard." Jordan kicks the toe of his boot into a grass tussock, dislodging part of it.

"Hey! You'd better watch—"

"Hang on, Jordan," says Ed. "We're in a national park, here. Things aren't like they are back on the farm."

Jacquie taps Pat on the elbow and enters the conversation. "Do you have your own farm?"

Jordan brightens. "Two sections. We won an environmental award last year, didn't we, Gina?"

"Yeah, we were pretty excited about that."

"I should think so," says Jacquie sweetly. "That's great to hear. All these kids are lucky to be up here with people who really care." She grins. "Now, since you're new in the park, I have to explain a couple of things. We've got caribou around here—"

She is interrupted by a girl who has walked over to listen. Other kids are following. "Caribou? Really? Caribou?"

Jacquie turns to her. "Definitely. We've seen them here before. And today we came within 30 metres of a grizzly bear."

"A grizzly bear?!" The kids are looking about, turning this way and that, instantly worried.

Jacquie plays on their fear. "It didn't bother us, but you never know. Were you with those kids who went over into the woods by themselves?"

"No, but *he* was." The girl points to one of the others. He shrinks away.

"Well, if I were you I'd stay close to camp."

"Oh, we will!"

By this time most of the other kids have arrived. There are a dozen of them, which is over the group-size limit in the backcountry of Jasper National Park. Reg starts to say something about that, but Jacquie catches his eye and he lets her continue uninterrupted.

"Okay. We understand your situation. Here you are, way up here, with all these kids. And you want to make sure they have a great time, right? Plus this is school, so you've got a unit to cover."

Ed, Gina and Jordan all nod. Ed says, "You sound like a teacher, Jacquie."

"Good guess! Diefenbaker Junior High. I look after the outdoor ed. program there. This isn't as bad as it seems, but we do need to sort out some stuff." She has their attention. The kids are quiet. "First thing is, you've got to have fun. This is a fabulous place, and there's lots to do. I can help you with that." The kids smile. "As soon as you have your tents up and your gear stowed and all your food hung up on the bear pole, I can show you this really neat place down by the lake."

One of the kids puts her hand up. "They won't let us go down to the lake, Mrs., uh . . ."

"Struzik. Mrs. Struzik. I'm not surprised, the way you're all acting. The first rule of the mountains is no running around without thinking. This is a big, scary, dangerous place."

"Oh, we know that, Mrs. Struzik. Jason, he already got a black eye last night. He, like, ran right into a tree." They all giggle, even Jason, who does, indeed, have a black eye.

"Good thing he didn't poke it out. So, okay, lesson learned, right?" They nod. "You want to have fun, you can have fun, but you've got to be safe, okay? Like over by the lake. And you see that big boulder over there? The one with the stack of stones on top? If you're good, and you're with me, you can climb all over it. But first you need to gather up all that junk lying around on the grass and get it organized. First thing, before a grizzly bear comes." Their hands fly to their mouths. "And even before that you need to get all your food, and I mean all of it, up the bear pole. Do you have food bags?"

"Just grocery-store bags," says Gina. "Would those work?"

"Not really. They're not very strong. But keep the food in the bags. Then you can tie the bags shut and put all the bags in three or four of the packs. You can hang up those packs, with just the food inside."

"If you've got a few plastic garbage bags I can show you how to cover the packs and keep them dry," Art adds.

"Yeah, that's one thing Ed made them bring lots of," Jordan offers.

"Good," Jacquie continues. "So right now all the kids should unpack their packs and bring all their food over here. Reg can show you how to hoist it up on the bear pole. Then they need to get out their sleeping bags and their sleeping pads and their clothes and stuff and get them arranged all tidy in their tents. And *then* we can go down by the lake."

"Yay!" One of the kids runs toward her tent. The others do the same. Soon the food bags are all piled on a table, Reg and Jordan are putting it into packs for hoisting, and the kids are hard at work organizing their belongings in their tents.

"Thank you very, very much," says Ed to Pat. "They really are good kids."

"Yeah, thanks," says Gina. "Sorry Jordan was kind of negative there."

"No problem," Pat replies. She's smiling. She looks over toward Jacquie, who's helping some of the girls get their tent in order. "Jacquie, there, she's great with kids. Absolutely great. They love being outdoors with her."

"We're lucky you guys came along."

Pat continues. "Now, about tonight. We're all tired. We need a good night's sleep. And that means you're going to have to keep these kids quiet."

"What time is lights out?" Ed asks.

"Ten o'clock. I don't care if they get their flashlights out and read quietly in their tents, but I really, really don't want them talking. It just gets louder and louder."

"We know," says Jordan, rolling his eyes. "We know all about that!"

Ben Gadd

"Do you have stoves to cook on?" asks Art.

"Yeah, but two of 'em don't work. We'll probably have to cook on a fire, even though it's not the best thing to do, like you said."

"Well, maybe you won't really need to. Can I see those stoves?"

"Sure. They just keep flaring up all the time."

"Well, maybe I can fix that."

Pat smiles again. "Art can fix just about anything." Jordan and Art walk away together. Art shows Jordan how to start the stoves correctly and soon they're working normally.

Jacquie comes back over. She has a little more to discuss with Ed. "One thing is that the boys will be peeing all over the place," she says. "They need to be told to use the biffy." She points to the toilet, a large, throne-like item of green plastic with a moulded-in privacy screen on one side. "And you need to tell them to raise the seat first. Some of them won't, of course, so Gina, you'll have to show the girls how to wipe off the seat with toilet paper before they sit down on the boys' pee."

"I was sort of hoping the boys *would* go to the bathroom in the woods . . ."

"The other thing is about food in the tents. The kids will tell you that they have all their food out of the tents tonight, but they won't. They'll forget about some candy in their pockets, or they'll be hiding something. So you'll have to check. You'll have to actually get in their tents and check through their stuff. There really is a grizzly in the valley, and the warden says it's a good bear—we didn't have any trouble with it—but you want to be super careful, just in case. It's not only for the kids. None of them are likely to get hurt. But if that bear gets some food from this camp, it'll be coming back, over and over again, every night, getting bolder and bolder. Eventually the warden will have to shoot it. And that would be a real shame."

She turns and speaks directly to Ed. "Can you sit them all down and tell them about that? Just before bed? About how it's really important to keep food away from bears, not just for our sake but because it could mean the bear getting shot? The wardens have a saying, and it's all too true. 'A fed bear is a dead bear.' Please tell them that."

"For sure. I wish I'd known that before. They'll listen when you put it that way."

"I know. Mine always have. Once they understand how serious it is." Jacquie moves toward their table. "Tea, anyone? I definitely need a cup. This thing down at the lake is going to be fun, but I need my tea first."

"I'll go with you," Gina says. "I'm kind of interested in the lake, too."

"Me, too," says Ed, "since I'm supposed to be their teacher. But hey, Jacquie, I defer to you. You're in charge. Uh—do you have any extra tea?"

Jacquie sighs. "Sure," she says, lighting her stove.

After tea, Reg and Jordan join Jacquie and the other adults as they go with the kids on their mini adventure down to the lake. Art naps. He goes to sleep with the sounds of happy children in his ears.

Bathing

"I need a bath, Reg." Jacquie and her husband have returned from doing their good deed with the students and are sitting under the tarp. "I hope those kids didn't notice the way I smelled."

Reg sniffs. "Aw, those kids had such a good time they wouldn't care if you smelled like a wolverine. Anyway, you don't stink any more than the rest of us."

"That's the problem. I'll bet we're all pretty bad and can't tell." She looks out across the meadow. "It's nice and warm out. Maybe I'll go hunt up that pool we found last time and dunk myself."

"Great idea," Reg says. "It's probably far enough away from all those kids. I'll tell Art and Pat where we're going."

Reg and Jacquie head into the woods. Ten minutes later they come to a stream, with a sizable pool invitingly located below a small waterfall. It's perfect, well hidden in the trees. No one is around. They strip down.

They've brought their cooking pot with them, and they use it to carry water from the stream more than 50 metres into the woods. They use a small container of biodegradable liquid soap to wash their faces, hair, arms, armpits, crotches and underwear. They do so well away from the pool, so as not to contaminate it with fecal matter, soap, insect repellent and sunscreen residue. They throw the soapy water into the trees, away from stream, then collect a pot of fresh water and rinse themselves. Free of pollutants, they wade into the pool.

"Hoo-wee!" Reg has stopped at the knee-deep point. "This is so cold! I believe I'll just splash myself a little . . ."

"Chicken!" Jacquie calls out. Already waist-deep, she leans forward and plunges in, swimming across the pool to a flat rock on the other side. Challenged, Reg does the same. He hauls himself out on the rock, spluttering and gasping.

"You do this to me every time, Jack." Reg is shaking the water out of his hair. "It must be a basic female pleasure, sending a guy's family jewels up into his armpits." Jacquie pushes him off the rock. They swim back to the other bank and dry off in the sun, no towels needed. They're now clean and fresh-smelling. When they return to camp, they'll tell Art, Pat and Shannon about the pool.

Dealing with difficult people

The sun goes down behind the Wall. Instantly the temperature drops five degrees. Out come the jackets, the tuques and the gloves. Some of the kids haven't brought enough warm clothing, and Ed makes them get into their sleeping bags until supper. At least they've had time to dry out after the storm, because some of them didn't have rain gear, either.

Having enjoyed Jacquie's company at the lake and the boulder, the kids are friendly and well behaved that evening. She's caught more flies with honey than with vinegar, a principle of social interaction that she has used many times in the wilds. She talks with Shannon about it.

"You know, Shannon, most people show decent manners in the backcountry. But for those few who don't, it's often the case that they're new. They're unsure of themselves."

"So they come on too strong, right? Like that Jordan guy did when we first met him?"

"Exactly. They have to assert themselves. I always try to act really friendly instead of jumping all over them. It kind of reassures them somehow. Then they loosen up and behave just fine. Provided they aren't drunk, of course. Did you ever see that tee-shirt that says, 'Instant jerk, just add beer'?"

"There's no hope for guys like that," Shannon says.

"No. I just stay out of their way and hope they don't fall over a cliff."

"Well, I wouldn't cry too much if they did . . ."

"Yes, you would," Jacquie replies. "That's the problem. We all would."

Northern lights

As night falls, the sky over Lillian Lakes is clear. The moon is about half-full, and Jacquie and Reg emerge from their tent in the wee hours, wanting to see the Wall by moonlight. They get more than they're expecting. The northern lights are spreading their drifting films of colour from horizon to horizon, the drapery especially impressive when it ripples pink and green over the icy summits. Jacquie remembers that Pat was hoping to get some photos of the aurora. She bends down to whisper into Art and Pat's tent.

"Hey, you guys. Wake up."

Art stops snoring. "Huh?"

"Northern lights. Really good."

"Oh, okay. You awake, Pat?"

"For sure. I'll be right out. Did someone tell Shannon?"

Soon the five friends are standing some distance away from the camp, where no one else will hear them, wearing every item of clothing they have. Pat has her tripod sitting on a boulder. She's shooting the best aurora, in the best location, that she has ever had the good fortune to photograph in her life.

"This is incredible," says Shannon. "It's worth it, getting up so late and standing around in the cold."

"Well, I won't be up much longer," says Jacquie. "I'm about frozen already."

"Imagine camping up here in winter," says Art.

"Do people actually do that?" asks Shannon.

"Oh, yeah," Reg replies. "In tents, too. This is a really popular ski trip."

"Wow. Hey, look—a shooting star!"

Splitting the group up safely

The next morning is just as cold as the one before, possibly more so. No one moves until the sun is melting the frost off the tents, and even so the kids are late getting up. Ed has said that they all have to head back today, because they took so long getting there.

"That's just as well," says Pat, over breakfast. She's eating a freeze-dried dinner instead of the usual breakfast fare, knowing that they have a long day ahead of them. "They all slept with the doors of their tents zipped up tight, and now their sleeping bags are wet. If they had to pack up and camp somewhere else tonight, they'd be cold and miserable."

Jacquie concurs. "Another good reason to plan for a day or two in one spot, don't you think? It gives you enough time for everything to dry out in your tent."

"So what's the plan for today?" asks Shannon.

"Staircase Meadows would be nice," Reg replies. "It depends on your ankle, I guess. How is it this morning?"

"Sore, but I can live with it."

Jacquie asks to take a look at it. Shannon removes her boot and peels down the sock. "It's not even terribly swollen. You really did get off lucky yesterday, Shannon."

"I know, I know. And I'm going to be really careful with it today."

Reg is looking at the map. "Hmmm. It might not be very wise for Shannon to go up into Staircase Meadows. It's 7 or 8 kilometres over to Caribou, and a side trip to the meadows would add four or five more. A lot of it's fairly steep. And it's on that rough little path, eh, Jacquie?"

"I agree. Maybe we shouldn't go up there."

"Well, I don't mind waiting somewhere for you," Shannon offers.

Reg considers. "Hmmm, maybe. We could leave our packs on the bear pole at Staircase Campground, go up to the meadows and back, and Shannon could wait for us there. Or she could go on to Caribou if she gets bored."

"Would it be safe for me to walk there by myself?"

"Um, maybe. But then you don't know the way . . ."

Art has an idea. "She could get in with a group going there. There's bound to be one. She could leave a note for us at the campground."

Jacquie thinks it over. "Yeah, that's possible. But she really should be sure of the route before she gets in with someone else, just in case. You know how people will tell you they know where they're going, but they really don't?"

Shannon has made up her mind. "I'll just wait for you at Staircase. If the weather gets bad I'll put up the tarp. I might do that anyway, just to practise those pop knots." She winks at Reg.

"Sounds like a plan," says Pat. They clean up, strike the tents, pack up and check their site. They're putting on their packs as the kids start arriving at the tables for breakfast. Ed, Jordan and Gina are with the first wave.

"Thanks for all your help, Jacquie," Ed says. "We learned a lot from you guys."

"Our pleasure," Jacquie replies. "Next time you won't have all this trouble."

"Next time we're going to go someplace easier!"

"It's a long haul back to Rutledge Hostel. Take care on the way out, okay? Keep the faster kids from getting ahead of the slower ones. Make everybody eat and drink enough. And take rests."

"We will. So long."

The five hikers leave the campground, waving goodbye to the kids, a couple of whom insist on giving Jacquie a hug. It's only a kilometre to the Staircase backcountry campground, with little elevation gain. No one else is there, but two of the four tent pads have closed-up tents on them.

"Looks like we won't be alone in the meadows," says Reg, opening a granola bar. "I'll bet these other folks are headed up there, too. I was kind of hoping to have it all to ourselves."

"Oh, it's a big place," says Jacquie. "There's room for everyone."

"True enough, Jack. Anyway, we can leave everything here except snacks and rain gear. How about we just hang the packs up with our tents and bags and stuff in them? And the food? Use the head-flaps for waist packs?"

"Definitely," Jacquie replies. "I was thinking the same thing. Go really light."

Shannon takes her pack off. "So I'll stay here, right?"

"If that's still okay with you."

"No problem. Can I have the tarp, just in case?" She looks at the sky. It's about half covered with puffy cumulus clouds, but none looks dark or threatening.

"Sure," says Art, reaching into his pack for the tarp. "You can use it as a sunshade if you like." He sets the tarp on the table and starts loosening the straps holding the head-flap onto his pack.

"Got your bear spray?"

"Are you kidding?"

Everyone except Shannon is hunting in their packs for fleece jackets and rain jackets, tuques and gloves. Pat and Art decide to share one full water bottle. Jacquie and Reg do the same. They carry the map and both GPS units—Reg sets a waypoint for this camp—a compass, one first-aid kit, some toilet paper and the poop-hole trowel. Reg and Art each have pepper spray. There isn't room in their head-flap packs for their jackets, so they tie these around their waists. They carry their big packs over to the bear pole, slip the rain covers over them and hoist them up. Shannon keeps her pack with her, since she will be on hand to guard it against any animals looking for food.

Reg clips his waist pack on over his fleece jacket and rain jacket. "Okay, we're off."

"What time can I expect you back?" Shannon asks.

"Oh, two or three hours. It's 10 o'clock now, so we should be back by, uh, noon or one. It's a fair way to Caribou, and we want to get there early like usual, so we shouldn't take much longer than that."

"I'll be here."

"If something happens and you have to take off, would you please leave us a note?" Jacquie asks.

"Sure. But I'm not going anywhere."

"Oh, you never know. It's better to get all the possibilities covered in advance. That way we'll all know what we're doing."

"Okay, but what if you're not back on time?"

"Well, we'll certainly try to be, but if not, then don't wait for us."

Art interjects. "Jacquie, I thought we all agreed that Shannon was going to wait for us here, no matter what."

"Ah, yes. You're right. Is that still okay with you, Shannon?"

"Sure."

"So," says Art, "just to make sure we all understand, we're going up the hill, back by one, and Shannon's going to wait here for us, even if we're late."

"Right," says Shannon. "And if I really have to go somewhere else I'll leave a note telling you where I've gone."

"Sounds good. Bye."

"Take care."

Art, Pat, Jacquie and Reg walk quickly away from camp, up the trail to the alpine meadows below Staircase Mountain. Shannon sighs, pulls out her sitting pad and a paperback novel and settles down under a tree to read.

Watching wildlife

At 12:50 the party reunites. "Ten minutes early," says Shannon to herself, looking at her watch as she notices the others coming into the camp-ground. She has enjoyed the solitude. She has been interrupted only once, by a couple from Australia who stopped to chat for a few minutes on their way to Lillian Lakes. To their mutual delight, Shannon was able to answer their questions about the Hermit Valley.

"Hi, Shannon!" Pat is grinning, clearly excited about something.

"Well, tell her, Pat," says Art. He, too, is all smiles.

"We got *this* close to a herd of caribou!" says Pat. "I couldn't believe it. We just sat there, really quietly, and they came right up. Two bulls, four cows, and—get this—three little ones!"

"That's really nice," says Shannon, wishing she had been there.

"And the photos! Here, look." Pat is fiddling with her camera, poking the tiny buttons to bring up the images for Shannon to view. "Have a look at this. I didn't even need my telephoto, that's how close we were."

They are, indeed, remarkable photos. The animals look completely relaxed, as if no humans were present. Shannon notices this. "How come they look so, you know, okay with you being there?"

Art answers. "That was the really cool part. They didn't *care* that we were there. We came over a rise, and there were those folks from the other tents, just sitting there. And there were all these caribou practically right beside them." Art is waving his arms. "And the people saw us and waved us over, which was kind of surprising. And we came over and sat down, too, and the caribou started to run away, and we said, 'We're sorry,' but they said, 'No, no, it's okay, they'll come back.' And they did. And we were all just sitting there, in plain view, and they came back. The other people were naturalists, and they knew what they were doing. They'd been hanging around there for like an hour, and they saw the caribou coming their way, and they realized that the caribou knew they were there, so they just stood there and waited for the animals to come over. And they did." Art stops to catch his breath.

Reg continues. "It's something I didn't know about watching animals. They told us about it. If you don't try to sneak up on them, if you just kind of sit around and look harmless, they're quite likely to come over and check you out. I've always made the mistake of acting like a predator—you know, sneaking along, ducking behind trees trying to get closer and so on. But if you *don't* act like a predator, the animals figure you're okay and go on about their business. Isn't that amazing?"

"It's like that Seton-watching thing," Shannon observes. She has been looking at Pat's digital photos while Reg has been telling her all this. She looks up. "Boy, I hope I get a chance to try that with caribou before the trip is up."

"Well, they told us it doesn't *always* work. And you have to be really patient, it takes hours and hours sometimes. And humans hardly ever do that, because we're always moving, eh? But it certainly worked this time. We were going to do a loop through the whole basin, and we just skipped that entirely to stay there and watch the caribou. It was absolutely amazing. Those other people are still up there."

"So you left to get back down here on time?"

"For sure. We told you when we'd be back, right? And we were jolly well going to be back."

Art adds, "And they told us one more thing. They told us that you can always tell when you're too close to an animal. It'll move away from you. Like those caribou. Pat wanted to get a really close photo of one of the babies, so she got up and took a few steps toward it. It didn't move. So she took a few steps more, and she must have crossed some kind of line in the sand, because the whole bunch got up and moved off about 10 metres."

"Yeah, I was sorry I did that," Pat says, looking down. "I thought I'd messed things up for everybody."

Art continues "One of them—that English guy, wasn't it, Pat? The one called Phil?"

"Yeah, it was Phil."

"Phil says, 'Not to worry. Come on back and watch what happens.' Pat came back, and they did, too."

Pat finishes the story. "So anyway, I learned something really important today. Wildlife will tell you when you're too close. You back off, and everything's cool again."

Shannon has been thinking. "Doesn't Parks Canada have a regulation about that, something about it being against the law to chase after animals? Not like you're hunting them, just with your camera?"

"You're right," says Reg, remembering the wording on a sign he has seen along the highway every time he and Jacquie have entered Jasper National Park. "'Unlawful to feed or approach wildlife' is how they put it. I mean, it's okay with them if you're watching an elk from 50 metres away, but I've seen the wardens ordering people back when they keep moving closer. Now I know why. It's basically harassment. It's unintentional, but it's still harassment."

"Right," says Jacquie. "In the park the animals come first."

"Hey, it's better than that," says Art. "In this park, the animals come to *you!*"

Horses on the trail

Art and Pat walk over to the bear pole to lower the packs. The group enjoys a late lunch at the tables. Then the head-flaps go back on the packs, and the hikers become backpackers again as they head for the Caribou Creek campground.

Along the way they pass a group of small cabins. Horses are tied in a corral. From here on, the trail is used heavily by horse parties and pack trains. The track is wide and muddy, and there's a strong smell of horse droppings and urine. Since the horses follow each other closely, stepping in the same places, their hoofs have produced long stretches of evenly spaced mud ridges across the trail—Reg calls it "corduroy"—and every ridge is just a little farther apart than a backpacker's stride. Every creek crossing is a mudhole.

Some horseback riders come toward them. The hikers step off the trail to let the horses pass. The wrangler at the front thanks them, and the guests smile and wave.

"How come we have to put up with this?" asks Shannon, after the last rider goes by, his horse leaving a pile of new droppings at her feet.

"Yeah, really," says Pat. "I was expecting some mud and horse crap, but this is awful. It's just plain unacceptable. They would never allow this down east. Most of the trails there you can't ride a horse on at all."

"Ah, but that's there and this is here," says Reg. "This is Alberta, where the Old West lives on. You're in *cowboy* country, *podnuh*, and we ain't gonna let you *ferget* it." He throws his head back. "Yahoo!"

"Seriously," Shannon continues, "does Parks Canada just let this go on?"

"Yup," Reg replies. "For years and years and years. Something about horses in the parks being a 'traditional use.'"

"Well, so was hunting. And logging and mining. And they got rid of that," Jacquie counters.

"Hey, I'm not defending it," Reg says. "I've written my share of letters to them about it."

Art has been thinking. "You know," he says, "I was down in California a few years ago—that trip you missed, Pat?—and they had this horse problem solved. Separate trails. Hikers on one trail, horses on another. Always."

"Now *that's* a good idea," says Reg.

"But it does mean more trails," Pat counters. "Is that such a good idea?"

"It's all so complicated—" Art begins.

"Or it could be like in Willmore Park," Jacquie says.

"Willmore?" asks Art. "Where's that?"

"It's the next park north of Jasper. Hardly anyone knows about it. But it's gorgeous."

"And they let horses go there?"

"That's basically *all* that goes there. You can hike if you like, but it's horse country. It always has been. No bridges across the rivers, nothing but outfitters' campgrounds, nothing for hikers at all, really."

"That sounds kind of unfair," Shannon comments.

"Yeah, it is in a way," Reg replies. "But I guess horse parties need a place to go, too, eh?"

"Not here, though," Pat says.

"You're right," Jacquie agrees. "Not here. Separate trails, separate parks, but not this."

Magic beans

As the party starts to move on, Pat's expression is grim. "This is making me crabby," she says. "Just plain crabby. I wish I could have a cup of coffee or something."

"Ooo, yes, coffee." Reg closes his eyes and sniffs. "What I wouldn't give for some joe right now . . ."

"Well, let's have some," says Shannon. She takes off her pack and pulls out her food bag.

Pat is baffled. "What? Right here on the trail? You want us to stop and make coffee?"

"We don't need to make anything." Shannon opens a small plastic bag and shakes out several marble-sized candies into her hand. She reaches toward Pat. "Here."

"What's this?" asks Reg.

"Magic beans," Shannon says, with a secretive smile. "Have a few, Reg."

"Magic beans?"

"Well, actually, they're just chocolate-coated coffee beans. I always have them with me in class. Those lectures can be *so* boring."

"Hey, instant caffeine!" Reg pops one of the candies into his mouth. "Oh, yum! I'm at Tim Hortons!"

Pat is grinning broadly. "What a great idea. What an absolutely *fantastic* idea!"

Shannon beams. The whole group is crowded around her, greedily accepting her "magic beans."

"Save enough for yourself," Jacquie reminds her.

"Oh, I have lots. You guys are so un-boring I haven't been needing them."

Unwelcome company, first aid

It's four o'clock in the afternoon. The chocolate-coated coffee beans have worked their magic, and the trail has taken the little group northward along the Wall, with world-class scenery all the way. The backpackers are now walking through the woods in the gentle valley of Caribou Creek, toward the backcountry campground there. Everyone who took the side trip to Staircase Meadows is tired.

"Are we almost there?" Pat asks.

"Just about," Jacquie replies. "I think I see the turnoff for the campground ahead."

"Good. We've had an incredible day, but I've enjoyed about as much of this as I can stand, as they say."

The others crack up.

"When we get to camp, I'm going to sit down under a tree and snooze for a few minutes before I do anything else," says Reg.

"Me, too," says Jacquie. She glances around, sizing up the weather. Nothing is coming over the Wall except more of the small, fluffy cumulus clouds that have been giving them patches of welcome shade all afternoon.

A few minutes later the five of them arrive in Caribou Creek Campground. "Ahhhh . . . time to relax," says Reg, as he slumps down against his pack, which he has leaned against a tree for a backrest. He starts peeling the wrapper from one of his favourite candy bars.

"Uh, hi."

Everyone looks toward the strange voice. It belongs to one of the two young men who passed them on their first day.

"Oh, no," says Pat under her breath. Then she notices that they look different. One of them has a sizable scab on his cheek and a bruise on his forehead. The other has his left arm in a sling. Their clothes are ripped in places, and one of their packs has a hole in it.

"What happened to you?!" Shannon blurts out.

"Oh, man, we're a mess," says the one with the sling. "I can't believe what happened."

"Well?"

"Okay. First of all, I've got to say that we are two of the dumbest guys in the mountains. No, no. We are *the* dumbest guys in the mountains . . ."

"Basically, we fell down a mountain," says the other.

"What?" Art is looking horrified.

"Yeah, we fell down a mountain. We thought we'd save time by going right over it. I mean, it looked real easy on the one side . . ."

"But the other side, man, that was a different story."

Art is shaking his head. "How did you fall?"

"There was this thing called a 'snow patch.'"

"Oh, I can guess. You figured you'd just slide down it, right?"

"Right. Only it got steeper and steeper, and there were all these boulders at the bottom, and—"

"And Matt damn near broke his arm, and it might actually be broken, but we won't know until we get back to Jasper, and I knocked myself out, and I've still got a headache that won't go away—"

"He was right out of it for a good day and a half," says Matt. "We just camped, boom, right there."

Jacquie walks over. "It's Jason, isn't it?" she asks, looking him over.

"Yes, ma'am," he replies. "You've got a good memory. Mine's the sh— mine's not so good since I whacked my head."

"Do you mind if I check you over? Just to see if you have a concussion or something?"

"Are you a doctor?"

"No, but I do have first-aid training."

"She's really good," says Shannon. "She fixed my ankle up after I twisted it."

"Okay, sure," says Jason. "Go ahead."

Jacquie notes that Jason's pupils are the same size. If one had been larger than the other, it would indicate swelling of the brain, a bad sign. She looks in his ears, checking for blood or other fluid from a possible fractured skull. She is relieved not to see any. "Did you throw up after the accident?"

"How did you know that?"

"Well, that often happens if you've had a concussion."

"Oh, I barfed, all right. So yeah, I must have, like, had a concussion."

"Probably. But you seem better now. When did this happen?"

"Uh—the day before yesterday. Right, Matt?"

"Yeah. But you didn't know what day it was at the time."

Jacquie nods. "Typical concussion. That headache will probably taper off. But you should see your doctor as soon as you get home."

"I will. How's Matt's arm?"

Jacquie moves on to the other hiker. He's trying to take his pack off with his good arm. Reg steps over to help him.

"Where's it hurt?" Jacquie asks.

"Right here," says Matt, pointing to his elbow. "It's really sore. Every time I move it, it just *kills.*"

Jacquie looks at the colour of Matt's skin, wondering whether he might be in shock. But his colour is good. "How do you feel, aside from the arm," she asks. "Dizzy?"

"No, not now," Matt replies. "I was kind of woozy for a while, but I'm okay now."

"It sounds like you might have had some shock. Have you been thirsty?"

"Yeah, but we've both been knockin' back the Gatorade pretty good."

"Good." She peers carefully into the sling, which has been made from a shirt. Blood is soaking through at Matt's elbow. She can see a large scrape and a lot of swelling. "Did you land on a rock?"

"Really hard. Really, really hard."

"Has it been bleeding a lot?"

"No. It just kind of oozes all the time."

"You should see the inside of his sleeping bag," says Jason.

Jacquie is thinking. "You know," she says, "this looks badly bruised. It might even be broken, like you said. Does it hurt much when you walk?"

"Not since we got a sling on it. But, yeah, it still hurts. I can do it okay, though, walk."

Jacquie is putting a new sling on Matt's arm, a proper sling made from one of the two triangular bandages she always carries.

"How about walking all the way out? Do you think you can do that?"

"Well, it would help to know how far it is, I guess."

Reg unsnaps the head-flap from his pack. "Hang on. I can tell you exactly." He unzips the map pocket under it and pulls out the route description, a few pages copied from the guidebook. "Eighteen kilometres to the Redstone Creek trailhead."

"Oh. We thought it was like, only five or six," says Matt. He turns to Jason. "I think we're going to be out another night, dude."

Jason sighs. "We've screwed up big time. I told my mom we'd be back today."

Matt looks worried. "Will they, like, send the wardens out after us?"

"Probably not until morning," Reg replies. "If your mom calls in about you, the wardens will most likely give you overnight to come out. They've learned not to just jump in the chopper and go looking right away. Most people who're late manage to make it out okay on their own."

Matt looks at the members of the Edmonton group. He looks down at his injury. "We, uh, Jason and me, we also got ourselves lost." He pauses. "And then this animal came around and got all our food. So we're kind of, like, like . . ."

"You're hungry, I'll bet," says Shannon, reaching into her pack. She hands each of them an energy bar.

"Oh, no, no," says Jason. "We couldn't accept that. This is all our own fault. That's you guys' food, there."

"I always carry extra," Shannon says, "and anyway I haven't been eating as much as I thought I would. So I've got plenty. Here."

The two young men gratefully accept the gift.

Last camp, fire-starting, burning trash (not)

Despite their fatigue, Art and Reg offer to hike the rest of the way out that day and call the warden service so that Matt can be flown to hospital, but Matt declines, saying that his elbow has lasted two days in its present condition and it isn't getting any worse. In fact, now that he's taken the aspirin Jacquie offered him, the injury is quite bearable. Jason has to do without aspirin, because of his head injury. Aspirin might encourage any bleeding in his skull. And anyway, the thought of rescue is clearly so mortifying to him that the subject is dropped.

It's decided that Matt and Jason will spend the night at the Caribou Creek campground. Since they haven't reserved space there, they pitch their tent on some packed-down ground, leaving the pads for people who have reservations.

Jason takes an interest in helping Art and Shannon string up the tarp. "What a great idea," he says, fingering the material. "This hardly weighs anything. We sure could've used one of these the night we had the storm. Eh, Matt?"

Matt, despite his injury, is trying to learn how to tie a pop knot. "These people know all kinds of cool stuff," he replies.

A couple of other hikers arrive at the campground. They wave hello. Everyone waves back.

Soon the tents are up, the sleeping bags are spread out inside to dry and fluff up before bedtime, and supper is on the way. The group has enough between them to give Matt and Jason a decent, if eclectic, meal. "Great smorg you guys put on," jokes Matt.

"Oh, wait!" Jacquie exclaims. "I just remembered. We've got that extra freeze-dry."

"Hey, that's right. This trip I didn't spill any." Reg pulls a pouch of pasta primavera from his food bag. "Here. You guys can split this, too."

Jason is waving the package away. "Oh, we couldn't . . ."

"Aw, c'mon. You're really hungry. I can tell."

"Well, if you're, like, sure you won't be needing it yourselves? I mean, we really, really appreciate all this."

After dinner the group relaxes on the sitting pads, enjoying the sunset over the Wall. As at their first camp, a deer arrives. It settles down on a knoll close by, chewing its cud.

"Last camp," says Reg. He sounds wistful, almost sad.

"Yeah. Tomorrow it'll be over," says Shannon. "This has been so great. I don't want it to end."

"Well, next time let's go for a week. No, eight days. Eight days is supposed to be perfect for the Boundary Glaciers Loop. That's the next one I'd like to do."

"Count me in."

Art is sitting a little way off from the others, binoculars in his hands, letting every moment in this magical place show him something memorable. Pat walks over to sit beside him. No one is saying much. Darkness will soon envelop the deep reds and purples above them, and every minute is to be savoured.

"Hey, we could have a fire tonight!"

It's Reg. He's pointing to something everyone has missed up to now: a small supply of sawn and split wood stacked between two trees. Parks Canada has installed two metal fireboxes in the campground and a large metal fire ring, indicating that campfires are allowed here. A posted message indicates that they're to be built only in the enclosures provided, and that only naturally fallen wood can be used. Standing trees aren't to be cut, and branches must not be broken off.

"Who could have left that wood here?" asks Art, rising to investigate.

"The warden, most likely," Reg replies. "They always seem to have a chainsaw on their horse, eh? For clearing the trail? I've watched 'em cutting up deadfall in campgrounds. And they leave it for us backpackers."

"Really?" says Jason. "That's cool. I figured that wardens were something you avoided."

"They are when you're breaking the rules," says Pat, pointedly.

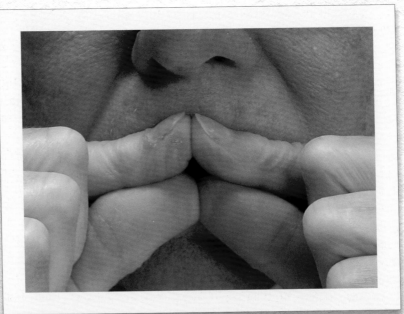

"Well, that was then and this is now," says Matt. "I've learned a thing or two on this trip."

Art is using his pocket-knife to split off some thin strips from one of the wood pieces. He sets the longest blade on his knife at a corner of a sawn end, then using another stick to tap the tip downward, he quickly produces some kindling without needing an axe.

"Hey, that was neat," says Shannon.

"A guy in northern Quebec showed us that," Art replies. He uses the knife to cut into the piece along its length, raising curls that will ignite easily.

Meanwhile Jacquie has been hunting for some tinder. She finds a reddish subalpine-fir twig that has broken off on its own—fair game—and has been lying on the ground long enough for the needles to die and dry. She places the twig in the centre of the fire-ring. Art adds the shaved kindling pieces, building them around the twig like a tiny log cabin. Around this he adds some of the smaller split pieces.

"Light the fuse?" Reg is holding out his butane lighter.

"Be my guest," Art replies. Reg works the lighter and touches it to the twig. It bursts into flame.

"Wow!" says Matt. "We used a lot of white gas trying to start ours."

"Yeah, and I lost all the hair on the back of my hand," says Jason. "Plus some of my eyebrows. We were *so* stupid."

"This stuff goes up even when it's damp," says Art. In moments the flames are rising and the fire is crackling, warm and inviting.

"Do you guys have one of these every night?" Jason asks.

"No," Jacquie replies, "we hardly ever do. We don't gather wood. The ecosystem here needs it for its own use."

"I can understand that," says Matt. "My science teacher from high school, he was way into all that eco stuff. Out here it makes sense."

"Or when somebody's cold and wet and just really needs to warm up," adds Reg. "We would make a fire for that."

"We sometimes have a fire when it seems kind of appropriate," Jacquie continues, "like tonight, since it's our last night out. And when there's plenty of wood lying around. Which there wouldn't be if someone hadn't laid this on for us, bless 'em."

"Speaking of which, we need more wood," says Art. No one has been watching the flames, and they're dying. Art brings over a few more pieces and adds them to the fire.

"Hey, I know a trick for making this catch quicker," says Jason. He leans close to the smouldering sticks, holding his hands near his mouth.

Suddenly the fire brightens.

"How did you do that?" asks Reg.

"It's called 'the diamond,'" Jason replies. "I learned it in camp when I was a kid. You make a little hole with your fingers and your thumbs, then you blow through it. Like this." Jason demonstrates.

"Like this?" Shannon tries the technique. Not much happens.

"You need to be closer. Blow hard. And kind of aim the air. That's what the diamond does. It aims the air."

Shannon tries again. Whoosh! The fire flares up. "Cool! I mean, hot!"

Matt has produced his trash bag. "We've got all these, like, soup wrappers and stuff. Is it okay to burn 'em up?"

Pat shakes her head. "Not really. They look like paper, but a lot of them actually have aluminum foil in them, and that doesn't burn up. It just lies there, looking tacky." She points out some bits of foil remaining in the firebox from attempts by previous campers to burn their garbage.

"You guys really think about everything," Matt says, closing his trash bag. "I'll bet you've been backpacking for a long, long time. And you really care."

"Well, it was good of you to ask before just tossing those wrappers in," Pat replies. She looks toward the two young men with a kind expression. "I'd say that you care, too."

Matt and Jason smile broadly.

Constellations

Later that evening, Art suggests that they do a little stargazing. Cups of hot chocolate in hand, the group moves away from the firelight in favour of the darkness 50 metres away from camp, in a small clearing. Pat offers to stay with the fire..

Shannon is excited. "Do you know about constellations? I'd really like to learn some of them."

Art points out the two that most people know—the Big Dipper and Orion—then he goes on to show them the "W" of Cassiopeia, the bright cluster of the Pleiades, the coal-scuttle shape of Auriga, the broad glowing band of the Milky Way and the bright star Vega about to set in the west. Then he reaches for his binoculars and takes a long look up.

"Anyone want to see the moons of Jupiter?" He hands the binoculars to Jason. "That's the planet over there, pretty high up. It's too bright to be a star, so it has to be a planet, which is how you find it. If you hold the binos really steady, you'll see tiny pinpoints of light close by."

Jason takes a while getting the binoculars lined up. Then: "Oh, wow! I've got 'em! That's too cool. Matt, you've got to see this." Jason pauses. "Oh, sorry, dude . . ."

"No worries. I'll try it when I've got two usable hands."

Reg sits with his knees pulled up, resting his elbows on them to steady his binoculars. "Hey, I can see three moons," he says. "No, wait. Four!" He looks over to Art. "Isn't that the most you can ever see? Without a scope?"

"Right. We're lucky tonight. Usually at least one's hidden behind the planet."

The aurora begins. It starts in the northeast, looking like searchlights shining up over the sawtooth horizon.

"This is earlier than last night," Art says. "It could be really good."

"And I'm going to miss it," says Jacquie. "I'm just too tired to get up at three again. In fact," she yawns, "I'm going to bed right now. See you all in the morning." She walks over to her tent.

"Good night, Jacquie."

"Good night, ma'am."

The others stay up later. The moon rises. Matt and Shannon talk quietly well into the night, as the northern lights grow brighter above them. Far in the distance, a pack of wolves begins to howl.

Over the pass and bound for home— with a stop for some enforcement

Next morning the group of seven breaks camp for the last time on this trip. They make their way gradually upward through the broad willow meadows along Caribou Creek to the windswept tundra of Redstone Pass. There they're reminded by Shannon about "All for one and one for all!" They clack their poles together by the summit marker, as Jason and Matt laugh and ask to join in a repeat performance.

A Parks Canada sign names the pass and indicates its elevation. This is all that's needed here, but other hikers have built a number of inukshuks—stacks of rocks that imitate the rock-stack markers used in the High Arctic—and Reg remarks on them. "This is some kind of fad, all this cairn-building," he says disdainfully. "I don't like it."

At that moment the warden arrives on her saddle horse, her pack-horse following obediently behind. After exchanging greetings, Reg points out the inukshuks.

"Those are new," says the warden. "They weren't here when I came by last week." She frowns. "We don't approve. Rocks get pulled up and moved. Some of those rocks might have been sitting there since the ice ages, and then somebody comes along and moves them just to gratify their ego. It's really a form of graffiti, as far as I'm concerned. Would one of you mind kicking those things over?"

Reg smiles smugly. Jason and Shannon attack the cairns.

"And scatter the stones around, okay? Kind of like they were just lying there?"

"You bet," says Jason. "This is kind of weird fun."

"Built by youth, destroyed by youth," says Pat. "The system works."

"Thanks for helping out," says the warden. Then she notices Matt's arm in a sling. "Hey, are you okay?"

"Uh, I am now," he replies. "We had some trouble back there . . ."

Jacquie speaks up. "I've got first-aid training. I've been looking after him. He seems like he can walk out okay on his own."

The warden dismounts to examine both the young men. Soon she knows the whole story. "Well, it looks to me like you're both okay to walk out. But I still have to call this in." She pulls out her radio. "May I have your full names, please? And your dates of birth, too."

"Oh, man. Here we go," says Jason under his breath.

The warden gets the information and moves off a little way to contact the park radio dispatcher in Jasper. They speak for a while. Then she comes back.

"May I see your permit, please?"

Jason is quick to reply. "We didn't get one," he admits. "We thought we were, like, too cool for that. But it kind of turned out that we are definitely not very cool about anything."

Reg intercedes. "You know, I think they made some mistakes. And they've learned their lesson, don't you think?"

The warden looks at Matt, then at Jason. "Well, I do have to give you guys a ticket."

Their eyes fall.

She tilts her hat back and smiles. "But it's just going to be a warning ticket this time. My guess is that you've already paid for your sins. And you have no previous infractions." She retrieves some forms from her saddlebag. "Matt, I need your mailing address. You, too, Jason." She fills in the forms and hands the men their copies. "Now—who should I get the dispatcher to call and report that you're okay?"

Jason's face lights up. "Oh, it would be so great if you could let my mom know!" He provides the phone number. The radio comes back out for a moment and, with the group's thanks ringing in her ears, the warden rides away.

Four hours later the backpackers will end their adventure at the Redstone Creek trailhead. There Matt and Jason will exchange phone numbers with the others. Art will retrieve his bicycle and pedal off down the road. After intersecting the highway, a few kilometres of easy riding will put him at the turnoff for Rutledge Road. He'll hide his bike in the woods again, stick out his thumb, and within 15 minutes he'll catch a ride to their jumping-off place. The couple who pick him up will be rewarded with Art's story of the Lillian Lakes Loop, an experience very different from their life in Don Mills. They'll delight in the idea of sleeping in the wilderness, and they'll shiver to think that the grizzly bear in the recounting may have walked right by Art and Pat's small tent in the night.

Seventy minutes after Art leaves the Redstone trailhead, he'll be back with Shannon's Subaru. In the meantime Jason and Matt will also have snagged a ride, theirs to Jasper for a trip to Seton Hospital and more phone calls. A couple of weeks later the two will show up at a meeting of the Capital Mountain Club, Matt's arm in a cast, to join up and begin a long, rewarding association with people who share their love of self-propelled outdoor adventure.

The summer following their Lillian Lakes trip, Pat, Art, Jacquie, Reg, Shannon and Matt will do the Boundary Glaciers Loop. In a few years Shannon will become president of the club. Art and Pat will write a hiking guidebook to Jasper National Park, illustrated with Pat's photos. Many years later, when all these people are too old to carry a backpack, they will have enriched their lives and given much to those around them, because they discovered the joy and beauty of putting one foot in front of the other in wild country.

The End

Kids and dogs

Entire books have been written on these subjects, so I'll keep this short and to the point. The skinny: yes, by all means take the kids. You'll be amazed at what they can do and how much fun they can be—when taken to the right sort of places and treated properly, of course. Dogs? Most are troublesome on the trail, in one way or another; you might want to leave yours behind. But again, this depends on where you take them and how you treat them.

Children in and of the wilderness

I have a treasured photo of my wife, Cia, on the trail to Boulder Camp in the Bugaboo Mountains of British Columbia. The picture was taken in 1970. I'm not in it, having remained in Calgary to write an excruciating university paper. Cia decided to evacuate the house, bless her, and in the photo you see her smiling, holding the hand of three-year-old Willy, who is looking tired. But where is little Toby, born just a few months earlier? Toby is in Cia's Kelty backpack, forming the top layer under the head-flap, sleeping.

As Cia discovered on that trip, you can take your kids—even wee infants—nearly anywhere. The hike to Boulder Camp turned out to be pretty tough, but my family had fun anyway. Of course, family

The kid may be tired, but a rest, a snack and a cuddle with the dog will do wonders

camping with the littles goes best if the location has certain amenities. Looking back at our experiences, our wish list is this:

- It's not a drive-to-your-campsite campground. You get there by taking a bus or walking in a short distance, no cars allowed. This kind of limited access keeps the party crowd out.

- Campsites are reservable. You needn't worry about showing up and finding that there's no room for you and your family.

- The campsite is kept clean, preventing conflicts with wildlife. A bear-proof stash is provided for food and used diapers (stored separately, you hope).

- Kitchen shelters are available, with wood heating for cold, wet mornings.

- Short trails lead to interesting places—streams, meadows, ponds, rocks—within a few kilometres of the campground.

- In case of emergency there is a campground supervisor on duty nearby at all time, or at least a telephone.

Rainer Schmid

Cia, Willy and baby Toby
(in the pack, asleep)

The kids loved such places and so did we. We brought our largest tent—not a huge, heavy car-camping tent, but one with ample rainy-day roominess—and plenty of food. After breakfast we would load up the necessary eats, diapers and toys, then we'd go explore a trail. The pace was set by Toby and Willy, each wearing a small pack with their favourite teddies peeking out. We adults carried everything else. We stopped often, sometimes every few metres, to examine a stone, a cone, a feather, a dropping, a caterpillar. On a good day we'd make 4 kilometres. We brought along a small tent to give us temporary shelter from weather or bugs no matter where we were. We kept the goodies flowing, measuring our progress by candy bars to the kilometre. We picked up our little boys and carried them whenever they asked. We coddled them terribly. Our motto was "Do what they want to do instead of what we want to do."

It turned out well. Both lads grew up loving the mountains as much as we do, delighting in the landscape and the ad-

Ben Gadd

Cia carrying Toby across Poboktan Creek in Jasper National Park

venture, showing stamina and courage as they accompanied us on real backpacking trips later on. Eventually there came a time when they carried the heavier packs, broke the ski trails, took the lead on the climbs. What we learned is that kids who're given a chance to enjoy the wilderness in their own way, with no pressure to perform or meet adult standards, will become excellent outdoorspeople when they grow up.

Contrast that with a scene we still witness all too often. Here's a little boy, tired and fussy. His dad is trying to make a man of him. "Nah, you can't be hungry again. Or thirsty. Now shut up and walk, Edgar. It's still a long way to the car." Poor Edgar; poor Dad. They've lost patience with each other, and Edgar is in the process of being turned off about the outdoors generally.

How much better it would be if, on that pivotal hike, Edgar had enough food and water in his tummy, wasn't expected to hike 10 kilometres in an afternoon and, perhaps most importantly, had been allowed to do something—anything—on the hike that was of interest to *him*. Kids have to play. For our family, the day's destination was a place in which the kids could have fun. The ideal location, from the boys' perspective, would have water to fall into, trees to fall out of, mud to get covered with, small animals to annoy . . . in other words, nearly any place in the mountains would do, as long as we adults saw this place through a child's eyes and let the children enjoy it in their own way. They always found enough to keep them occupied. Our job was to watch them carefully and step in as required when the water was too deep, the trees too tall, the mess too large, the animals pestered too much, etc.

Before you get the impression that Cia and I were selfless saints about all this, I should point out that we got to do things of interest to us, too. Do you want to know our secret? We'd invite someone else along, often a relative who was willing to look after the kids for a day while we went off to climb a mountain together.

Some safety advice for families:

- Always keep a close eye on children in the wilds. If a two-year-old wanders only 50 metres into the woods alone, that child may never be seen again. Children have been carried off by cougars and dragged away by coyotes when the parents left the scene briefly (the animals were waiting). Watch your kids even more closely than you do at home.

- Be sure that your kids know and remember what to do if they should get separated from you. Tell them, "If you get lost, stay right where you are. *We will find you!* Shout a lot, so we can hear you. You can yell our names. Whoever comes along will be a friend, even if it's someone you don't know. That's because in the mountains everyone is a friend. So don't hide. Come right out and say, 'Hello. I'm lost.'"

- There are places where you really need to keep your kids close: near cliffs and along dangerous rivers, for example. Some trails have hazardous sections that go on for kilometres. Holding a child's hand on a single-track trail for those sorts of distances is impractical, so when our boys were little Cia and I found another method. Approaching a continuously hazardous stretch, we'd say, "Let's rope up!" Our kids understood this, having been on a climbing rope before, so they were happy to accept the bowlines we snugged around their middles. To them, it meant, "Something cool ahead!" We'd all tie in together, a short distance apart, like a party of mountaineers. If one of the kids had slipped—and I can't recall this ever actually happening—we could easily have hauled them back onto the trail. If one of us slipped, though, we might all have tumbled into the gorge. The thought of this made for extra-careful footwork on our part.

- Kids are often on the ground, so check them over for ticks a couple of times a day, looking especially carefully in their hair.

- Don't let your kids play with ground squirrels. Cute as these little animals are, some species have fleas that can carry bubonic plague. Yep, you read that right: the Black Death. Entire ground-squirrel colonies can be infested with these fleas. You read occasionally of a human fatality, with the cause attributed to exposure to ground squirrels and failure to recognize the flu-like symptoms in time. Before you panic about this, be aware that the squirrels must be in very close contact with a human to pass on the fleas. If you don't attract rodents into your lap with food, there's little danger.

Bear in mind that losing track of a child may occur unexpectedly, and it needn't be your fault. A family may find itself on the run from an attacking moose, say, or tossed out of a canoe, and in such a situation it may not be possible to keep everyone together. When the danger is over and a child is missing, the parents can only hope that the child remembers to stay put, hug a tree and call out repeatedly until found.

Dogs

Should you take your dog with you on the trail? That really depends on the dog and the trail. Canadian dog-owners are fortunate that so few places are off-limits. In American national parks, dogs are generally banned on trails.

Assuming that the place you have in mind is legal, and supposing that your dog is well-mannered, meaning that it obeys, stays close, doesn't chase animals, leaves skunks and porcupines alone, gets along well with other dogs and strangers . . .

That's a long list. How many dogs are like that? Not very many. Should all others be left at home? Rationally, yes. It certainly makes a hike less complicated. However, Spot's beautiful brown eyes aren't so easy to resist. We humans love our pets and want to take them everywhere.

Before you cave in to Spot, consider this. The Canadian wilds are dangerous to dogs, full of swift rivers, big cliffs and protective moose mothers, protective bear mothers, cougars, coyotes—the list goes on. Spot's first backpacking trip may be his last, if not for the danger to Spot then for the trouble it causes Spot's people in pulling the quills out of his nose or trying to get Flower's odour off him.

Fortunately this is a conundrum with a high-tech solution. It's called the **leash,** the perfect piece of equipment for dogs that aren't quite perfect. A leash, plus a collar that won't slip off (try the new limited-slip collars—these aren't choke chains—available in pet shops), will keep Spot and the skunk a safe distance apart. In lots of places leashing is a requirement.

If it is, please, please be a good dog-owner and obey the law. My wife and I like to take our blue-heeler-something-or-other cross on the trails around Jasper. Bo is not completely reliable as a companion, and park regulations require that all dogs be leashed at all times. For both reasons, we keep Bo clipped on. But lots of other dog owners don't. They let their dogs attack ours, chase the elk, kill birds, snarl at us and so on. It's all very unfair. Where's a warden when you need one?

Dogs have been known to run ahead of their owners, harass a grizzly bear and then run back for protection with the enraged bear in pursuit. The result can be tragic for all concerned.

Ben Gadd

Dog leashed between two hikers, the perfect position for your pet on the trail

Some dogs move off the trail to poop, while others insist on going right in the centre of the path. Few Canadian jurisdictions require that dog droppings be picked up in wilderness areas, but it's just common courtesy to move your dog's waste far enough off the trail to prevent anyone from walking in it.

As for leashes, the retractable ones are very good for trail use. The dog can make five-metre sorties but not longer ones, and the leash seldom tangles because it reels itself in as the dog comes back. When the dog stops to sniff and piddle—ours is obsessed with this and does it about every 10 metres—you can often keep walking, because the dog learns to break off and catch up before the leash reaches its full extension and jerks it along. For walking with poles, I can put the handle of the leash through the waist belt on my pack. This works pretty well, except when something bolts into the woods beside us and Bo fires off after it. When he hits the end of the leash, I get spun sideways.

For backpacking with your dog, you can buy cute doggy saddlebags and make Spot carry his own dog food. This usually works fine, as long as the carriers stay on the dog, but *be sure to waterproof the load.* Wrap everything well in plastic bags or use bags designed for boating. Most dogs love to get into the creek on a hot afternoon and few announce their intention to do so (yet another reason to keep your dog on the leash).

Make sure that your dog gets enough to drink. On a hot afternoon, most dogs need water every kilometre or two. When my wife and I are going to be on a trail with few slurping spots, we carry lots of water for our dog and pour it into a spiffy fabric dog bowl that weighs hardly anything. It clips onto a pack and dries out between uses. If you can't find one of these at your local pet store, check online for one.

Dogs, like people, can contract giardiasis and then spread it around in their poop. You may wish to give your dog only water from home or treat its drinking water the same as you treat your own.

Dogs that are kept in urban backyards typically have rather soft pads on their feet. On day two of a week-long outing, you may find your otherwise doughty Doberman limping along on bloody paws. The best solution is to let a dog build up its calluses before putting them to the test, but if that's not possible, then you can buy dog booties made expressly for this.

Bedtime can be awkward on a canine-friendly backpacking trip. Your giant Newfoundland will take over the centre of the tent, pushing you and your alpha mate to the sides, perhaps putting a claw through your Therm-a-Rest pad and ripping out the mosquito netting when a deer wanders into camp at 3:00 a.m. One solution is to use a tent with a vestibule big enough to give the dog sufficient shelter, close to you but not in with you. A piece of blue foam, which is cheap and light, makes a fine doggie sleeping pad. A nearby tree can serve as a strong night-time tie-in point. Of course, you still have to teach the dog not to paw at the mosquito netting.

If your dog tangles with a porcupine, and you can't take the dog to the vet, you may have to pull the quills yourself, especially quills in the mouth and tongue. These prevent a dog from eating. The good news is that quill wounds rarely infect. Porcupines produce natural antibiotics that coat their quills, thereby protecting one another during mating and fights. To pull quills, you may have to muzzle the dog. I say "may have to" instead of "will have to" because I remember watching one dog sit patiently and passively as its owner yanked quills out of its mouth!

Start by asking the dog to sit. Cover its eyes briefly with your hand as you grab a quill with your trusty multi-tool pliers (page 116). The dog will jerk back, and the quill will come out. Repeat.

If your dog is not this cooperative (some would say "not this stupid"), you may have to put on heavy gloves—or thicken a light pair by donning extras—and go after in-the-mouth quills by force. Your companions can help hold the dog. Quills in the lips and cheeks are more easily pushed through than pulled out. Clip the ends off these to make it easier on the dog. But don't clip any quills that must be pulled outward. The story about clipping quills to "let the air out" isn't true. Clipping the ends just causes them to fray, making them more difficult to grip.

A **lightweight muzzle** can be a huge help if you need to remove quills from elsewhere on a struggling dog. You could also use tape, being careful to ensure that the dog can still breathe. (To remove porcupine quills from your child, you may not need the muzzle and gloves. But on the other hand, you may.)

If your dog is sprayed by a skunk, too bad. Beyond rinsing its eyes with lots of water—a direct hit there is very irritating—there's little you can do about the odour until you get home. At that point you can wash the dog in the concoction promulgated widely on the web these days (see next page) and supposedly much better than the previously popular tomato-juice treatment, which never worked very well.

Skunk-spray remedy

4 cups	hydrogen peroxide 3% solution	1 L
¼ cup	baking soda	60 mL
1 tsp	dishwashing detergent	5 mL
	No water is used	

You may find kits with these ingredients in a pet store. If Spot has previous skunk experience and a short memory, you would be wise to keep one on hand.

Wear rubber gloves when you're mixing and applying this compound. Mix the constituents in an open container such as a bucket, not a plastic bottle, which could explode because the combination produces copious amounts of oxygen. It's this oxygen that breaks down the stinky thiol compounds in skunk spray, so use the solution right away, before most of the oxygen is wasted. The detergent takes out the oils.

Knead the mixture into the dog's fur well, getting someone else to hold a washcloth over its eyes, nose and mouth. You might want to wear safety goggles yourself. Leave the stuff on the dog for 10 minutes to do its work. Then rinse well in lukewarm water, not very warm water, which can be harmful to pets.

Hiking off-trail: "Leave No Trace"

Thus far, what I've described in this book applies best in situations with well-used trails and hikers' campgrounds, whether officially maintained or not. Most hiking and backpacking in Canada is done in such places. But what if you're venturing into the sort of wilderness in which few people travel, where the trails are used mainly by wildlife and the campgrounds are just places in which it's physically possible to camp? You can go to such places without doing lasting harm to them if you practise leave-no-trace hiking and backpacking. **Leave No Trace Canada** is dedicated to this idea (www.leavenotrace.ca).[1]

---

1   The international headquarters is the Leave No Trace Center for Outdoor Ethics, Box 997, Boulder, CO 80306, 1-800-332-4100, www.lnt.org.

The Leave No Trace premise is an optimistic one: that humans can move through the wilderness without damaging it. Of course, we can't go anywhere without inflicting some kind of wear and tear. We're large land animals. We can't help but leave footprints in soft and dusty ground. We break and trample vegetation without intending to as we move about. The grass packs down overnight under our tents. The trick is to minimize all this, leaving no signs of passage that endure for more than a few days and allowing enough time between visits for the wilderness to recover.

Here are the seven principles of Leave No Trace:

1. Plan Ahead and Prepare
2. Travel and Camp on Durable Surfaces
3. Dispose of Waste Properly
4. Leave What You Find
5. Minimize Campfire Impacts
6. Respect Wildlife
7. Be Considerate of Other Visitors

I have taken these principles and combined them with what I've learned since my youthful days of hacking the branches off spruce trees for bedding. The result is the following extended list of leave-no-trace rules you should try to observe in pristine Canadian wilderness. Really, these are things to keep in mind wherever you go in the wilds. A place that has been worn and abused can always benefit from better care.

- For any trip in the outdoors, observe that wonderful motto "Take only pictures and leave only footprints." You may find places in which even footprints or the touch of a hand are too much: a mossy place behind a waterfall, a spider's web, a tussock covered with wildflowers, a delicate mineral deposit. Need we walk on everything, touch everything? No. Can we view some things from a respectful distance and be satisfied? Of course.

- Here's another famous motto: "If you can pack it in, you can pack it out," meaning "Don't leave any garbage." As a step beyond being careful not to litter, we should pick up and carry out any litter we find. These are the rules throughout Antarctica. They should be applied in the Canadian wilderness, too. (Be aware, though, that very old litter—older than 50 years—may have historical value and should be left alone. As a rule, if something looks old it probably

Pristine wilderness in the Gataga River area, northern Rockies

is old. So in line with that wonderful Newfoundland expression, "Leave 'er lay where Jesus flang 'er!")

- Avoid walking on soil crust, also termed "cryptogamic soil," "microbiotic crust" or "cryptobiotic crust." This is a thin ground cover of tiny intergrown mosses, lichens and fungi, fragile and easily broken up by boots. Usually associated with deserts, biotic crust is very common in mountainous areas of Canada at all elevations, but especially above the treeline, where it forms part of the alpine tundra. You'll see it beyond the northern treeline, on the arctic tundra, too. Where biotic crust is disturbed, erosion quickly follows. Try not to step on it.

- Consider your boot soles. Soft rubber soles with shallow tread, like those on runners and light hiking boots, are less damaging than hard rubber soles with deep tread, like those on mountaineering boots.

- On land that's free of human disturbance, we ought not to collect anything—wildflowers, edible plants, rocks, pieces of wood, the fish or the animals, whether for sport or for food—because it all has its place out there and we shouldn't be taking it for our own use. We have shopping malls from which to supply ourselves. The wilderness does not.

- When you're examining something, bring your eye to it rather than bringing it to your eye. Stoop down and examine that wildflower instead of picking it. Rather than catching that butterfly or frog, use your binoculars to look at it from a few metres away. (For this you'll want binoculars that focus closely.) Have you ever picked up a stone, only to find a colony of insects underneath? Perhaps you tried to replace the stone carefully, but chances are you weren't able to get it back in exactly the same position, leaving the little darlings in a fix, and you probably squashed some of them anyway. Better not to have moved that rock at all. "Leave 'er lay . . ."

- As a general rule, give wildlife plenty of room. That's not just because an animal might be dangerous—it certainly could be—but mainly because it needs to carry on its life without dodging the likes of us all the time. Nearly every creature has to

Soil crust in the Canadian Rockies

Ben Gadd

spend practically all its time simply trying to survive. We shouldn't make life any harder for it, just so we can get a better photo. If an animal moves away from you, you've come too close. Back off. In the national parks, it's against the law to "approach wildlife."

- Behave in ways that wildlife find predictable. Animals aren't stupid: the first rule of natural history is that everything out there is smarter than we think it is. The critters watching you from their hiding places have probably seen humans before. We look and act like large predators, with our eyes on the fronts of our heads and our big teeth showing every time we smile, so animals that are truly wild are afraid of us. They know from observation that we're active along trails during the day, and inactive and settled into camps at night. Unless habituated to our food—see below—animals learn to stay off trails used by humans during hiking hours. They avoid known campsites after dark. The flip side of this is that animals such as bears will be using the trails at night and checking out our tent sites after we leave in the morning. To reduce stress for people and bears alike, we should be where we are expected to be. Avoid hiking in the evening, especially at dusk and just before dawn, when many animals are on the move to and from feeding areas. Camp at locations used by other parties.

- Visit the same pristine place no more than once or twice a season. This is perhaps the most important point. It takes only a few trips per summer along the same route, or a few camps per summer in the same spot, to establish the human footprint. I've done this myself, without intending to, and I know it's true. Walking through the same untracked meadow four times in one season with a group of 10 other people beat the grass down into a path that was followed by other parties. Within two years there was an established trail. So now, when I'm going to any particular back-of-beyond valley, I limit my guided trips to no more than two in a season. I may even skip several years entirely.

- Travel in small groups of no more than six. The larger the group, the greater the potential impact can be, especially when some members aren't well-versed in Leave No Trace. A single well-trained person does the least damage, of course, but it's advisable to have companions in the backcountry in case of emergency.

Perhaps the perfect number is four: two people to head out if rescue is required, leaving one to stay with the person needing assistance.

• Whenever possible, use an established path—often an animal track—for walking. Animal paths tend to disappear in meadows, where the animals spread out to graze. Your herd, too, should spread out, and you probably will anyway, as you look for the continuation of the path.

Hikers using the Leave No Trace method of hiking in trail-less terrain

- If there is no established path, spread out to prevent starting one. This is how you should walk in alpine meadows and mossy forest areas.

- In snowy areas, walk on the snow instead of on the soggy ground that surrounds summer snow patches.

- No one needs to be told to avoid walking in the mud, and leaving tracks on the muddy shore of an alpine lake is to be avoided, but if you're using a trail with a muddy section, the advice is just the opposite: stay on the trail. This one is particularly difficult for most of us to accept, because we hate getting our feet wet *(continued on page 278)*

Sticks used as directional markers

Slinging food bags from trees to keep food away from bears

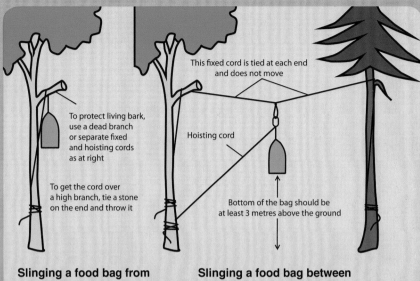

This fixed cord is tied at each end and does not move

To protect living bark, use a dead branch or separate fixed and hoisting cords as at right

Hoisting cord

To get the cord over a high branch, tie a stone on the end and throw it

Bottom of the bag should be at least 3 metres above the ground

Slinging a food bag from a branch is fairly secure

Slinging a food bag between two trees is more secure

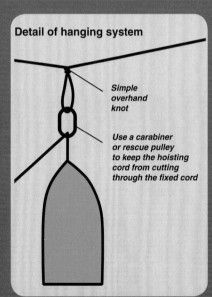

Detail of hanging system

Simple overhand knot

Use a carabiner or rescue pulley to keep the hoisting cord from cutting through the fixed cord

The rope is tied low to one tree, goes over a branch, across to the other tree and down, where it's also tied. There is a loop in the centre of the rope, between the two trees. A rescue pulley is clipped on there with a small carabiner. The free end of the rope runs up through the pulley and down to the bag. A loop in the rope is tied to the tree, keeping the bag suspended. This rig does minimal damage to the tree branches, because the pulling is on the carabiner. Once secured, the rope over the branches doesn't move much. Remember to hang your food bag at least 3 metres off the ground and at least 1 metre from the trunk or the nearest branch.

and caked, but really we should walk in the mud rather than on the vegetation beside the trail. Walking on the vegetation will widen the path and the mudhole. Resist the urge and slog on.

- Here's an alternative for when a trail is a real mess for some distance, and you're getting mud down into your boots and you've bloody well had enough: move well off the track to the right or left—at least 10 metres—and walk through the woods. In a group, spread out while doing this. Chances are the bad section of trail will dry in a few days and others won't need to do this, so no new trail will be created.

- In trail-less country, walk around vegetation instead of thrashing through it. When you do have to make your way through the shrubbery, push it gently aside rather than breaking it under your boots. Don't try to make passage easier for anyone else.

- Avoid marking your route with flagging tape, cairns (stacks of rocks) and whatnot. If you really need to indicate where you made a turn or which way it is to your camp, use three sticks to form an arrow or leave a stick or two propped against a tree. Dismantle these markers when you're finished with them.

- Camp in places that can take it, such as spots with strong turf. Bedrock slabs are pretty much human-proof, although some kinds of rock lichens are sensitive to being camped upon. If an otherwise pristine area has a heavily used campsite—common in places reached mainly by aircraft or boats—pitch your tent there so as not to spread the human presence to other locations nearby.

- Even though gravelly campsites along rivers and lakes recover quickly from use, we should really camp well away from water, at least 100 metres. This is partly to avoid polluting, but it's also for the benefit of wildlife. Animals often travel along streamcourses and lakeshores, and we should allow them room to get by. They need to pass your camp without having to alter their route and undergo the accompanying stress. (Somewhere I have read something along the lines of "Would you like a bunch of noisy, dangerous-looking, foul-smelling Martians camping in your driveway?")

- When you're tenting in a pristine site, use a slightly different route to your water source each time to avoid producing a trail down to the creek. Reduce the number of trips by using a water bag to carry lots of water back to camp per trip.

- Rather than engineering a super-comfortable tent site, be prepared to put up with some lumpiness under your sleeping pad. If you absolutely must pull up a rock to make a tent site usable, do so gently and replace the rock when you leave.

- There's no need to dig a drainage trench around your tent. The floor of a good backpacking tent doesn't leak (you may have to apply seam-sealer), and there should be enough freeboard at the entrance to keep rain-wash from flowing in.

- If you're hanging your food from a tree, be as gentle as possible. Throw the rope attached to a stone rather than climbing up the tree. Rather than injuring a live tree by pulling a rope over a branch, find a dead tree that's leaning to one side. If you must use a live tree, put an overhand loop into the rope and use that loop to attach a carabiner or rescue pulley through which the actual food-hanging rope will be drawn. You pull the main rope over the branch only once, then you anchor it at the base. Same sort of thing for heavy-duty food-hanging rigs, in which a rope runs between two trees with several food bags centred on it.

- Poop in individual cat-holes 15–20 centimetres deep and 10–15 centimetres across. (See page 204.) If the group has four or more persons, dig a single larger, deeper hole for camp use. Save the turf if there is any and replace it when you leave. Don't bury toilet paper and tampons; animals may dig them up. Pack this stuff out with you in a sturdy zip-lock bag. In Canada there are a few places that require packing out the poop along with the paper. When called upon to do so (in all caves, for example), please comply.

- Urinating doesn't usually present health issues, because urine is nearly always sterile,[2] so ordinarily you needn't bury urine or go very far away from water to pee. However, urine contains urea, which is a nitrogen-rich fertilizer. Urine is beneficial to vegetation

---

2   Hepatitis can be transmitted in urine, but this is rare.

in small quantities, but it attracts wildlife, especially deer, who lick it for its salt content. If you pee on delicate vegetation such as moss, animals will scratch at it, causing damage. Try to pick surfaces that won't be damaged in this way. Rocky spots and areas of deadfall are good, as are the trunks of large trees.

- Don't throw any food away. If you plan your meals carefully you should be able to eat everything you cook with no leftovers. Pack out anything you just can't eat. Human food is terribly addictive for wildlife, especially bears, which will seek it voraciously if exposed to it. And food-habituated bears cause trouble. They're often shot for their actions, a sad ending to a problem that begins with human carelessness. A fed bear really is a dead bear.

- Wash your pots, cups and dishes as little as possible. Supper is typically the messiest meal of the day, so keep it tidy by eating freeze-dried food if your allergies and dietary requirements permit it. Freeze-dried food requires only the addition of hot water and can be eaten directly from the bag, eliminating the need to wash out a pot gunked up with macaroni and cheese. Try freeze-dried food for breakfast, too, or eat instant porridge, instant beans and rice or other things that can be rehydrated right in your cup. Lick that cup clean!

  I like to finish a meal with hot chocolate or Postum, strongly flavoured beverages that can go into the cup on top of whatever flavour was in there before. Drink the last drop, pour in a little drinking water for a rinse if you like, then drink the rinse, too. If you have to dispose of the last bit of a hot drink, dilute it with water and fling it away from camp. Pack out used tea bags.

- Dipping your whole body into a stream or lake is not encouraged under Leave No Trace's guidelines, but the organization sees little harm in swimming in a sizable stream or in a large lake in a place that sees very little human use over the course of a summer. Except for your crotch, no other part of your body—hair, feet, underarms—is likely to cause contamination just because it's smelly. If you wish to bathe, first wash your bum well away from the shore to keep fresh fecal matter out of the water. Wash off insect repellent and sunscreen to prevent the introduction of chemicals. Remember that soap will also pollute a water body. If you want a full-body wash, not just a dip or a swim, you should wash and rinse at least 50 metres from the source. Use as little soap as possible. Spread your wash water and rinse water widely as you toss it out.

- All garbage must be packed out, including apple cores and orange peels. The seeds of apples, cherries and most other Canadian orchard fruits are naturally poisonous with protective cyanide compounds. These fruits don't normally grow in the places most of us hike, so the local rodents aren't familiar with them. Don't give a chipmunk the opportunity to make a fatal mistake. Orange peels almost always contain dye, and like other citrus peelings they tend to lie around unscavenged when thrown away. The general rule is that if the food isn't native to the place in which you're eating it, make sure that none of it gets left around, not even parts you consider inedible. The easiest solution is to eat dried fruit in the wilderness.

- Canada's forests are complex ecosystems in which all wood plays a part. Living trees, dead but still-standing trees, dead limbs on living trees, trees that have fallen, downed branches, rotting logs and stumps—all this is important in the lives of a myriad of forest organisms that eat it directly or indirectly, use it for shelter, perch on it, climb up on it to escape predators and so on. When you build a fire, you deprive the local ecosystem of something quite important. Further, you risk burning up that ecosystem if your fire gets away from you.

  For all these reasons, I think that fires in pristine places should not be built unless a fire is absolutely necessary for emergency warmth. In a campground setting, with an established firepit or firebox and cut firewood provided, a fire is not as harmful and can make for a delightful evening every now and again.

- If you must make a fire, try to do so in a rocky place. If the fire must be built in a vegetated spot, cut out a piece of turf and replace the turf when the fire is out. Extinguish a fire by pouring water on it until everything is cold to the touch. Spread the ashes around and brush the surface clean. Don't surround the fire with stones; they'll get permanently blackened. The next group will identify the spot as a firepit and build another fire there, thinking that it's okay. It's not.

- Don't burn food wrappers. Pack out all your trash, even items that appear to be burnable. Many wrappers are lined with foil, which doesn't burn unless a fire is very hot. Even so, if you sift through the ashes you may find bits of foil left behind.

- Move your camp often, preferably every day. The longer you stay in a place, the more wear and tear accumulates and the longer it takes to disappear. If your site is at all evident, another party coming along may see it and use it themselves, further establishing the footprint. It's better to make a no-trace camp than a some-trace camp, which will eventually become a permanent site.

- When breaking camp, make a determined effort to remove all signs that you were there. Check extra-carefully for bits of trash or food. In dusty, gravelly or muddy sites, remove your footprints by brushing them with your hand or a branch found on the ground. Put back any rocks or downed branches you moved. Go over any paths you made through the grass and gently brush these, too. It helps in land recovery.

- If you're in grizzly-bear country you need to make noise to let the bears know that you're coming. But that's really the only time that repetitive shouting is necessary in the wilderness. At other times, keep your voice to a normal, conversational volume. Why spook all the wildlife in the valley when you don't need to? They won't appreciate it. Nor will anyone else in the area. Noise is a form of pollution.

Lastly, and in light of all the foregoing, consider this: to carry out low-impact hiking and camping effectively, you have to know what you're doing. You need prior experience in the outdoors, preferably with people who practise leave-no-trace principles. Before heading into a sensitive place you should be familiar with the techniques needed to protect it from your passage, or you should go with people who do and be willing to learn from them. Otherwise you should stick to well-travelled parts of the outdoors.

Safety and emergencies

After 45 years of knocking about in the wilds unscathed, in 2004 I fell off a mountain. It happened unexpectedly, while I was scrambling along an easy ridge, unroped. Fortunately I tumbled only 10 metres, but that was enough for a broken wrist, a head injury and 25 stitches. However, it could have been a lot worse, in which case you would be reading a book by a different author.

Like most aging mountain climbers, I have lost friends and acquaintances to the heights. Most of those accidents were the result of taking chances, pushing too hard, not paying enough attention—which is what caused my fall—or being in the wrong place at the wrong time.

Hiking and backpacking are inherently much less dangerous than mountaineering, but being miserably cold on the trail or slightly banged up in camp are points on the same continuum. Comfort is at one end; death is at the other. Here's how to stay in the safe part of the curve:

- Approach this pastime cautiously. If you're new to hiking and backpacking in the Canadian outdoors, then get into it gradually. Go on short outings to safe places at first. Learn the basics. Tackle the longer, more difficult outings later, when you've acquired enough expertise.

- Go with people you know and trust. How many times have you heard of some group that met with an accident because of incompetent leadership? Or no leadership, meaning no one who knew how to guide the party properly when leadership became essential? You need to be in the company of people who clearly know what they're doing. Take a backpacking course. Join a reputable hiking club. Hire a qualified guide. In a few years, you may be the one leading, and by that time you'll do an admirable job.

- Stay with the group. Many a hike has gone wrong when the group split up. It often happens like this: Frank and Richard get out ahead of Eileen, Sharon and the kids. At a trail junction, the guys take a left. The others, who weren't there to see this, take a right. The two groups spend the rest of the day looking for each other. *Keep the entire party together and in sight at all times.* Especially keep the kids in sight, and among kids, especially keep young teenagers in sight. They have a remarkable talent for straying off the path.

When you come to a trail intersection, make absolutely sure that everyone is with you before going on. As I pointed out earlier, a group is only as fast as its slowest member. And there's a good reason for this. A slow member of the party will tell the others, "You go ahead. I'll catch up." Nope. The distance between the slow hiker and the others will just keep increasing. The rest of the party should be prepared to slow the pace. If the group must wait for someone to catch up, be sure to give that person some time to rest before everyone moves on together and at a more moderate speed.

- Carry creature comforts and navigational aids. In my pack I always have the "20 essentials" (see page 350) required to protect myself from the weather, to take care of thirst and hunger, to keep from getting lost and to deal with minor injuries or equipment failures. Carrying the right stuff is second nature to those who spend a lot of time in the outdoors, but for the inexperienced it's not. A couple from Ontario, enjoying their first visit to the Rockies, may intend to walk for an hour. They carry no jackets, no water, no lunch, no sunburn protection, no insect repellent, no map and no matches. Because they're having fun, they push on and on. Eventually they find themselves 10 kilometres from the car, above the treeline and drenched, stuck in a cold and frightening thunderstorm. This is a common experience, and although seldom fatal it's certainly unpleasant. Lots of people who stride unprepared into the Canadian wilds are quickly humbled as they discover that the northern wilderness is tougher than they thought. Next time these folks will come better prepared, more knowledgeable and better equipped. In similar weather they'll fare much better, snug in their warm jackets, eating their lunches in comfort as they wait out the storm inside the trail shelter that was mentioned in the guidebook they brought. Each region of this huge and varied country has its own set of hazards. You would be wise to check out unfamiliar territory before plunging in.

- Know when to turn around. What if that blister on your heel is starting to get infected? Turn around and go home while you can still walk. What if half a metre of snow falls in mid-August, and the slope ahead is steep? Don't cross; it might slide. Turn back. What if 5 centimetres of rain fell last night and the river is way up and you have to ford it? Don't. Hunker down and wait for the level to drop. What if thunder is rolling through the mountains and the trail is climbing above the treeline? Don't go up there until the storm has passed. You get the idea.

- Think before you do something dumb. Let's suppose that everybody is stripping down to jump off the rock into the river, and nobody has been there before. Should you join in the fun? No way. That water looks deep—although unseen rocks may lurk—and it's clearly swift and cold. Or how about this: everybody is drinking the water from the river without precautions because somebody said it was safe. Should you? No. These days, any untreated water in North America is suspect. The kids want to roll that big rock over the edge? Nosiree; someone might be down there. It's a long way back to the car along the trail, but you could get there a lot more directly if you just went straight down this mountainside, right? Wrong. Hidden from view below is an impassable cliff. The best advice about making snap decisions comes from Mom: "When in doubt, don't."

- Leave word. Tell someone back home where you're going and when you expect to be back. Leave thorough and accurate information about your trip. Write the following down and leave the note with a responsible person:

1. Who's going? List names and phone numbers.
2. Where, exactly, are you going? Name the area, the trail(s), the route, the destination.
3. Where will the car be parked? Write down the make and the licence number.
4. When do you expect to be back? Give a reasonable return time, with some built-in extra.
5. Who should be called if you don't show up? Leave the phone number for the proper agency.

This information will be of great help to the authorities if they have to look for you. In the national parks, you may also want to use the voluntary safety-registration system in addition to the required overnight camping permits.

Common things that go wrong on Canadian trails

If you've taken the foregoing section to heart, the common screw-ups listed here are unlikely to happen to you. You'll have put into practice the main point of this whole section of the book: avoid getting into trouble in the first place.

But what if, you know, something just kind of happens? Like when I fell off that mountain. Such an emergency is serious albeit rare. It requires the response outlined on pages 310–311.

For the more common situations and minor injuries one encounters while hiking and backpacking, here's how to handle them. You might even want to copy these pages and slip them into your pack, just in case.

Getting separated and lost

Lost? Not you. No, you just weren't sure of exactly where you were. You just got "turned around" for a while, after you got so far ahead of Sally and the others. How come they couldn't keep up, anyway? Wimps. They had the map, of course. And Mike had done this trail before. Okay, it was probably dumb of you to keep going past those two Y-junctions. You probably took the wrong one. Then the trail you found yourself on by accident joined a bigger trail, and soon you bumped into someone who explained how to get back to the car. The rest were waiting for you there, unable to hide their irritation. Still, they were glad to see you. You made a mess of the outing, but you got back in one piece.

This kind of thing happens all the time. If you're the person who became separated and lost, *stop the first person you meet and ask for directions*. Do this even if you're male.

Of course, spoken directions have a way of being wrong. "You can't miss it" is one of the Three Great Lies (along with "Your cheque is in the mail" and "I won't tell anyone"). So ask for directions from another person as soon as you can, to see if the two sources agree. If they don't, try a third, and so on. If you're hiking in well-travelled country, this method will almost always get you home.

If it doesn't, perhaps a **cell call** will. It might be wise to bring that phone with you, even though you don't intend to use it. These days you can often receive a signal in areas that were once technology-free havens. To prevent an intrusive call when you're trying to enjoy a carefree walk in the wilds, just keep it turned off until you need it.

It's always a good idea to carry a map and a GPS unit in country you're not familiar with. Before you start walking, remember to tell that wonderful electronic gadget to store the location of the parking lot. (Or your hotel if you're exploring a strange city.) It takes only a moment to set the waypoint. Then take another minute to study the map. What's the general layout of the trails in the area? Where does your route fit in? As you go along, haul out the map from time to time and trace your progress, using topographic features such as streams crossed, lakes passed, hills traversed, etc. If you're not sure where you are along the route, turn on the GPS and find out.

No map or GPS? But you do have a compass? Alas, for most people a compass is seldom useful. Hiking routes are complex, and your average hiker hits the limit of their compass-working skill when they've learned in which direction north lies. Uh, now what? Beelining the proper direction to the car by compass, even if you know which direction to go, rarely works anyway. There always seems to be something in the way: a canyon, a river (where the heck was the bridge?), a high ridge, a cliff, a swamp . . . You're going to be falling back on the ask-someone method. Next time, remember to bring that map and GPS.

But let's take the worst-case scenario. You have no map, GPS unit or compass. You're all alone in the wilderness, completely lost, far from help of any kind, in a dense forest. You didn't leave word with anyone. You're an idiot. Years from now they'll find your bones. As Jim Deegan wrote in his poem "Game Warden Lament"[3] back in 1954:

Now do this act before you freeze;
let it be the final thing—
cross your arms and legs so you'll skid out
behind a saddle horse in the spring.

However, my guess is that you don't want to wait that long to be found. Here is what the search-and-rescue people recommend that you do to prevent it:

- Find a reasonably comfortable spot near water and stay put until someone comes for you.

- Build a fire. Don't set the whole forest ablaze, but build one big enough and smoky enough to attract attention. (This is a great

---

3 From *Timberline Tales: Folklore in Verse of the Canadian Rockies*, Coyote Books, Canmore, Alberta, 1994.

approach during fire bans. You'll get a ticket, but your smoke will be spotted and you'll be saved.)

- It takes at least 40 days to starve to death. Rather than wander around for five of them until you stumble over a cliff and get killed, use the time wisely. For example, collect more wood. If you don't have a tent, improve your kip by making a lean-to.

- See if you can catch a fish, but don't drown while trying.

My wife once took a course from famed Alberta woodsman and survival instructor Mors Kochanski, author of *Northern Bushcraft*,[4] who told the class that most of what he was about to show them was entertainment, to keep them in one place, busy and out of trouble while the search was underway.

Spending a night out unexpectedly

There you are, hiking alone in the woods after dark—okay, you thought you'd be back sooner—on a cloudy night with no moon. But you have your headlamp. No problem; it's only a couple of hours to the car. Then the batteries run down, and you have no spares. You can't see a thing. You fumble along for a while, going by the feel of the trail under your feet, until you take a couple of headers over roots and rocks and decide that it would be better to just sit tight until someone with a working headlamp comes along. But they don't. You're going to be out all night, alone.

You might have been stupid about trying to walk too far that day, and you were definitely stupid about not having fresh batteries in your headlamp, but you've been smart enough to bring the 20 essentials (page 250), including warm clothing, a tuque and gloves, and, ah yes, a lighter.

No need for a fire yet. The evening is still fairly warm. You put on your extra layers and settle down beside the trail, leaning against a tree. You try calling home on your cell phone. No go; you're too far from the nearest tower. Angie's going to be very worried. You check your food bag. Well, you've got a candy bar, some veggies and a handful of gorp. You swish your water bottle around. It sounds like there are at least a couple of swallows in there. You eat most of the food and drink most of the water. This nourishment will help to keep you warm.

---

4   Now out of print, but the classic survival guide of its time.

The night drags on oh-so-slowly. The temperature drops. Your feet begin to get cold. You empty out your pack, loosen your shoes and slip your legs into the pack. Again, you've been smart: it's a nice, tall pack with a sleeve that pulls up over your knees. Your feet warm up. You drift off to sleep, awakening every hour or so. Something big comes down the trail, passing so close you can hear it breathing. You have no idea what it was, but it scared the hell out of you. At least it didn't walk on you, despite the fact that your feet were right in the middle of the path. You change position to move your legs out of the way, in case it decides to come back.

You doze again. When next you wake, it's in the blue-grey light of incipient dawn. You stretch out the stiffness, nibble your remaining gorp, take that last swig of water and hit the trail for home. You never did need to make a fire.

An hour later you try your cell phone again. This time you have a signal. Angie is most happy to hear from you.

The lesson: Always be prepared to spend a night out. You may have to.

When someone doesn't show up as expected

Angie has waited up for you until all hours. Sure, she's worried. She also knows that you left late for the hike and may have been caught after dark on a moonless night, alone. She knows that you had a headlamp, but she's already guessed that the batteries were low, because you've both been using it all summer, and now it's August, and even though it's an LED-type light that goes for a long time, it must be nearly out of juice.

In other words, she has the scenario rather well figured out. She knows that you have warm clothing and a lighter. She's given up hope of getting a call from you, but she knows that you're no fool, that you'll probably settle in somewhere and wait for dawn. She doesn't dial 9-1-1 in a panic and demand that the authorities begin looking for you. They won't. They know that nearly everyone who is overdue shows up just fine the next morning, so they wait until noon. Angie decides to wait until 10:00 a.m., when you'll surely have called from the trailhead or from wherever you got within cell range. You do, of course.

If the deadline had passed and Angie had not received a call from you, then she would have been quite right to report you as missing. Whom should she have called? If you'd been hiking in a national or provincial park, she should have called that park. Otherwise, call 9-1-1.

Exhaustion

Things go wrong when people are tired and hungry. They make poor decisions. Things go very wrong when people are so tired and hungry that they cannot go any farther. To avoid this, keep your body fed and watered. Stop to rest. Most important, know how far you, personally, can walk in a day. And don't overdo it.

When someone does overdo it, though, you need to lighten that person's load, feed them, make them drink, let them rest awhile and see if you can get them moving again. Or, if this isn't working and you have the gear, just stop and camp right there. You'd be surprised, though, how a cup of tea or a few chocolate-covered coffee beans can perk up an exhausted hiker. Sometimes the exhaustion is mental. The person is discouraged, perhaps a little scared. "Everyone else is doing okay but me!" The destination seems too far away. A little personal attention, plus some food and drink, is usually all it takes to save the day.

Dehydration

Thirst sneaks up on you, especially in cool weather. This may not be something you think of as a problem, but consider this: even mild dehydration affects your balance and coordination significantly. It makes any malady worse. So, as the athletes like to say, "Stay *hydrated!*"

When we're hiking hard on a hot day we expect to drink a lot of water and usually we do. But when we're making the same effort on a chilly day we still need to drink water, not as much but more than seems necessary. Make a point of hauling out the water bottle whenever you stop for a rest or a snack. You should be peeing fairly often, at least once every hour or two. If you haven't emptied your bladder all morning, you have to be dehydrated. (For more on getting enough to drink, turn back to page 149.)

Hypothermia

Hypothermia, defined as the inability to keep the body core warm enough, afflicts Canadians more commonly in summer than in winter.

Say what?

Yes. In winter, we northerners prepare properly for a day outdoors. In the summer we sometimes don't. In winter we venture forth in longies and woollies, with extra layers in the pack, knowing that the winter cold in this part of the world can easily kill us. In the warm season, though, which is deliriously short, we act as heedless as summer-crazed hares. We fling ourselves at the landscape in shorts, tee-shirt and sandals. Then it begins to rain, and the temperature drops to the single digits, and the wind comes up, and our friends hear about us on the evening news.

Normal body temperature is 37°C. Technically, you're suffering from hypothermia (previously known as **exposure**) when you have a core body temperature that has dropped to 35°C or lower. Your body can't keep itself warm. You shiver. Your movements slow down. You become uncoordinated. Your brain function is failing, which explains why you may not take the correct course of action, which is to put on another layer of insulating clothing, hopefully dry. If no additional insulation is available, you have to get to someplace warm, and right away. In another hour your core temperature may drop below 32°C, rendering you helpless. At 28°C your heart will stop.

So it's always wise to tuck a fleece jacket into your pack, plus something waterproof to keep the fleece dry and doing its job. If you just don't have enough clothing of the right type, and you're starting to shiver, head home. Fast. If someone with you shows signs of hypothermia, and the necessary additional warm layer isn't available, get *them* home as quickly as possible.

What if you're on day three of a backpack, far from the car heater, and someone is becoming hypothermic? The onset is sneaky. Victims of hypothermia aren't rational and don't ask for help. They'll often *refuse* help. In the two cases I've had to deal with, one required nothing more than an extra jacket, a snack and a drink—hunger and dehydration exacerbate hypothermia—before we were back at camp, where dry clothing in a dry sleeping bag, suitably pre-warmed by someone else, did the trick. A couple of hot water bottles (regular water bottles filled with hot water and tightly capped) provided ongoing heat. In the other case, we stopped and camped where we were. The hypothermic person was placed in a sleeping bag with another person for an hour and given food and warm drinks. Soon he was better.

The first case was mild, the second moderate. If hypothermia becomes severe, rewarming is best done in hospital, where intravenous fluids can be used and a heart-stopping surge of cold blood can be prevented. Backpacking can take you a long distance from the nearest hospital. So the bottom line is this: don't let hypothermia go beyond the mild stage. As soon as you see someone shivering, do something about it.

Heat exhaustion, heat stroke

Here we have the opposite of hypothermia: the body is overheated. Think southern Okanagan Valley or southern Ontario in July.

In the case of **heat exhaustion,** the body's near-surface blood vessels are expanded to their maximum diameter to shed heat. This dilation reduces blood pressure, which affects the brain. A victim may faint. The skin is cool, clammy and pale. Get that person into the shade and give them cool liquids to replace the large amount of moisture that has been lost to sweating.

Heat stroke, also called "sunstroke," is different and more serious. It's an emergency. The core body temperature is rising above 41°C. Blood-vessel dilation and sweating cannot control it. The skin is hot and pink rather than pale and clammy. The heart is pounding. The victim is confused. You have to cool that person quickly or they'll die. The best outdoor treatment is immersion in a cool, shady water body, taking care not to let the person's head go under. If full immersion is not possible, get the person into the shade and splash their upper body and head with cool water.

Asthma

Exercise-induced asthma—difficulty breathing because the bronchial tubes are narrowed by spasm and clogged with thick mucus—is becoming increasingly common in Canada. Most young people with this condition know they have it and carry an inhaler that dilates their bronchi before or during an attack, but adults who have never been diagnosed often suffer without medication.

Starting a hike vigorously can bring on asthma in anyone subject to it. Stopping suddenly soon after a rapid start is the worst situation. A victim will cough, wheeze and have difficulty speaking. They may become angry, lashing out at other members of the party for walking too fast.

A severe asthma attack is life-threatening. The person cannot get enough air into their lungs to maintain consciousness, in which case mouth-to-mouth rescue breathing will be needed. This will be difficult because of the bronchial spasm.

To avoid triggering asthma, begin any walk slowly. Build up speed gradually, and—this is very important—*don't stop for at least 15 minutes.* Better yet, walk for a half-hour before stopping.

First aid for asthma when the victim has no inhaler: the person should sit down and consciously attempt to control their breathing, making it regular and deep. Exhaling through pursed lips usually helps. If the air is cool, which makes asthma worse, it can be warmed by breathing through a loosely wadded sweater, a fleece jacket or a hat. Loosen clothing on the upper body. A cup of strong black tea can also help, because it contains **theophylline,** known to ease bronchial spasm. When the victim has recovered enough to move on, start very slowly and keep going at a gentle pace. Chances are the person will soon feel much better.

People with asthma should drink enough water to keep the body well hydrated, which makes mucus less tenacious.

Lightning

It's not so much that lightning can kill you—it most certainly can, although the odds are very slim that you'll be struck—it's that being threatened by lightning is scary, no fun at all. This is an experience best avoided.

Avoid it by keeping an eye on the sky. If the clouds are dark and you hear thunder approaching, seek a low, well-wooded place. Lightning strikes most often wherever things stick up from the landscape—mountains, rocks, trees, buildings, towers, bridges, lighthouses, boats' masts. During an electrical storm you need to avoid ridges and passes above the treeline. You should stay out of meadows or open fields at any elevation, because you don't want to be the tallest thing in the clearing. If there's only a single tree in a large open area, don't stand under it. This is how golfers get killed by lightning. Avoid an empty beach during a thunderstorm.

Does metal attract lightning? No, not even pointy metal items such as walking poles and umbrellas. There is no need to run from your pack just because it has a metal frame or metal stays. Having said that, metal certainly does conduct high-voltage electricity, and if you're struck, any metal on your body will probably burn you. So if lightning is hitting very close by, it makes sense to set your pack and walking poles aside. Remove any change in your pockets, along with your pocket-knife. Take off any metal objects around your neck or wrists and remove your glasses if the frames are metal.

To protect yourself in an exposed position, search out the lowest spot you can and crouch in it. Don't lie down or sit down; a close strike will send currents along the ground. Keep your feet under you. Just your boot soles should touch the ground.

If someone is injured by lightning, it will not be dangerous for you to touch them. If the person is unconscious, check immediately for heartbeat and breathing—electricity can stop both—and begin rescue breathing or full CPR immediately if required.

A lightning strike is survivable (the North American death rate from strikes in open situations and under trees is about 50 percent), but anyonestruck even moderately is likely to suffer burns and heart irregularities for some time. They should go to hospital as soon as possible.

Difficult stream crossings

Streams never look as deep as they are. You wade out a couple of metres, and water that looked to be barely over your boot-tops is up to your thighs. Whoa! Don't lose your footing and get swept away!

Here's a good method for fording a knee-deep stream.

- Take a good look at the crossing point before you start. Is it safe? Ideal fords are shallow and flat underfoot, typically in places where the river has spread out and is running slowly. Bad fords are in constricted, fast-running places with boulders and deep pools.

- Wade across singly, or just a few persons at a time in a big group, leaving others on the shore to watch. The watchers should have their packs off, so they can quickly dash out and help you if you fall, grabbing your pack or whatever else might be floating away. A pack that gets loose in a rushing stream can go a long way in a short time.

- Wear shorts, or strip to your underwear.

- Take off your boots, stow your socks in your pack and put on your wading shoes or your sandals. (Be glad you brought them. Those rocks are sharp underfoot!) No wading shoes? Have to wear your boots? Take out the insoles and don't wear your socks. The boots will dry out faster inside if, after wading, you put on dry socks atop dry insoles.

- Tie your empty boots securely together with their laces, about 20 centimetres apart. Flip up the head-flap on your pack and slip the joined laces under it, so a boot sits on each side of the pack, well up on it, close to your back and not swinging around. Close the head-flap over the laces to secure the boots.

- Walking poles provide good stability in the currents. If the poles are adjustable, lengthen them so you can probe for deep pools ahead.

- Wear your pack with the waist belt and chest-strap unbuckled, in case you slip and fall in the water, in which case you may need to get out of that pack quickly.

- With your poles ahead of you, offering four-footed balance, start across. Take your time, even if the water is painfully cold; you need to plant your feet carefully.

- If the water deepens to your knees and the current becomes strong, turn so that you're facing upstream. Move sideways, leaning into the flow, bracing with your poles.

- If you're swept away, point your feet downstream. If your pack is pulling you under, get rid of it. Use your feet to ward off rocks. Backstroke vigorously to slow your forward speed, and work your way over to the shore—*the shore you came from, if you were the first one trying to cross.* You don't want to be the only one on the far side of a dangerous crossing.

If the water is swift and hip-deep, you're quite likely to lose your footing. It's better not to cross water more than thigh-deep, especially if the water is very cold. You're risking more than a drenched pack. Carried into even deeper, swifter water, or over a waterfall or under a submerged tree, you may drown.

Sometimes a large group can link arms and cross deep water safely, but it's better to search up and down the river for a safer ford. If you can't find one, you might wait for the water level to drop, as it often does in glacier-fed mountain streams after the mid-afternoon rush of meltwater goes by. Such streams are much lower in the early morning.

Trouble with large animals

Depending on where in Canada you're walking, the critters living there may be of concern. This country has a lot of wildlife, some of it large and toothy, large and antlered, etc.

We humans are primates, with instinctive climbing ability. If you've ever climbed quickly to escape danger—up a tree, over a fence, onto a rock or a vehicle or a structure—you know this to be true. When a large animal is coming toward you with intent—a bear, a farmer's bull, an elk, a moose—your reflex action will probably be to climb the nearest object that looks tall enough. Can't argue with that. It works.

It's better, though, to avoid such situations. As always in the wilds, *keep your eyes and ears open,* aware of what is going on around you. Too many people walk right into trouble, chatting heedlessly with their friends, paying no attention to what's standing in the trail ahead, just beyond the rise. It might be bigger than you are, and it might have attitude.

Bears aren't to be trifled with. They can and sometimes do kill humans. There are three species of bears in Canada: black bears, grizzly bears and, in the North, polar bears. Here's what every backpacker should know about them.

First, and this applies to all three species when you're hiking and camping in their habitat, *you have to keep them from getting into your food.* Even if you fail to take the proper precautions with cooking, food storage and garbage, and no bear arrives while you're there, you can bet that it will arrive later. If it finds something to eat, it will return to the site repeatedly looking for more. And perhaps another party will be there. Or perhaps the other party made the initial mess and your group is the one having to deal with the bear. Not good either way.

Second, you want to avoid them. You especially want to avoid polar bears, which are by far the most predatory and dangerous species. Fortunately you're less likely to encounter polar bears than black bears or grizzlies. With grizzly bears and black bears, letting them know that you're coming is important. With polar bears, *not* letting them know that you're coming is important. Don't get confused over this.

Third, you need to know what species you're dealing with.

In eastern Canada, **black bears** and people have been living near one another for a long time, which has made the bears understandably shy, considering how we treat them. When we show up, they're inclined to fade into the shadows. That's good. Still, if black bears are known to frequent the area, be careful with your food, keep an eye on the kids, and don't let your dog chase a bear into the bush. The dog may be hurt, or it may kill a cub.

Black bears have been known to attack us as prey. It's a rare event, but it happens. A black bear will sometimes stalk a human, following more and more closely, trying to get up close behind, then running at the intended victim, head low, in an attempt to knock the person down. In such a case, showing submission is obviously the wrong thing to do. The bear may make the kill. Experience has shown that it's better to fight back. Luckily for us, black bears seldom press an attack very far. If you show that you'll not be taken easily, a black bear is likely to be repelled. You can get your message across by using your pepper spray (if the first blast doesn't do the job, perhaps an-other will), striking the bear with your walking poles, throwing stones at it, kicking it, shouting and screaming.

Better yet, chase the bear away before it gets to the point of mounting an attack. For this, there's strength in numbers. I've heard of cases in which a group of campers has gone after a black bear that was hanging around the camp and dosed it with pepper spray. This was strong negative conditioning, and it was probably good for the bear. The message was "Don't mess with humans. They're worse than skunks." We can only hope that a bear treated like this is a quick study and stays out of trouble in future. Otherwise it will certainly wind up dead, shot by the authorities after proving itself a dangerous nuisance.

In western Canada we also have **grizzly bears,**[5] which are more likely to attack us than black bears are. Why the difference? Grizzly bears are primarily ground-dwellers, while black bears are agile tree-climbers. When a black bear feels threatened, it climbs to escape. A female black bear can send her cubs up a tree very quickly, then go up there herself. A female grizzly bear, however, must defend herself and her cubs on the ground. Any grizzly will defend its feeding area or a carcass it's consuming. Their reputation for fierceness is quite justified.

A grizzly bear's best defence is a good offence, so a grizzly is more likely to charge you than a black bear is. If this happens, I hope that you've seen the bear's advance and are safely up a tree rather than being charged, but if you're on the ground then it's somewhat reassuring to know that most of the time such charges are bluffs. The bear stops a couple of metres away. It treats you as it would another big, powerful predator, seeming to know that a fight between the two of you would leave both parties injured. For wild animals, any injury except for a very

5 The grizzly bear of North America and the brown bear of Europe and northern Asia are the same species, *Ursus arctos.* Thus, a grizzly is properly termed "brown bear," but for the purposes of this book I use "grizzly bear" because that name is more commonly used in Canada.

Protective postures to take during a grizzly bear attack

minor one usually leads to death. With this in mind, play your role as a tough character but one who is not interested in a scrap. If you show no alarm but move away slowly, not shouting or staring at the bear—these are interpreted as signs of aggression—then statistics show that the bear is unlikely to actually attack. Move off facing sideways, just as a bear often does in leaving an encounter, each party keeping an eye on the other but not threateningly so, then go your separate ways.

If you are attacked by a grizzly bear, Stephen Herrero[6] and other experts advise being submissive, to show the bear that you mean no harm. If you do this, your chance of escaping injury is good. Research has shown that these animals can moderate the force they use during an attack and have done so when the victim remains still and non-confrontational. In such cases the victim may receive a non-lethal bite or two and then be left alone.

Two postures have been shown to be effective during an attack: lying prone with your hands behind your neck, or curling up on the ground. In either case, lie very still. The bear will probably withdraw. Grizzlies, unlike black bears, seldom attack us as prey. They attack us as competitors. Once they realize that we're not after their food or their babies, that we're submissive to them, they leave us alone.

If a bear of either species makes contact with you, however, statistics also show that a blast of **pepper spray** is your best response. An attack may come very quickly, with no warning. If you carry pepper spray, keep it where it's instantly accessible. In studies of using pepper spray on charging grizzly bears, a shot full in the face has nearly always turned the bear around. Black bears seem to be less sensitive to pepper spray, but they're also easier to repel, as discussed above.

Should you carry a gun in black-bear or grizzly country? This is unlawful in national parks and many other places. Where it is allowed, though, few hikers pack firearms. These weapons are heavy. The carrier must be trained to use them, otherwise they risk lethal mishaps to themselves and those around them. The usual error, though, is that a bear is killed unnecessarily, and that's a sad thing.

If you're attacked and you have no pepper spray, or if the pepper spray fails to deter the bear, you need to know which species of bear you're facing so that you can respond in the correct way. Both species can be black, brown, sometimes very pale, and similar in size. But nearly all black bears have a contrasting white chest patch, while grizzlies don't. You can positively identify a grizzly bear by its short snout, small ears, shoulder hump and—especially—its long claws, which stick out well beyond the fur on its front feet as it approaches. A black bear has a long snout, large ears and shorter claws, which typically don't show much beyond the fur on the front feet.

---

6   Stephen Herrero is the author of *Bear Attacks: Their Causes and Avoidance*, Lyons Press, 2002. This book is frightening but essential reading for anyone who wishes to understand the issue.

Hiking with dogs can be hazardous in bear country, as discussed earlier.

Having said all this about grizzly bears and black bears, I have to conclude with the following: your chances of being hurt by one in Canada are very slim—you're more likely to be hurt by a falling tree. There is no record of a group of six or more hikers being attacked by a grizzly bear.

When grizzlies or black bears may be present, let them know you're in the area by shouting often, especially when you're going upwind in brushy areas along streams, rivers or lakeshores. If you do see a bear, bunch up and give it plenty of room as you pass. (See page 229.)

Do not, however, make a lot of noise in **polar-bear** country. These animals are attracted to unfamiliar sounds. The largest bears in North America and the most carnivorous, they have caused many human deaths and are a serious threat along Canada's northern coast and in the Arctic Islands. Summer is nonetheless the safest time of year to venture into polar-bear territory, especially the month of July, when many of these bears are inactive and asleep (**estivating**) in order to get through the period when there's no sea ice. Polar bears hunt mainly on the ice, and when there isn't any they prefer estivation to hunting on land.

The authorities in Nunavut recommend not camping on beaches or anywhere close to the sea. As per hiking in grizzly-bear country, it's wise to travel in groups of six or more. If signs of polar bears—tracks, droppings, scavenged carcasses—are found, leave the area immediately. And quietly.

The jury is out on the effectiveness of pepper spray in deterring polar bears, but carrying it can't hurt. Also recommended are trip-wires or motion detectors around your camp, to alert you to the presence of a bold bear on the prowl.

Many parties carry firearms in coastal areas, sometimes even in the northern national parks despite the potentially heavy penalties for doing so. Parks Canada's policy seems strangely muted about this. I checked the agency's web pages for the various northern parks in which polar bears live and found the same in all: firearms are simply not mentioned in the safety information about polar bears. Yet people wishing to backpack there will certainly want to know. We need clear information on this topic.

Since there no trees from which to hang your food at arctic latitudes, you may wish to keep it in 10-litre **bear-proof containers** such as the Backpacker's Cache sold by MEC for this purpose. Made of tough, slippery ABS plastic with smooth edges, and too large for even a polar bear to get its jaws around, these containers are also useful for protecting food from grizzly bears in alpine areas south of the treeline. Bear-proof containers are necessarily heavy—the Backpacker's Cache weighs 1.27 kilograms—and they cost over $70 each, but when your own safety and that of such a glorious creature as a polar bear are at stake (remember, *a fed bear is a dead bear*), then this is clearly the way to go.

Other animals that you might want to avoid include **moose,** which kill humans, and themselves, mainly by colliding with vehicles at night. These huge creatures are difficult to see because of their dark colouring, and they're a serious hazard to hikers driving to and from their trailheads in wilder parts of the country. Slow down, especially near dawn and dusk. Moose do sometimes attack hikers and backpackers. The bulls can be quite dangerous during rutting season, meaning late summer and throughout fall, and the cows will attack in defence of their young at any time of year but especially in the early part of the summer when their calves are small. Moose fight mainly by rearing up and striking out with their front hooves, as members of the deer family generally do. Don't let an encounter get this far. Give these animals lots of space any time you see one.

Elk can be dangerous to hikers in the same way that moose are—attacks by rutting stags and by hinds protecting their young[7]—so they require the same kind of attentive hiking in places where they're found. The rutting season is, again, late summer and fall, and females with young are touchy until late summer. The same can be said of **mule deer** and **white-tailed deer,** although attacks are rare.

If you're charged by an elk, waving something at it is a good defence. I've waved a white plastic grocery bag to good effect in and around Jasper, where elk frequent the town and sometimes try to intimidate people. The park wardens chase the elk away from places in which they're not wanted by tying strips of flagging tape to hockey sticks and going after them—a very Canadian form of harassment.

Keep clear of **bison** if you're hiking in Wood Buffalo National Park or Elk Island National Park, Alberta. The largest animals in North America, bison aren't particularly aggressive, but you don't want to annoy them. Stay well away from their babies.

Cougars, also called mountain lions, pumas and panthers, seem to be hurting us more often these days than in the past. This is likely

---

7   Note the proper terms for male and female elk: "stag" and "hind." "Bull" and "cow" aren't correct. Neither is "elk," actually. In Europe this is the term for the moose. We should really be saying "red deer" or the official Canadian term "wapiti." Just thought you might like to know.

to do with our increasing numbers in their habitat. Perhaps they're responding to this invasion of their range, but whatever the reason, the stats on fatalities from cougar attacks indicate that if you're small in stature and alone, your chances of attack have increased.

In places known for the presence of cougars—inquire locally, especially in southwestern Alberta and southern British Columbia generally—you're wise to travel with others and stay close together. A cougar hunts by stealth, often lying in wait, and an attack can be lightning fast. Attacks also seem to come in the form of prey-testing, in which the animal walks right up and takes a whack at you with its claws. Pick up a big stick and fight back. Throw rocks. Like black bears, cougars can be repelled. They don't have the size and strength of bears. Anecdotal evidence suggests that pepper spray is highly effective against them.

Animals that you might think ought to be dangerous but rarely are include wolverines (the biggest members of the weasel family), wolves (dangerous only in captivity or when habituated to humans by being fed), mountain goats, bighorn sheep and caribou.

Animals that you might not think of as dangerous but sometimes are include coyotes (known to bite people who feed them and then withdraw food), beavers and muskrats ("It came right out of the swamp at me!"), raccoons, deer mice (droppings can carry hanta-virus), Columbian ground squirrels (fleas can carry bubonic plague—see page 266), great horned owls (sometimes they rip people's scalps at night, apparently mistaking human hair or furry-looking tuques for rodent prey) and that least predictable of all animals, the family dog.

The animal most likely to injure your dog is the porcupine. (See page 269.)

Treating common injuries

This section is no substitute for a proper first-aid course, which any outdoorsperson should take. It's good for every member of a group of hikers/backpackers to know some first aid. If only one member is trained, what if that person is hurt and unable to advise the others about what to do?

If you haven't learned standard first aid, or if you've let your certificate lapse (it should be refreshed every three years), two days of basic instruction can save a companion's life. First-aid courses at all levels of interest are offered by St. John Ambulance, the Canadian Red Cross and other properly accredited organizations. Call today! To find out where you can take a course, got to www.sja.ca or www.redcross.ca.

Blisters

The most common injury in hiking, blisters are an absolute pain in the, uh, heel. Which is where they usually occur. Not only do blisters turn hiking into misery, they also tend to become infected, which is potentially disabling. You really want to avoid getting them in the first place. Buy shoes and boots that fit properly (see page 33). Wearing two pairs of socks, the inner pair lighter than the outer and turned inside out so the smooth side is against your skin, may help. More important, put enough kilometres on your footwear ahead of a long hike to get your feet properly toughened. See the section on preparing yourself, page 24.

At the first sign of a blister, meaning a spot on your foot that starts to complain, fix it. No one likes to draw attention to their own problems, so you'll be tempted to ignore the pain and keep walking. Don't. Get that sock off, let the skin dry for a few minutes, then carefully stick on a blister pad, smoothing it and stretching it as required to cover curved places without bunching or wrinkles. The gel-type, all-in-one pads offered by Band-Aid, Spenco and kindly old Dr. Scholl are terrific. There's no need for cutting little doughnut-shaped pieces out of moleskin and covering them with tape, etc. Gel pads even work pretty well once the hot spot has become a visible, fluid-filled blister.

Ben Gadd

Fix that "hot spot" on your heel before it looks like this!

Should you poke a blister to drain it? The prevailing advice is not to, for fear of infection. Usually a blister opens up on its own anyway. When that happens, it's a good idea to wash the spot well and let it dry before covering it up with a blister pad.

Sunburn

In the short term, a bad sunburn will spoil an outing. In the long term, it will increase your risk of skin cancer. Dark-skinned people aren't exempt from sunburn.

For all these reasons, keep your shirt on, wear a hat with a broad brim and use sunscreen of at least SPF 30 on any skin that's left bare. You can buy sun-protective, long-sleeved shirts and long pants made of wonderfully light, cool material. Check out www.nozone.bc.ca, www .sunprotectiveclothing.com or www.sun-togs.com.

Be aware that a tee-shirt may not protect your shoulders and back as well as you think it should, especially if the fabric is thin. If you're hiking around water or on snow, ultraviolet light reflected upward from it can burn you under your nose and chin, around your eyes and on your earlobes (ouch!).

Okay, despite all these warnings, you've gone and done it. Your back throbs with every heartbeat. The tops and backs of your legs feel like they're on fire. What can you do? Wet cloths help, and so do painkillers. But that's about it. However, look on the bright side: 30 years from now, you'll be enriching the dermatologists who will be removing your precancerous lesions.

Other burns

Look closely at the people you see along the trail. The ones clearly missing hand-hair and parts of their eyebrows may have recently experienced adventures in stove-lighting and naphtha-assisted fire-starting. White gas is dangerous stuff!

We should see fewer burns from stove fuel as the years roll by and safer LPG stoves supplant the old liquid-fuelled models, any of which can become a Molotov cocktail in the wrong hands. Learn to operate your stove competently at home—practise outdoors—before you take it camping.

First aid for any burn is *quick* immersion in cold water. This is where the frigid streams and lakes found in so much of our country offer an advantage. Keep the burned part in the water for at least five minutes. By cooling a burn pronto, the tissue-killing effects of the injury are minimized and the inflammatory response is reduced. You have less pain and heal faster. So do take the time to properly cool a burn injury.

After that, if it's a small burn and not very serious—nothing more than reddening and a small blister, say—all you need do is wash it with soap and safe water to prevent infection, cover it with a light dressing and keep it clean. You should be able to continue your hike as planned.

Larger, deeper burns—blisters over the entire back of your hand, say, or patches of crisped or blackened flesh—are serious injuries and very prone to infection. You don't want to develop **septicemia** (blood

Treating a burn in a stream by cooling it

poisoning) when you're several days away from the highway. Head home and get medical attention immediately.

Stings and bites

Canada is mercifully short on dangerously venomous insects, spiders and snakes, but we do have honeybees, bumblebees, hornets (yellow jackets) and other kinds of stinging wasps, as well as a few spiders that pack a punch. The black widow is found in southern British Columbia, and the hobo spider is found nearly anywhere. We also have a couple of species of rattlesnakes, both near the limits of their range and seldom seen.

To avoid being stung or bitten by any of these, be cautious when handling firewood or picking up objects on the ground. Don't poke your bare hands into dark hollows. Listen for buzzing around you in brushy places and in flowery meadows. Be wary when entering abandoned structures. Wear shoes or boots instead of sandals. Keep your head covered. Check locally to see if there are poisonous spiders or snakes in the area.

If you've ever experienced instant chest stuffiness and/or trouble breathing after an insect sting, you should consult a doctor. You may have had an anaphylactic reaction. It may be worse next time, even life-threatening. Your doctor may prescribe an **epinephrine auto-injection kit,** plus antihistamine pills.

A good on-trail treatment for an insect sting is to immerse the site in cold water or cover it with a cool cloth until the pain subsides. Extract the stinger if it's still in the skin by lightly scraping it off with a knife blade or credit card. (Pulling it out with tweezers may empty any remaining venom in the attached sack into your skin.) Wash the spot with soap and safe water. There's no need to cover it. Spider bites are more troublesome, not immediately after the bite but days or weeks later, when you may find the spot failing to heal. Go to the doctor.

Despite our good fortune in Canada of having so few nasty biters and stingers, we do have world-class **mosquitoes.** We're used to them, and for most of us the occasional bite is a minor inconvenience. However, visitors from Europe and other parts of the world in which mosquitoes aren't troublesome may react to a bite with a big, itchy welt. If a mosquito-country newbie is going to be walking with you, it might be wise to suggest that they bring some bug-bite ointment with them. The itching can be relieved somewhat by an old folk remedy I learned from my wife: use your fingernail or thumbnail to indent the skin over the bite, then make another, similar indentation at 90 degrees to the first, so that you have a little cross over the bite. This works surprisingly well.

Nowadays, with potentially fatal **West Nile virus**[8] a possibility in much of southern Canada, it's better not to be bitten. In buggy places, wear clothing that's tightly woven and mosquito-proof. Long sleeves and long pants are advised, with cuffs buttoned tightly and trousers tucked into socks. Add gloves and a head net, and you may not require any smelly DEET-based repellent.

Blackflies and their larger biting relatives the **deerflies** and **horseflies** aren't known to carry disease in Canada, but a blackfly bite near an eye can swell grotesquely. Blackflies are surprisingly good at crawling under cuffs and getting around other barriers. Their favourite target area is your hairline, especially on the back of the neck and on or around the ears. (I typically get nailed on my earlobes, of all places.) It's a stealth attack. Most people don't feel a thing as the fly chews a tiny wound in the skin and laps the blood from it. For some reason you feel the need to touch your neck. Your hand comes away bloody. Too late; the fly has flown. The little red dot of a bite takes a week to heal and itches the whole time. Every time you pick the scab, it bleeds. When blackflies

---

8   The symptoms are flu-like at first but can progress to lethal encephalitis and meningitis. You can find more information at www.phac-aspc.gc.ca/wn-no/.

are around, DEET may be your only reliable defence. Applying it just under your hat-brim may be enough to keep these wee beasties from biting you.

DEET will also repel **ticks.** Tiny black-legged ticks of the genus *Ixodes* can carry **Lyme disease.** The infectious agent, *Borrelia burgdorferi,* has been reported in tick saliva right across southern Canada. **Rocky Mountain spotted fever** can be acquired well east or west of the Rockies. The carrier, the Rocky Mountain wood tick (*Dermacentor andersoni*), is found from central British Columbia to central Saskatchewan. Ticks are also known to cause **tick paralysis,** a serious motor-nerve condition brought on by other agents in a tick's saliva. Tick spit can make you sick!

Inquire locally as to whether or not it's tick season in the place you intend to walk. If it is, at the end of each day you should check well for them. Look especially in your hair, behind your ears and in places where your clothing fits rather tightly, such as under belts and bra straps.

Ticks don't drop from trees. They get on you from low-growing vegetation, particularly grasses and short shrubs, then they crawl up. The more time you spend lounging around in meadows and brushy places during tick season, the more risk you take on.

Luckily they're slow-moving. In most cases you have several hours in which to find and remove a tick before it selects a location on your body and begins to feed. Contrary to folklore, the whole tick doesn't dig in. Just the tiny mouthparts are inserted into the skin.

To remove a tick, don't just pull it off your skin quickly. The mouthparts may remain in place, possibly leading to infection. Applying heat or chemicals—including liquor—is not a good idea, either. These usually just kill the tick, again leaving the mouthparts imbedded. If you pull slowly and gently, trying not to squeeze the tick, it will gradually withdraw its mouthparts, which is what you want it to do. There are handy tools for this. Perhaps the lightest and simplest that has been shown to be effective is the inexpensive Pro-Tick Remedy (see page 131 for photo). If the mouthparts remain, remove them like you would a splinter (see next page).

Scrapes and cuts

Prevention first. It's all too obvious: if you fall down in the rocks with a heavy pack on your back, and you're wearing shorts and a tee-shirt, you're going to get scraped up. If you have to push your way through heavy brush in that sort of attire, you're going to get scratched up. This is why I wear long pants—the type with zip-off lower legs—and a long-sleeved shirt in such places. When skin damage is a possibility, I cover my skin.

The usual first aid for scrapes and small cuts is to let the injury bleed for a while, to allow your protective bodily fluids to bathe the site. Then wash the area with soap and safe water. A puncture wound that doesn't bleed should be encouraged to do so by light massage. Cover a scrape with a dressing to keep it clean. Bandage a cut. Change either dressing every day.

Deep cuts and lacerations become infected easily in the dirty outdoor environment. Go home and get medical attention.

Splinters

You grabbed a rose bush by mistake. Ow! Swiss Army knife to the rescue. With its small tweezers you pick out the spines. But dang it, there's one tiny prickle you can't find, and it goes bzzt on a nerve ending every time you brush it against something. The solution is to brush the surface of your palm with the edge of the blade, and the invisible spine will pop out. Sometimes the edge of a credit card will work, too.

You shoved a sliver under your nail. Oooo, that hurt. But again, the tweezers had it out quickly. Then—you're having a bad day—you get a real beauty of a splinter wedged into your finger, and it breaks off just under the skin. Tweezers can't get it. You'll have to dig for it. In your first-aid kit you have a sewing needle. You wash around the splinter with soap and safe water. You flame the needle with your lighter (hold the tip briefly just above the top of the flame, so the needle doesn't get covered in soot) and go after the splinter. When the end is exposed, you flame your tweezers—they, too, need to be sterilized to work in what is now an open wound—and the splinter comes out. Ahhhh. Wash the spot again and put a small Band-Aid over it.

Sprains

Very stiff, very heavy boots, like those meant for mountaineering, provide some protection against a turned ankle. But not as much as you might imagine. I once received a sprain while wearing mountaineering boots. Besides, stiff footwear is so uncomfortable for hiking that few people choose to wear it.

The best way to avoid spraining your ankle is to keep your eyes on the trail ahead. Take small steps, especially when going downhill with a heavy pack. Don't walk pigeon-toed. If you feel an ankle starting to turn under, get your weight off it instantly and roll to that side. Your pack will probably protect you as you fall.

If you turn the ankle under anyway, the intensity and duration of the pain provides a clue to the severity of the injury. A truly sprained ankle hurts like hell. You can't put any weight on it after the initial pain subsides, and it remains that way hours after the incident, swelling up considerably. If so, your trip is definitely over. That ankle needs to be immobilized for several days, and you need to get it x-rayed. Let's hope you're not too far from the road when the injury occurs. Your friends can carry your gear out, with you limping along on walking poles. It may help to shorten the pole on your injured side enough to let you rest the heel of your hand on it and let it take most of your weight.

On the other hand, if the pain subsides rapidly and you can weight the joint within a few minutes, the sprain may be mild. I have a weak right ankle and have experienced this degree of sprain twice on backpacking trips. In a couple of days my ankle has been sufficiently recovered to enable me to carry on normally.

However, what appears to be a mild sprain may actually be more severe. Recently a backpacker on one of my guided outings turned his ankle on the first day of a week-long trip. The pain was not too great, the swelling was moderate, and he was able to weight the ankle soon after the injury. So he decided to continue. As the days passed, he was walking better and better. But the pain lingered after the trip was over, and an x-ray of the ankle revealed a spiral fracture of the fibula—the smaller of the two lower leg bones.

For a turned-under ankle, whether slightly injured or severely sprained, you can soak the foot in cold water—a bag of snow from a summer snowbank is an excellent substitute for ice—to reduce the swelling. Soak it or ice it for ten minutes, then let it sit for ten minutes. Repeat this cycle several times. After that, you may get further comfort by wrapping the ankle in an elastic bandage (Tensor bandage). Or, if you're wearing stout boots, you could put the boot back on instead of using the bandage. This offers good protection and some support to the injured ankle. You need to maintain adequate circulation in your foot, so if the boot feels too tight, you'd be wise to substitute a protective camp shoe or wading shoe over an elastic bandage. And really, given what I now know about the potential seriousness of apparently minor ankle injuries, you should get to the doctor as soon as possible, regardless of how mild the sprain feels.

Responding to an emergency

As any guide does, I constantly monitor the safety and comfort of those in my care, considering their individual situations and conditions, the strength of the group, the state of the environment we are in at that time (weather, distance to travel, time of day, potential hazards), what sort of mishap might occur at that location and what I might have to do about it. How I wish that everyone else in the group had similar concerns!

However, accidents and medical emergencies have a way of just happening, if not to your group then to someone else's, and you may be the one who has to deal with one. In any wilderness situation that requires emergency response, here's a good general three-step plan:

1. Ensure that unaffected members of the party are safe, removing yourselves from danger if necessary.

   - If the scene is clearly dangerous, don't try to rescue the victim(s). You may be the next person requiring rescue. Contact the authorities. If someone has a GPS unit, that person can use it to determine the exact location. Set a waypoint for it. If carrying a cell phone, try dialling 9-1-1. If you're out of range, send two reliable party members (preferably three, if two others can remain with you) out for help. Make sure that they have the cell phone and the GPS unit with the waypoint.

   - Maintain order at the scene until help arrives. If you can't do much for the victim(s), make sure the rest of the group remains okay.

2. If the situation seems safe, the group should stay together while carefully ascertaining the condition of the affected person(s). If outside help is clearly going to be needed, contact the authorities as above. While waiting for them to arrive, continue to look after the victim(s). Stay calm and maintain order.

   - Attend immediately to anyone in obvious life-threatening difficulty (e.g., not breathing, no heartbeat, severe bleeding, in danger of falling, pinned, drowning), using help from any other qualified member(s) of the party.

- Then attend to anyone else in need of help.

3. If the situation seems not to require outside help—that is, the injury is obviously minor—attend to the victim(s) until they have recovered enough to move ably on their own, perhaps even continuing with the trip. Or, if they're not able to continue, help them to reach medical attention. In the process, everyone should stick together to maintain group strength, share the load, lend clothing and food, etc.

As a guide, I provide a basically similar list of my own emergency-response sequence to institutional clients who need such information from me for their insurance agencies. My list has never been rejected. You might want to copy the list and carry it with you.

See also the **first-aid reminder card** I carry affixed to the lid of my first-aid kit (page 130).

Hiking and backpacking in selected regions

What's it like to take a walk along the Newfoundland coast or on the Gaspé peninsula? In this section you'll find an overview of the conditions hikers and backpackers may encounter in selected regions of the country, as well as brief descriptions of Canada's two interprovincial trails.

Detailed information about specific hiking areas and trails is beyond the scope of this book, so if you decide to pay a visit to an area you're not familiar with, you should do some research of your own. A good place to start is the Internet, searching under such keywords as "hiking," "backpacking" or "trails," plus whatever geographic names you can supply.

For example, when I used Google to search "hiking trails" and "Northwest Territories," the search engine found several excellent websites, including one devoted to the remote and challenging Canol Heritage Trail. The Canada Trails website (www.canadatrails.ca) also popped up, which had me clicking on the Pangnirtung Pass route in Ayuittuq National Park. Pangnirtung Pass looked interesting, so I went to the link for Parks Canada's Ayuittuq website. There was the phone number for the park information centre. Within a few minutes of beginning my search I was speaking with someone who could answer any question I might have. Such are the wonders of the World Wide Web.

Outdoor-equipment stores such as Mountain Equipment Co-op stock maps and trail guidebooks. So do friends-of-the-park stores in national-park and provincial-park information centres. A good guide-book can mean the difference between a great hike and a wasted weekend.

MEC stores are also great places to ask for specific information. Many MEC employees are accomplished hikers and backpackers who know their regions well. If you're planning a hike at, say, Lake Louise, then drop by the MEC store in Calgary, where you have a good chance of finding someone who has hiked the very trail you're interested in. MEC staff and their friends across the country have been an invaluable help in compiling the information in this chapter. My sincere thanks to them, and to all the other hikers and backpackers across the country who shared stories about Canada's wonderfully varied landscapes and climates, and about the wide range of adventures you can experience on so many thousands of kilometres of trails. Maybe one day I'll be able to enjoy a classic backpack in each region of our huge and diverse land. Or—and this would be the ultimate—maybe I'll get the chance to walk right across the nation on the National Trail or the Trans Canada Trail.

Ah, we Canadians are so lucky to live here!

High Arctic

You may have the wrong idea about Canada's arctic islands. I certainly did, until I talked with Jerry Kobalenko, author of *The Horizontal Everest: Extreme Journeys on Ellesmere Island*.[9] He assured me that this is an inviting place to go hiking and backpacking. The weather is decent and the terrain is easy. You're a long way from the nearest medical attention, though, and that's a sobering thought, but aside from polar bears (read on) the Arctic is pretty benign. Given reasonable fitness and a good guide, even a novice hiker can have a great time. The difficulty is in *getting there*.

Access is by air charter and that ranges from the expensive—about $2,500 a person (round trip) to get to Devon Island, the closest high-arctic destination—to the extremely expensive—$30,000 charter fee for a Twin Otter to Quttinirpaaq National Park on northern Ellesmere Island. Few of us have that kind of cash to spend on a holiday, and that's good: the fewer humans tramping about in the Far North's fragile ecology, the better. Not that you have to feel guilty about walking the mind-bogglingly huge amount of wilderness here. It's the perfect place in which to apply Leave No Trace ethics and tech-

---

9   Published by Soho Press, New York (www.sohopress.com). Not a guidebook per se, Jerry's book provides an excellent description of what it's like to be on foot in the High Arctic.

niques (page 270). Be especially careful not to disturb any cultural or historical artifacts, including litter that has clearly been lying there for a long time. It may have historical significance. Removing anything is unlawful.

The High Arctic's mountainous areas are the more interesting places to go. Yet seldom will you find a cliff or a canyon in the way of your walk. Nor will you find any trees blocking your view. The walking is usually on tundra, which is surprisingly dry; there are few marshy areas. There are rivers to cross, and no bridges, but while the water is very cold, the river channels are shallow and braided, not deep—except during periods of warm, sunny weather, which increases melt and brings river levels up.

In summer the sun is up around the clock. You sleep when you need to, or when your watch tells you that it's time to try. The sun is low in the sky, like having morning or afternoon all day. Photographers, note that there's no harsh midday light in the Far North!

The hiking season runs from the third week of June until the third week of August, when the frost returns. Snow can fall at any time in

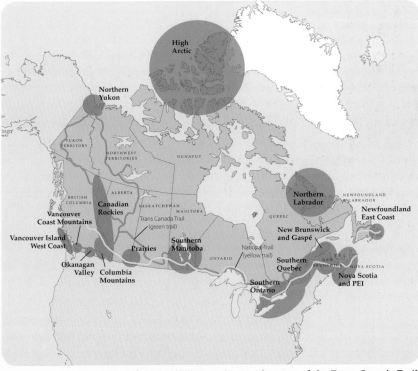

Map showing hiking regions and routes of the Trans Canada Trail,
National Trail and Canadian section of Appalachian Trail

the intervening months, but usually it doesn't stick, and if it does it melts quickly in the nearly continuous sunlight. An average daily high for late July is about 5°C. The overnight low is in the single digits but above freezing. A warm day might reach 10°C.

Rain is not common. This is the land where those renowned arctic high-pressure cells are born, and several weeks can go by without any precipitation. When it comes it's often in the form of cold mist and drizzle. There are no thunderstorms, no heavy downpours and not a lot of wind. Still, when it gets to blowing, the breeze can be quite strong in this treeless place.

The High Arctic is practically bug-free. Blackflies and ticks can't survive here, and you'll find very few of our National Insect. The main problem animal is the polar bear, and it's a serious threat. Polar bears can kill you, and given the chance they're likely to try. Pepper spray is anecdotally known to have been effective in stopping attacks, but at time of writing we're still waiting for the results of a thorough study. A lot of groups carry firearms. If you do, though, you must be properly trained in their use; a rifle is just as dangerous to you as it is to a bear. It's better to just avoid bear encounters entirely. Polar bears tend to stay close to the coast, so the further inland you are the safer you are. Announcing your presence by yelling just attracts polar bears, so don't behave as you might in the Canadian Rockies. Keep the noise down.

There are very few trails, not even paths used by animals. What animals? Small, widely scattered herds of muskoxen don't leave much in the way of trails. You have to be able to find your own way from point to point. There are no guidebooks yet, but good topographic maps are available. This location is so close to the magnetic north pole that a compass is useless. Bring a GPS unit and know how to use it.

A few outdoor operators have built some roofed accommodation for their clients, but otherwise you'll be camping in your tent. It should be a good, solid tent, able to withstand infrequent but potentially fierce windstorms. Camping is informal and unregulated. You need to secure a permit in national-park areas, but you stay where you please.

The size of your group is controlled mostly by the size of the aircraft you're using. You'll want to gather the number of people needed to fill the plane, so as to get the per-person price down to something approaching reasonable. Once you arrive, you can split up into small groups of three or four, numbers that work very well. Because the region is so isolated, each person must be healthy, competent enough for the trip(s) planned and a reliable party member.

You'll need good gear that isn't going to fail—you're a long way from home, remember. Bring tough, dependable boots. It's wise to be well-versed in first aid and to have a better-than-average kit with you. In case of disaster, or more often just to stay in touch with your pickup pilot in iffy weather, most groups carry satellite phones.

Northern Labrador

We're speaking here of the Torngat Mountains, the highest range east of the Rockies in mainland Canada. (There are higher mountains in the Arctic Islands.) Now a new national park, the Torngats offer exceptionally wild, isolated and challenging hiking and backpacking. You'll need experience, fitness and skill to enjoy this place.

The climate is high-mountain, rugged, glacial and—despite being at the same latitude as northern British Columbia—near-arctic to boot. Icebergs float in the fjords. There are no trees. There are no trails or campgrounds in Torngat Mountains National Park Reserve, no human conveniences at all.

Yet the weather in summer can be surprisingly warm and pleasant. Daytime highs can reach into the 20s, although the constant wind makes it seem cooler. Be aware, though, that the weather can turn suddenly foul, with rain, fog, blowing snow and winds that can flatten a camp in moments. You'll need a very strong mountaineering-type tent. Guy it out well.

If you have a good eye for route-finding you can avoid the cliffs and travel this country with ease, but be prepared for big ups and downs: the elevation gain from the valleys and fjords to the upland plateaus is over 1,000 metres, with peaks rising higher yet. Yes, you can stay in the valleys, hiking over flowery tundra and enjoying the caribou, which are abundant, but the heights will call you. In the high eastern part of the range it's a harsh, frost-shattered yet exquisite wilderness. (How true it is that difficult places are also beautiful places.)

You'll want sturdy all-leather boots that won't come apart a day after the charter flight or the boat drops you off for a week or two. Bring wading shoes for crossing the many small streams, most of which have rocky bottoms. Overnight lows can drop below freezing even in July, so bring a sleeping bag good to $-5\,°C$, a couple of warm layers (fleece, down jacket), a tuque and gloves. Be prepared for winter in summer.

The season here starts in early July, with the warmer weather falling between mid-July and mid-August. By the end of August overnight temperatures are dipping below freezing routinely. However, a

September visit can bring exceptionally rewarding days on the tundra, in its briefly brilliant fall colours.

Mosquitoes and blackflies live here, but they're not as numerous or persistent as they are farther south, and the wind provides relief on buggy days. Still, you might want to bring a head net and repellent.

Along the sea and in the low-elevation valleys, polar bears are a hazard. They're on land throughout the summer, and they're dangerous, sometimes preying on people. Occasionally they have been seen far inland and at high elevations. You must be vigilant at all times. Avoid the Atlantic shore, despite its beauty. Move inland and up to higher elevations to camp. You should know how to behave in polar-bear country, and you should have recommended bear deterrents with you. Practise using them. Only beneficiaries of the Labrador Inuit Land Claim and Nunavik Inuit Land Claim may carry firearms. It is highly recommended that you employ the services of an Inuit guide. For more information, go to www.pc.gc.ca/pn-np/nl/torngats/ (see also pages 296 and 300).

Black bears live here, too—this population may be the only one in the world to live north of the treeline—so be watchful of them. Store your food in bear-proof containers to keep either species of bear from getting hooked on human food and eventually winding up being shot as a dangerous nuisance. Bring several days' worth of extra food with you, in case your planned pickup is delayed due to bad weather.

Park or not, the Torngat region is the homeland of the Labrador Inuit people and is managed under their land-claims agreement. The area is rich in cultural history. Artifacts and sites should not be touched. As in other national parks, you must register with the park office before starting your hike.

Getting to the Torngats is expensive, no matter how you go. Access is by scheduled jet from Montreal to Kuujjuaq, Quebec (on Ungava Bay), or by scheduled prop aircraft from Happy Valley–Goose Bay to Nain, then on by charter flight or boat to one fjord or another in the Torngats. A number of outfitters offer trips to the area.

Northern Yukon

From Old Crow north to the Arctic Ocean, at the northern tip of the Yukon Territory, you're in isolated country at and beyond the northern treeline. Two national parks, Vuntut and Ivvavik, protect a mountainous yet gentle land that's essential habitat for the great Porcupine caribou herd.

These parks encompass a great variety of terrain, from foothills and high ridges to the arctic coastal plain and the shore of the Beaufort Sea. Despite its high latitude, the place has never been glaciated, so there are few sizable lakes. The landscape is mostly covered with tundra and low-growing willows. The slopes aren't very steep, and cliffs and canyons are rare, so the walking is generally straightforward. Rivers and the occasional stand of tall, over-your-head willows are the main challenges. Be prepared for long stretches of ankle-breaking tussocks: flimsy, basketball-sized mounds of vegetation. Walking poles help.

There are no trails that have been built and maintained by humans, and no established campgrounds, but the caribou have their own trail network. When a problem looms ahead, following a caribou path will often lead you past it.

The only town in the region is Old Crow, which is accessible by air via regularly scheduled flights from Whitehorse. However, most parties find it more convenient to charter a small plane with tundra wheels or floats from the town of Inuvik, situated at the end of the Dempster Highway. A good group size is three, the number of passengers in such an aircraft. There are few suitable landing places, unless you're going in by helicopter, which is very expensive. Most groups carry a satellite phone and use it mainly to speak with the charter company when it's time to be picked up.

This is a land of extremes. Summer conditions begin in early June, when the snow cover is mostly gone, but by mid-August the snow is falling again. During July, maximum temperatures can be as high as

Leanne Allison & Karsten Heuer

Backpacking in the Northern Yukon

32°C, and since the sun is up around the clock (yep, it's 24 hours of daylight in summer), things don't cool off much. Fortunately the air is dry.

Despite the likelihood of sweltering temperatures, you'll need warm clothing (tuque, gloves, medium fleece, long underwear, down jacket, waterproof/breathable rain gear) and a sleeping bag good to –5°C or –10°C, because cold storms can move in quickly from the coast and send the temperature plummeting to below freezing. This can happen two days out of seven. The wind is nearly constant in this region, fair weather or foul, so coupled with an arctic maritime storm—driving rain, snow, fog—conditions can be quite rough. Hypothermia is a real danger. You'll need a solid tent for shelter on bad days and a light-coloured tarp (your best choice is an aluminized, reflective model) to use as a sunshade in hot, sunny conditions.

The mosquitoes can be thick here, especially in the first half of July. Before this period you get some grace, and again in mid-August, but head nets are essential, as well as tightly woven, bug-proof clothing. If you're properly dressed, you won't need much repellent. Blackflies are around but not particularly noisome; the quick-biting deerflies are worse, as are the tiny no-see-um sandflies that appear late in the summer.

Grizzly bears live in the northern Yukon, and polar bears sometimes frequent coastal areas, although rarely in the summer. You may have trouble with grizzlies when you're near caribou, which are bear food. Bring pepper spray and sing out loud to let the bears know that you're coming. Should you carry a gun? The usual cautions apply, and firearms aren't permitted in the parks.

Since there are no trees from which to hang food out of reach of bears overnight, you'll have to dangle it over a cliff or from a big boulder, neither of which is common here. You can use bear-proof food containers (see page 300), but they're heavy. An alternative approach is counterintuitive but has worked well for recent backpackers: store your food in tightly sealed bags that don't spread the odour around and keep them in your tent at night. Only a very bold bear would dare go after them, but sleep lightly and keep the bear-blast handy.

Other animals that can give you trouble are jaegers ("YAY-gurs"), large birds that dive-bomb anything approaching their nests, and ground squirrels, which nibble food bags.

The main hazards in this region, though, are river crossings. Permanently frozen ground lies just under the surface, so runoff from storms is sudden and massive, swelling the streams very quickly. You'd best bide your time on the bank until the level drops, which doesn't take long.

All in all, this is a place for people who know what they're doing. If you're inexperienced, be sure that you have a competent leader.

There's no hiking guidebook available at time of writing, but the national parks can provide good information when you acquire the permits you'll need if you're planning to travel within their boundaries. Use the Parks Canada website (www.pc.gc.ca) to find contact info for Vuntut and Ivvavik.

Also recommended: *Being Caribou*, by Karsten Heuer. Not a guidebook, this account of following the Porcupine caribou herd through the northern Yukon to its calving grounds in Alaska is a Canadian adventure classic—as is Leanne Allison's video of the journey, also called *Being Caribou*.[10]

West coast of Vancouver Island

This section deals mainly with the world-famous West Coast Trail, a six-day seaside slog in the rain and the mud. Well, during some trips it can seem that way. Whenever you're in the woods, you're in the mud. But rain falls, on average, only one day out of six in July and August, and perhaps three days out of six earlier or later in the season. The more you can walk the beach, the less mud you'll have to contend with, and the fewer huge fallen trees you'll have to climb over and balance across 2 metres off the ground. This is a difficult route, and it's definitely not for beginners. It can be very trying.

Your well-earned reward is complete immersion, so to speak, in a great coastal ecosystem. Big Pacific waves wash up on a shore that offers a bit of everything—beaches, cliffs, rocks, wind-twisted trees, tidal pools and inlets. It all fronts a classic British Columbia temperate rainforest of huge cedars and hemlocks, mysterious and exquisitely beautiful in ghostly fog.

The West Coast Trail runs for 75 kilometres on the west side of Vancouver Island between Bamfield on the north and Port Renfrew on the south—more precisely, between Pachena Bay and Gordon River, neither of which can be reached by simply driving up to the trailhead. Buy an up-to-date guidebook and inquire locally.

The trail lies within Pacific Rim National Park Reserve and is administered by Parks Canada, which regulates its use to 60 persons in total

---

10   The book is published by McClelland & Stewart (www.mcclelland.com). The video can be ordered through Leanne and Karsten's website, www.necessaryjourneys.ca.

starting from either end each day. With 360 or so hikers strungout over six segments during busy periods, you'll certainly be seeing other folks on this trail. Spring and fall are less crowded, but to be assured of a spot between June 15 and September 15 you'll want to book as far ahead as possible. And be prepared to pay. A Parks Canada permit was $128.75 in 2007, with a reservation fee of $24.75 tacked on by their agent, SNBC (1-800-435-5622), plus $30 in ferry fees payable at the trailhead.

You can, however, camp where you please. A storm can pin you down at any point, but in good weather nearly everyone uses the same campgrounds. They can be crowded, and there are no reservations, so you should arrive early.

A key recommendation for the West Coast Trail is to avoid trying to cover too many kilometres in a day. Getting overtired leads to accidents and mistakes, like falling off a log. Parks Canada averages 80–100 evacuations over a season (which may explain the steep permit fee), and falls are the number-one cause. Walking poles will help prevent slips. Another hazard is that bugbear of seaside walking—the Big Wave. Don't go out on the rocks, close to the surf. You may be swept away.

The season has fixed opening and closing dates of May 1 and September 30, coinciding with the annual better-weather window and enough park staff to handle things properly. During July and August,

Parks Canada

West Coast Trail

the warmer months, daily high temperatures are in the upper teens and may reach the lower 20s in this cool maritime climate. Evenings are fairly warm, with overnight lows around 10°C. There's no need for a heavy sleeping bag, but do take a synthetic-fill one. The place is very damp, and down will get soggy. A medium-weight fleece will do for warmth. Gore-Tex rain gear will quickly wet out. You might as well go with a fully coated rain jacket and rain pants, both made of strong fabric that won't snag and tear while you're crawling across yet another shattered tree.

You'll want to wear synthetic fabrics generally, which dry quickly, rather than cotton. The wind makes shorts and short sleeves uncomfortably cool on the beaches, but things can get muggy in the woods, so zip-off pantlegs and button-up sleeves are good. Notwithstanding the above, I know of one couple who hit the West Coast Trail during a hot stretch and walked the whole thing in the nude.

They still needed boots, though. The trail is very rough and muddy, with lots of rocks and roots. Over-the-ankle footwear is recommended. Your boots will get soaked and stay wet, so consider using Gore-Tex socks inside them for comfort. It's also nice to have a pair of lightweight camp shoes or sandals to slip on when the day is done.

For shelter, it's not the bugs you need to worry about—there are very few troublesome insects, and the wind keeps them off you—it's the storms. These are real screamers, with buckets of horizontal rain flung at your tent. Bring a solid model with guying-out loops and a fly that reaches to the ground. A tarp won't cut it in a west-coast blow.

The most dangerous animal here is the cougar. Several attacks have occurred in the park, luckily none fatal to date. Bears and mice will get into your food, so Parks Canada has supplied metal lockers at all the main camps. Will humans get into your car while you're away from it for the better part of a week? This seldom happens. There is protected parking at one end of the trail and a well-watched lot at the other.

For hikers who can't get enough of this kind of backpacking, or, alternatively, are tired of the West Coast Trail, the new Juan de Fuca Marine Trail runs 47 kilometres southward from Port Renfrew to Jordan River. It's not in a national park, so the fees are much lower: $6 per person per night. For more information go to www.juandefucamarinetrail.com.

Some popular trail guides for this walk and others on Vancouver Island include *The West Coast Trail and Other Great Hikes*, by Tim Leadem, and *Hiking on the Edge: West Coast Trail–Juan de Fuca Trail*, by Ian Gill and David Nunuk.

Coast Mountains in the Vancouver area

Vancouverites have all the luck: a mild climate—if a bit wet—and proximity to a cluster of mountainous provincial parks loaded with great hiking trails. Wow!

Of course, the people of Vancouver do use those trails, sometimes in great numbers, so you'll find them crowded on summer weekends. If you want solitude in this region, put some distance between yourself and the city, or do your walking midweek. The famous (infamous?) Grouse Grind, an incredibly steep 2.9-kilometre-long trail/stairway running 853 metres up the face of Grouse Mountain, is so popular that it can seem like one long line of people, start to finish.

As is true of the Pacific Coast Ranges generally, this is a very rugged area, with big elevation gains and losses. You'll need to be fit. Fortunately, once you get fit you can stay that way, because it's possible to hike here year-round. Winter is cool and rainy, with gusty storms, but there is seldom snow at lower elevations. Spring and summer are lovely, with far less rain than people from other parts of Canada might assume. From early May through September, big high-pressure cells off the coast can keep things sunny for weeks on end. Expect highs in the upper 20s in the valleys and in the lower 20s higher up. Hot days can get into the 30s, but they're normally rather dry and quite bearable. Further, Coast Range trails are in Coast Range forest, so you'll be shaded by big trees.

This is a terrific area for hikers and backpackers of all abilities. Access to trailheads is easy by car, and even by city bus in some cases. The more popular trails are well built and well maintained, with markings to help you find your way. However, this is no substitute for a good map. The woods are dense and wild, and it's easy to get lost. Given the number of people out and about on any given weekend, Vancouver-area search-and-rescue groups are busy. If you're new to Coast Range hiking, bring a GPS unit to keep track of where you are, and maybe bring that cell phone, too.

Streams and rivers are bridged. You'll seldom have to share a trail with horses. And here's a pleasant surprise: the bugs are not nearly as bad here as you might have come to expect in other parts of BC. Still, mosquitoes can be aggravating in June and again in August. Blackflies, deerflies, horseflies, ticks—they're all here, with Lyme disease reported nearby in the Lower Mainland. In boggy areas you'll want tightly woven clothing and repellent, although most people get by without head nets.

You won't be troubled by poisonous spiders, poisonous snakes or poison ivy, but spiny blackberry bushes and devil's club lie in wait beside the trail. Cougar sightings are on the rise in British Columbia, with incidents having been reported in the Lower Mainland area, so watch for any posted warnings.

Severe storms are rare here, because the area is shielded from the open Pacific by Vancouver Island, but some recent whoppers may indicate a trend to more violent weather. It tends to be frontal, meaning that it can come in hard, and when the rain arrives it often stays for more than a day. So bring what you need for walking in the wet. An umbrella works well, because typically there is not much wind pushing those showers along.

Approach shoes are very popular here and rightly so, given the generally good walking surfaces and the long climbs, in which case every gram you can take off your footwear counts. Walking poles provide more uphill power. Long pants and long-sleeved shirts of light, mosquito-proof nylon work well during buggy periods. Zip-off pantlegs are popular.

Since storms are generally mild, your tent can be light. Big trees provide good support for hammocks, which you'll see in use here. But be aware that if storminess increases in the years ahead, so will fatalities from being under one of those big trees when it comes down.

Tarps, too, are popular in the Lower Mainland in non-buggy times. Synthetic-fill sleeping bags are recommended for the damp climate. If you're camping at fairly low elevations, a light fleece jacket will do for the morning and evening. Bears, raccoons and squirrels will all be keen on sharing your food, so keep the cookies out of the tent and string everything up at night.

Be sure to check into making reservations for on-trail campgrounds as they tend to be crowded. Even for day-hiking, you may have to pay for parking; this is British Columbia, land of the user fee. It's also the land of the parking-lot break-in, so don't leave anything valuable in your vehicle. However, as in the rest of Canada there is practically no violent crime on the trails, even those close to the city.

Two recent trail guides to popular hikes in the Vancouver area are *Easy Hiking around Vancouver: An All-Season Guide*, by Jean Cousins, and *103 Hikes in Southwestern British Columbia*, by Jack Bryceland, Mary Macaree and David Macaree. Check the Vancouver outdoor shops and bookstores for others.

Okanagan Valley

For a warm, dry-feet hiking experience, try the Okanagan area of southern British Columbia. Around Keremeos and Osoyoos, for example, the climate is downright desert-like. In a typical year you can walk snow-free through the winter months if you stay at low elevations. The trees are scattered, making for very sunny outings.

Come late March, things are already greening up and the days are warm enough for walking in summer clothing. It's tempting to wear light shoes, and a lot of Okanagan hikers do, but watch your step: there is cactus here. And rattlesnakes.

At middle elevations the snow does pile up in the woods, delaying the hiking season until May. But by early June you can be enjoying the high country sooner than in the Columbia Mountains and Rockies to the east.

The enormous forest fires of 2003 did a lot of damage in this part of British Columbia, especially along the Kettle Valley rails-to-trails hiking and biking routes. These abandoned roadbeds lost many trestles in the fires, which will need to be rebuilt before they're fully functioning trails again. Check locally to see how this is going.

In July the place really heats up, forest fires or no, with daytime highs well into the 30s in the valleys. The mercury hits 40°C in the southern Okanagan most every summer. In that sort of weather you'll want to escape to the heights of Cathedral Provincial Park or Manning Provincial Park, where the temperature will be in the 20s at treeline. You can continue to walk the alpine meadows there through September and into October, even into November in some years.

Access to popular trailheads is easy, usually by car from secondary roads. If your vehicle can navigate the many logging roads in the area, you can work your way far into the wilds. This is regrettable in many ways, but the upside is that it spreads the human beings around—and there are many of them in this part of Canada—rather than concentrating them in a few easily accessible parks. On a long weekend in summer you'll probably find the trails surprisingly uncrowded.

For backpacking, this is a mild and friendly place. It makes for a light pack, because you can leave your woollies at home. Rain is a sometime thing, with weeks of continuously good weather being the summer norm. You may wish to play it safe and carry your tent in case of a storm, but here it's possible to actually sleep out under the stars with little fear of getting drenched overnight. Your sleeping bag need keep you warm only to 10°C, and a sweater or a light fleece jacket is all you need to deal with the evening chill.

So far so good, but what about the insects? Yes, you'll want to sleep behind netting in June and July, when the mosquitoes and blackflies are busy, but by mid-August the bug season is over. A simple tarp will do. And what about those rattlesnakes? Will they crawl into bed with you? This is highly unlikely, and anyway they're found only at very low elevations.

In fact, this may be the hassle-free-camping capital of Canada. You'll rarely see a bear, the local rodents seem uninterested in gnawing holes in your food bag, and on most public land you can camp where you please at no charge. The main hazard is also the joy of the region: the heat. Be sure to carry enough water.

Many of the through-going trails are on old railway grades, and even in burned areas these continue to provide the easiest walking. B&Bs in small towns along these routes cater to hikers and bicyclists. Just remember to bring good sun protection and enough money to enjoy the fresh fruit and the local wines.

Some current guidebooks to popular Okanagan hiking areas: *Okanagan Trips and Trails*, by Judie Steeves and Murphy Shewchuk, and *The Similkameen Hiking Guide*, edited by Macdonald Burbridge. Perhaps guidebooks for areas within the recent fires have been updated to reflect the changes wrought. As always, stop at local bookshops and sporting-goods stores in hope of finding homey guidebooks to specific areas.

Columbia Mountains

East of the Okanagan Valley in southeastern BC lie the Columbia Mountains—the Purcells, Selkirks, Monashees and Cariboos—of the province's interior wet belt.

In places where the forest hasn't been logged too heavily (this is a region with a lot of cut-over mountainsides), you'll walk through groves of big cedars, hemlocks and Douglas firs. Large ferns and tall shrubs dot the lush, mossy forest floor. Look out for impenetrable patches of devil's club, the botanical version of *T. rex*. These things are covered with spines that can snag you nastily along a narrow, brushy trail, of which there are many in the Columbia Mountains.

In contrast with the tough going below the treeline, the high country of the Columbia Mountains is exquisite. Nowhere else in the country will you find alpine meadows as breathtakingly flower-rich as the ones you'll see here. But first you have to get there. Trails up through the dense bush of the middle slopes are few and steep. Most of them begin as logging roads, which overgrow quickly after the crews leave. For this reason, a lot of hiking is done in the area's national and provincial parks. At Mt. Revelstoke National Park, for example, a good paved road takes you right to the meadows.

At low elevations around Revelstoke, Creston and Nelson, the hiking season starts in late April or early May. This is deep-snow country, so for hiking higher up you'll have to wait until early July—in some years even into August—before the trails are clear. But the fall is mild, and you can walk well into October.

It rains a lot here in the warm months, sometimes day after day. Prepare to be soaked by wet trailside vegetation brushing against you. You'll need good rain gear and boots that can take the moisture. Try wearing Gore-Tex socks inside your boots.

Trail surfaces are damp most of the time, which is not a problem on well-maintained paths in the parks, but elsewhere you'll be dealing with mud, slippery rocks, equally slippery logs felled across roaring streams you won't want to fall into . . . the whole gamut of primitive, difficult hiking. For this you'll need strong footwear, walking poles, accurate navigational aids (map and GPS) and directions from locals who know the area well. So much of the Columbia Mountains is unsettled that there is great potential for long backcountry treks, and some people do them, but they have to be skilled, tough and resourceful. Beginners should stick to well-travelled routes. This is not the place to overestimate your abilities.

Mosquitoes and blackflies are certainly present, but the numbers vary a lot depending on where you are. Glacier National Park is surprisingly un-buggy, while nearby Mt. Revelstoke National Park has an annual late-summer plague of horseflies.

The weather tends to stay put for several days at a time in the Columbia Mountains, meaning that a week of showers may be followed by a week of dry, sunny days. Daily midsummer highs are often well into the 30s at low elevations, and in the 20s higher up. Overnight lows average around 15°C in the valleys, and it's considerably cooler near the treeline. If you're on a backpacking trip with camps at a variety of elevations, you'll need a sleeping bag good to the single digits for chilly nights. It should open right to the foot for ventilation on warm evenings.

Black bears and grizzly bears both live here, so be prepared to protect your food. Some of the parks provide bear-proof storage, but ask ahead of your trip to find out whether or not you'll need to bring your own food-slinging rope.

The usual mountain-hiking hazards apply in this region—falling over cliffs, being caught above the treeline in electrical storms, getting hypothermic in a cold rain—with the additional danger of being caught in a June avalanche. The usual accident of this sort occurs while crossing a steep gully well down the mountain from the origin of the avalanche far above, where the snow is still deep and prone to slide.

For guidebooks, check out *Glacier Country: A Guide to Mt. Revelstoke and Glacier National Parks*, by John Woods; *Don't Waste Your Time in the West Kootenays*, by Cathy and Craig Copland; *Hiking Yoho, Kootenay, Glacier and Mt. Revelstoke National Parks*, by Michelle Gurney and Kathy Howe; *Mountain Footsteps: Hikes in the East Kootenay of Southeastern British Columbia*, by Cathy Strong, and *Valleys and Vistas*, by Monty Horton. *Footloose in the Columbias* is a Parks Canada pocket hiking guide available in English, French and German.

Canadian Rockies

From Waterton Lakes National Park to the wilderness provincial parks of northeastern British Columbia, and from the foothills on the east to the Rocky Mountain Trench on the west, the Rockies are perhaps Canada's best-known region for hiking and backpacking. No fewer than seven interlocking national and provincial parks—Banff, Jasper, Yoho, Kootenay, Robson, Hamber and Assiniboine—make up a World Heritage Site. They attract walkers from many countries every summer. What can these folks expect to find?

The landscape variety is staggering. At the southern end of the range you can walk in prairie-style grasslands, smack up against the colourful billion-year-old rock of the Waterton area. The craggy limestone peaks of the front ranges from Crowsnest Pass to Jasper have a lot in common with parts of the Alps, and the paths are just as challenging. Along the Continental Divide, huge mountains and great icefields provide the backdrop for national-park trails that go on and on, day after day, some of them for distances of over 100 kilometres without crossing a single road.

This can be 100 kilometres of mudholes, horse poop and flies, because the Rockies are commercial-outfitter country. Still, within the national parks the trails are generally well maintained. You can reserve a tent pad in a different campsite each night, and the rivers are bridged. North of Jasper National Park the experience becomes wilder, with few maintained trails or campgrounds. The rivers remain unbridged, and no warden is going to be looking out for you. Here you're really on your own.

Wherever you go in the Rockies, the mountains will make you work hard, with long uphill sections over high passes. Glacially fed rivers rise a great deal during the afternoon heat. An easy ford in the morning can be uncrossable at 3:00 p.m.

The Rockies are a land of big animals—grizzly bears, cougars, wolves, elk, moose, mountain goats, caribou—that can grace your photographs one day and raise the hair on the back of your neck the next.

For all these reasons, you should approach the Rockies with the respect they deserve. Be prepared! For anything!

The season begins in mid-April, when the ground dries out at lower elevations. Green-up happens in mid-May, but the spring is often stormy and chilly here, with snow falling well into June, which is often a miserably rainy month. The higher passes can be plugged with snow until early July, when the backpacking season really gets going. The warmest period is from mid-July until mid-August, with average daytime highs around Banff and Jasper in the mid-20s and overnight lows in the single digits. Heat waves can reach into the 30s. But the rain always comes down cold, and above the treeline it can change to sleet and snow even in midsummer. August is the thunderstorm season. You should treat the prospect of lightning seriously on any trail that reaches the land above the trees. In unsettled weather, you'll want to be safely down in the woods in the middle of the afternoon, when the thunder often rolls.

By mid-August, if you're camped at treeline you might find a skiff of ice in a pot of water left out overnight. A week of bad weather is a regular occurrence late in August or early in September, with rain turning to snow, but the subsequent autumn can be lovely: yellow aspen groves, no more bugs, and trails and campgrounds largely free of summer crowds. Halloween has a spooky way of bringing the first real snowfall of the season. By mid-November everything is frozen up and it's time to trade your hiking boots for skis.

Insects in this area include wood ticks in April and May, mosquitoes in June and July, blackflies in August and yellow-jacket hornets at picnic tables in late summer. As elsewhere in this bug-rich country, the farther north you go the more trouble the mosquitoes are. A head net may make your evenings more pleasant north of the Peace River.

Hiking in the Selkirk Mountains, Glacier National Park, BC

Black bears will want your supper, so in the national and provincial parks be sure to use whatever has been provided to keep your food safe. The usual stash is a bear pole for hanging up food, or metal lockers for stashing it. Outside the parks you're on your own. Getting food up off the ground at least 3 metres still seems to be the best approach. In some campsites, red squirrels get into food that has been hung up; placing it in a plastic tub with a lid keeps them out.

For camps at and above the treeline, where grizzly bears may come by, you have the choice of packing food in bear-proof containers (see pages 145 and 300) or hoping to find a nearby cliff or a big boulder over which you can sling your food bag on a length of rope. Sometimes the only option is to keep food close by, just outside your tent, where only a very bold bear will attempt to take it. Sleep with one eye open and keep the pepper spray close at hand. (See page 296 for more on bears.)

Other creatures to be wary of are female elk and moose with their young, and male elk and moose in the fall rutting period (late August through October). Bighorn rams look tough, but they save their head-butting for each other, not us. Female sheep, though, can gang up on your dog and kill it. Female deer, elk and moose can do the job all by themselves. Cougar attacks are becoming more frequent, and there has been one known fatality in recent years.

As elsewhere in Canada, light hiking boots are popular in the Rockies for backpacking. However, low temperatures at higher elevations make wearing low boots and runners a chilly experience in wet weather. Consider a pair of leather hiking boots—not the really heavy, mountaineering ones—and buy them big enough to hold both a light pair of socks and a heavy pair. Walking poles are in vogue, and internal-frame packs are far more popular than external-frame packs. The afternoons can be warm enough for shorts, but with the cool evenings and the bugs it's a good idea to pack a pair of long pants or wear zip-offs. If you're planning to spend a lot of time above the treeline, lightweight long underwear will keep your lower half, including your feet, warmer in the windy mist. Longies also provide sleeping comfort when you're camping in the high country.

After August, once bug season is over, a tarp may be all the shelter you need at low elevations. Higher up, though, where the wind is stronger, you'll want a proper backpacking tent.

The more popular day-hiking trails around the Big Three resort areas of the Rockies—Banff/Canmore, Jasper and especially Lake Louise—are busy all summer, busier than many a solitude-loving hiker would find acceptable. These trails are justifiably popular, being gorgeous beyond words, so you might want to suppress your claustrophobia and blend in with the crowds oo-ing and ah-ing over the scenery. It's worth it! But if you're willing to choose a walk that starts well away from the postcard centres, or if you head out overnight, you'll find the Rockies lightly peopled and mostly unspoiled.

Violent crime is rare in the Rockies, but Banff is famous for overnight theft from cars, and every now and again there's a wave of break-ins at

Hiking in the Canadian Rockies near
Buller Pass, Kananaskis Country

trailhead parking lots where cars tend to be left for several days. The lot for the Berg Lake Trail at Mt. Robson is one of these. Park elsewhere nearby if you can, in a place that sees lots of activity around the clock, and lock everything you're leaving behind in the trunk. No one has ever stolen anything from me when I've left my tent zipped up in the backcountry and gone away for the day. Let's hope it stays that way.

There are so many hiking and backpacking guidebooks to the Canadian Rockies that I couldn't begin to list them here. A few of my favourites are *The Canadian Rockies Trail Guide*, by Brian Patton and Bart Robinson; *Classic Hikes in the Canadian Rockies*, by Graeme Pole; the two-volume *Kananaskis Country Trail Guide*, by Gillean Daffern; the park-by-park guidebooks authored by Don Beers (he gives lots of interesting historical info, too); and Mike Potter's uncannily accurate guidebooks.

Prairies

Hiking and backpacking on the grassy prairies of southeastern Alberta and southwestern Saskatchewan? Who would do that? It must be boring.

Not at all. It's just different. Whereas in the mountains it's the middle-range views that count—the peaks ahead, the river beside you—on the prairies it's the very near and the very far distant. There are no trees and no mountains, so you can see forever. Watching the changing light on the Sweetgrass Hills many leagues away in northern Montana is a classic prairie pleasure, as is watching the huge, ever-changing prairie sky. There's a lot that can be of interest close at hand, too, such as wildflowers, small birds and insects, but in the middle distance you're going to see mainly, well, grass.

For middle-distance diversion you need to follow a major prairie river valley, such as that of the Milk River, the South Saskatchewan or the Red Deer. These rivers have cut their way down into layers of sandstone and shale that have eroded into incredible badlands topography. Small side valleys—locals call them "coulees"—feed into the larger valleys and also provide interesting variation in the landscape. A wonderful way to travel this country is by canoe, stopping to explore on foot.

Two attractions of the prairies have little to do with the scenery. The first is the season, which starts early for western Canada: in late April or early May, while the mountain passes are still snowbound. Southeast of Calgary you'll find pleasant temperatures (daytime highs

The constant wind rustles the grasses near Red Rock Coulee
Natural Area, 30 km south of Seven Persons, AB

in the mid-20s) and wildflowers in bloom. The best time to go is from Victoria Day until late June. The other attraction is that you'll see very few other people out there.

Access is by car, although this is not the usual drive to a trailhead. The nearest towns are generally rather far away—like half-a-tank-of-gas-from-the-nearest-filling-station far away—on little prairie roads that criss-cross and can easily lead you astray. This is how you run out of fuel on the prairies. You have to know where you're going. Work it out in advance and maybe use your GPS to get you to the jumping-off point. Further, if your planned hike is on leased or private land, you should have contacted the owner ahead of time to get permission. Usually it's freely given. Show respect by leaving open gates open and closed gates closed behind you. Don't trample crops, and give livestock plenty of room so as not to stress them.

Unless you're hiking in one of the protected areas there (Grasslands National Park, provincial parks such as Cypress Hills, Dinosaur or Writing-on-Stone), your hike probably won't begin at a proper trailhead. The parks have developed trails, interesting scenery, campgrounds and the like. But that's not true prairie hiking. If you want to do this thing for real, you have to hoof it across a lot of calf-high grass from minor drainage to minor drainage, with an occasional prairie pothole (a shallow natural lake or reservoir) as a destination.

By mid-July, things have heated up and dried out. Daytime highs are in the upper 30s and the flowering season is over. The landscape goes brown. By late July it's even hotter, and you might as well be in Phoenix, Arizona. Still, the walking is easy. It seldom rains, except for the odd thunderstorm—lightning is a hazard out here—and the overnight lows in May and June rarely drop below 10°C.

There is little water available on the prairies, so be prepared to carry several litres for a day's hike in warm weather. Begin your hike early, around 6:00 or 7:00 a.m. when the temperature is cool and the birdsong is at its best. In the heat of midday you might set up a light tarp as a sunshade—you'll have to carry poles—and snooze under it. With luck the afternoon breeze will keep the mosquitoes away. You then continue your walk later on, when the sun is less punishing.

You'll need clothing for cool and warm temperatures all in the same day. Pants with zip-off legs are good for this. Gaiters will protect your ankles and calves from the grass and other prairie vegetation, which can be quite rough, even inflicting cuts.

Does this style of hiking remind you of something? Minus the grass, hiking in the deserts of the American Southwest is an apt comparison. We even have a few rattlesnakes and small scorpions. You needn't shake out your boots, though. Hardly anyone gets bitten or stung. But you shouldn't be reaching into ground-squirrel holes, because you might be nailed by a resident black widow spider, the only real danger from wildlife to be found out here. The mosquitoes can be bad in May and June, despite the apparent absence of water for them to breed in, and wood ticks are plentiful in April and early May. Sandflies—small biting flies—can be a nuisance at times.

Wildlife is surprisingly plentiful on the prairies. You'll almost surely see pronghorns, which are truly at home on the range. (Contrary to popular belief, the pronghorn is not actually a species of antelope. The only member of the family Antilocapridae, this animal has no close relatives.) In the brushier coulees, look for elk, deer and even moose. The sky is home to many hawks, especially Swainson's and ferruginous hawks. Sparrows and other small birds sing from the grass. Marshes shelter a dozen kinds of ducks, and in the fall migration some water bodies host geese by the tens of thousands. Richardson's ground squirrels go "tweep!" as you drive by, but they're quite uncommon away from the roads. Grasslands National Park has true prairie dogs. Stalking all these birds and rodents are coyotes and red foxes. There are no bears from which to protect your food, but you won't be cooking it over an open fire. It's stoves only in this understandably fire-wary country.

There is cactus here, hiding in the grass. Watch out for three small *Opuntia* species that are difficult to see as you walk. You'll need leather boots because the spines go right through boots with fabric panels.

Prairie-hiking aficionados, and admittedly they are few, recommend that you get into this pastime by hiking the established trails in the parks first. You can then use one of those parks as a base for hikes farther afield, staying in the park campground at night. Eventually you may find areas that you want to explore for days on end, doing proper backpacking.

For more on all this, consult *A Hiker's Guide to the Northern Plains*, by Ken Ludwig, and the Parks Canada web pages for Grasslands, www .pc.gc.ca/grasslands/. The park provides an excellent publication, *Grasslands National Park Field Guide*.

Southern Manitoba

It's usual to think of southern Manitoba as flat, but you'll also find interesting, hilly terrain with a lot of variety in vegetation and landforms. You'll walk through aspen woods, conifer stands and grassy meadows, and pass by rivers, lakes and wetlands. There are areas of deep boreal forest, too. Riding Mountain National Park and Whiteshell Provincial Park are popular and typical places for hiking and backpacking in this part of Canada. Whiteshell offers the beauty of the Canadian Shield.

Trails in Manitoba's protected areas are generally easy to travel and well maintained. Uphill sections tend to be short with no long climbs to high passes, the rivers are almost always bridged or easy to ford, and there are backpackers' campgrounds. In some parks you can camp where you please, but it's first-come, first-served. Inquire locally for the most accurate information.

The hiking season here begins in mid-to-late April, when the snow has cleared. By Victoria Day everything has greened up and temperatures are approaching summer norms. July and August are the warmer months, with daytime temperatures in the mid-20s. Hot afternoons can reach into the upper 30s. Overnight lows are around 10°C, although heat waves can keep the temperature above 20°C around the clock. By late September the days have cooled. By late October, snow is on the ground and few people are backpacking.

The weather is generally mild in summer, but this area is also famous for rip-roaring thunderstorms that will have you running from the lightning and hail. Expect to see rain on about three days out of seven, but it won't last all day. Most precipitation is in the form of short showers. The rain is cool—refreshing on a hot day—but seldom feels very cold. Mist and fog are rare. It rarely snows in June and never in July or August.

Mosquitoes can give you trouble all summer here, although less so in August. Instead of using a lot of insect repellent, consider wearing tightly woven, bug-proof clothing and packing a head net. At dusk, the buggiest time of day, you'll want to be camped in a breezy place with your mosquito netting zipped. Blackflies aren't particularly bothersome here, at least not in comparison to the mosquitoes. Check yourself daily for wood ticks in April and May.

The only other creatures likely to give you problems are black bears. These are rarely aggressive, but you need to store food overnight in the metal bear boxes provided in the parks. Elsewhere, hanging food in trees seems to work. In the fall, be wary of rutting moose.

The terrain is not particularly rough in southern Manitoba, and light hiking boots are currently popular for backpacking. For day hikes, a lot of people wear shoes rather than boots. Walking poles are rapidly gaining in popularity.

You'll need long pants and a long-sleeved shirt to ward off mosquitoes in the evenings, which can be cool enough to require a light fleece jacket. A tuque and light gloves will offer further protection from bugs, although they're seldom necessary for warmth.

Given the severe thunderstorms and the need for mosquito netting in this part of the country, a tarp isn't really enough shelter. You'll want a tent with good ventilation for hot nights. Sleeping bags need to be good down to 10°C from late June through August, and good down to freezing if you're pushing the season.

Trails close to Winnipeg are popular and can be busy, but if you're willing to drive a couple of hours or walk a few kilometres into the wilds you'll find things delightfully uncrowded. Even on a long summer weekend, parts of Riding Mountain and Whiteshell offer hikes and backpacking routes along which you'll see only maybe 10 people in a day. Theft and crime of all sorts are quite rare, and solo hikers have little to fear.

A good general hiking guidebook to this large area is *Hiking the Heartland*, by the Prairie Pathfinders of Winnipeg. Check locally for more specific guides.

Southern Ontario

For many hikers and backpackers in Toronto, London, Hamilton and elsewhere on the Niagara Peninsula, the famous Bruce Trail is a classic and representative route in this region. It's 800 kilometres of four-star trail linking St. Catharines at the southern end with the northern tip of the Bruce Peninsula on Georgian Bay. The dominant landscape feature here is the nearly continuous limestone cliff of the Niagara Escarpment, which provides the main attraction of the trail: scenic overviews.

Southwest of the escarpment the landscape is pretty flat. To the northeast, beyond Barrie and Peterborough, you're on the Canadian Shield, which is hilly and forested, and rich in lakes and wetlands, rivers and streams. Ottawa/Hull-area hikers have easy access to Gatineau Park, across the river in Quebec.

Trails in southern Ontario are generally easy to walk. The terrain can be steep and rocky here and there, especially in the Shield country, but overall the hiking is not very rough. Rivers and streams are bridged. There are many established, maintained campgrounds, and in some places you can reserve sites in them, but for most campgrounds it's first-come, first-served. Keep this in mind if you're anticipating a fall weekend on the Bruce Trail, when all forms of accommodation fill up early in the day.

The hiking season begins in late April. By mid-June the wildflowers are in bloom—the famed trilliums are very attractive—and backpacking is quite pleasant. Daytime highs are reaching into the upper 20s, with overnight lows around 10°C. In July a hot day can reach the upper 30s, complete with high humidity, and without an afternoon rain shower the night can be uncomfortably hot as well. Heat exhaustion is the main hazard in this part of Canada. Drink plenty of water. As elsewhere, pump-filter it or treat it to guard against pathogens.

In any given week you might have a day or two with rain. Afternoon thunderstorms in August produce downpours, sometimes with hail, but a full day of rain is rare. Morning mist is fairly common and is a lovely sight across the many lakes in the Shield region.

By late August the days are cooling off, the nights are getting down into the single digits, and there are fewer people on the trails. In mid-September the fall-colour season starts, and suddenly the woods are busy again, this time with leaf-peepers. Who wouldn't be one? The hardwood forests are glorious, full of the bright-red maples that attract camera-laden hikers from all over the world. The nights are chilly, but the days are pleasantly warm and the bugs are gone. By mid-October the show is winding down, and by the end of the month winter is nigh.

As for bugs, this is the land of plenty. West Nile virus is here, so take precautions. Mosquitoes come out in mid-May and one species or another is active all summer, especially at dusk. Blackflies are an even worse problem, but only in May and June. In August the deerflies and horseflies show up. Ouch!

At times, all this demands either a lot of DEET repellent or armour. You might want to pack a head net and a bug jacket made of tightly woven fabric and netting, with a netting hood. For this clothing, and for your tent, you'll want no-see-um netting, with holes too small to admit these tiny biting flies.

On the upside, at least you won't be troubled by poisonous spiders, of which there are few. The small Massasauga rattlesnake can inflict a painful although non-lethal bite. Rare to the point of being officially endangered, it lives in marshy areas and is active mainly at night.

If you're sensitive to poison ivy and poison oak, take care in this region where they grow in abundance. Thorny blackberry and raspberry bushes grow close to the edges of many trails. People who wear shorts may wish to wear gaiters for protection.

Pants with zip-off lower legs, a long-sleeved shirt to slip on over your tee-shirt and a sweater or light fleece jacket for evening coolness are useful additions to your pack. Few backpackers carry tuques or gloves for additional warmth until late in the season, although light gloves are good for keeping the bugs from biting your hands in camp. As elsewhere in Canada, a waterproof/breathable jacket and pants are recommended for rainy days. For better ventilation plus pack coverage, some people use ponchos.

The combination of generally easy walking and warm weather makes light footwear practical in southern Ontario. In fact, the trend in this region is to go with minimal gear in general. After bug season, many backpackers choose to sleep under a tarp rather than in a tent.

Internal-frame packs are popular, as are walking poles. A sleeping bag good to about 10°C is fine for midsummer use; one good to a few degrees below freezing will see you through to the end of fall, but be prepared for discomfort on hot nights. The humidity tends to make tents drippy inside, so choose one with excellent ventilation. Your sleeping bag will probably get damp anyway, so you might want to choose synthetic fill, which dries quicker.

The farther north you go in Ontario, the more bears there will be. Some parks provide bear-proof food lockers for visitors on foot. In other places you'll have to hang your food up for the night. Raccoons are common and not particularly adept at getting into food bags hung between trees, but they'll quickly claim food or food bags left unattended in the open or in a tent. The tree squirrels in some campgrounds are famous for their raiding ability. Inquire locally for the latest in defences.

This is the most populous part of the country, and along parts of the Bruce Trail you'll see hundreds of people on a summer weekend. Try to plan your trips for midweek, or be prepared for crowded camping, in which case small groups will be able to find camping space more easily than large groups will.

Here's an alternative to consider. In southern Ontario you're seldom far from a highway or a town, so you can do extended walking tours in very civilized fashion, staying in B&Bs instead of camping.

To escape humanity in general, head for the eastern and northern shores of Georgian Bay, or the north shores of Lake Huron and Lake Superior, where you can walk for day after day in wild surroundings. Killarney Provincial Park, southwest of Sudbury, is renowned for this kind of experience.

Like other parts of Canada, southern Ontario is not known for on-trail theft and violence. Stuff left in a tent for the day is unlikely to be stolen, but car break-ins are rather frequent. Try not to bring valuables that have to wait for you at the trailhead. If you must bring them, keep them locked in the trunk.

Good general hiking guides to this area include *Hiking Ontario's Heartland,* by Shirley Teasdale; *The Bruce Trail Reference,* the authoritative guide to the whole trail by the Bruce Trail Association (www .brucetrail.org); and *The Hike It Bike It Walk It Drive It Guide to Ottawa, the Gatineau, Kingston and Beyond,* by Ann Campbell.

Southern Quebec

The southern part of the province, with Montreal and Quebec City as centres, offers great variety in landscape and challenge. You can go for easy sea-level strolls along the St. Lawrence River or take on the tough and isolated International Appalachian Trail in the Chic-Choc Mountains (Monts Chic-Chocs) of the Gaspé Peninsula. Alpine tundra can be found only 150 kilometres north of Quebec City, in Grands-Jardins Provincial Park. Northwest of Hull/Ottawa you have the Canadian Shield.

The large wildlife reserves and provincial parks north of Montreal and Quebec City look inviting on the map, and some of the parks have fine day-hiking routes, but they're mainly canoe country and extended foot travel isn't really encouraged. However, the potential for multi-day trail routes is huge, and demand is growing.

For backpacking, La Mauricie National Park is popular, with its well-maintained trails and hikers' campgrounds. Saguenay Provincial Park also comes highly recommended, and north of Quebec City, in the Baie-Saint-Paul area, you can hike the multi-day Sentier des Caps de Charlevoix along the St. Lawrence, with whale-watching a possibility. In much of the province, trailside camping is unregulated and primitive. It's best to inquire locally.

You can hike in late April south of the St. Lawrence, but elsewhere the season really begins in mid-May, when the trails have dried out sufficiently after the abundant Quebec snow has melted. Sometimes muddy conditions prevail well into June. Daytime temperatures in July and August are typically in the 20s in shady woods, reaching into the 30s out in the open. July tends to be rainy one day and hot the next, with high humidity, sometimes making for miserable conditions. Fall colour, which is spectacular here, brings a delightful extension to the hiking season from late September through mid-October. By November the snow is on the ground to stay.

Backpackers will find summer nights mild in southern Quebec, with temperatures seldom lower than 10°C. Bring a fleece jacket. At higher elevations in the Chic-Chocs you may need a cap and gloves for warmth in the evening or the early morning.

The area does have thunderstorms, but usually the rain is showery and not very cold. As in the Shield country of Ontario, the morning mist around lakes and along the St. Lawrence is a treat.

Be prepared for lots of bugs, especially north of the St. Lawrence. The mosquitoes and blackflies are thick here in May and June, making for pretty unpleasant hiking and camping when the wind is too light to keep them down. By August you'll be seeing far fewer, and the October fall-colour season is wonderfully bug-free. Lyme disease is known in Quebec, so check yourself daily for the small ticks that may carry it. This is not poisonous-snake country. Black bears are present in most of the area, but you'll seldom see them. Raccoons and squirrels are more of a problem. Keep your food slung between two trees at night. Watch out for poison ivy and poison oak along the trails.

Quebec hikers tend to walk mainly in shorts. For footwear, you can get away with walking shoes on many trails, but for the higher, tougher routes you'll want light hiking boots.

An excellent all-round guidebook to Quebec trails is *Répertoire des lieux de marche au Québec*, by the Fédération québécoise de la marche.

You can order it from their website (in French only), www.fqmarche .qc.ca/bipede.asp.

New Brunswick and the Gaspé Peninsula

In this part of the country, within a few hundred kilometres you can experience two very different landscapes—the Appalachian Mountains and the Atlantic coast—plus the three different cultures of English-speaking Canada, Acadia and Quebec (toss in Maine, too). Enjoy!

Mountains first. The trails in northwestern New Brunswick and the Gaspé Peninsula of Quebec offer a great range of difficulty and commitment, from pleasant day hikes around Mt. Carleton to tough, isolated stretches in Forillon National Park and the parc national de la Gaspésie (Gaspésie National Park). You should gauge your level of ability carefully and do some research before diving in.

The "IAT"—the international section of the Appalachian Trail, meaning the Canadian section—runs through northwestern New Brunswick along the river valleys of the St. John and the Tobique. Here you'll find varied walking (at time of writing, much of it's along roads) through rolling, rural landscapes and past small towns, culminating in Mount Carleton Provincial Park and its 820-metre summit, the highest in the province. From there north it's deep-woods, boreal-forest country. As you move up the Gaspé Peninsula, you hit the wildest, most demanding portion of the entire trail, US or Canadian. The higher peaks rise above the treeline. For some sections you may have to carry up to two weeks of food. But the trail is nice and new, with many fine campsites.

It's possible to start hiking the New Brunswick valley floors in April, but trails along the higher Gaspé ridges can be snowbound into early June. Inquire locally. Be prepared for mosquitoes and blackflies in late spring and early summer, and into August at higher elevations. Also be mindful of the wide temperature range that comes with a wide range in elevation. In the valleys, expect daily highs in the mid-to-upper 20s and overnight lows around 10°C, but considerably cooler higher up. As elsewhere in eastern Canada, the fall colours are glorious here, and the weather can be mild well into October.

When the weather is hot inland, head for the sea. In fact, you can walk to the sea along the popular Dobson Trail from Moncton to Fundy National Park. It takes about three days. You can extend this trip through the park for two more days, then keep going southwestward along the Fundy Footpath for more than a week of fine hiking.

Hiking in New Brunswick

Fundy protects some of the better sea cliffs, tidal flats and salt marshes in this part of Canada. You'll also find trails that take you into the coastal forest, through lovely mixed coniferous and deciduous groves with mossy bogs frequented by moose and deer. The underlying soil is shallow, and heavy lugged boots are hard on it, so the park recommends light footwear with shallow tread—recognizing that good grip is still important. Kouchibouguac National Park is quite different. It's a sandy coastal plain, offering level walking through the woods, great for short family strolls.

Mosquitoes and blackflies are seldom a nuisance right at the shore, but they can be bad only 100 metres inland, especially at dusk in early summer. Black bears are shy in the Maritimes, but in some areas you may have to protect your food from them—and from raccoons. Seek out local advice.

The greatest danger here is forest fire. Much of New Brunswick and the Gaspé are heavily wooded, and large forest fires are a possibility all summer. If you're backpacking, plan on using your stove only.

Maritime storms can be cold and blustery, so if you're backpacking overnight in Fundy you should be prepared for wind-driven rain and temperatures that can dip below 10°C in July. Hurricanes are a possibility in New Brunswick in the fall, but they've been less damaging here than they have been in Nova Scotia and Newfoundland. The tide in the Bay of Fundy may be the highest in the world, but in the park it comes in slowly, so it's okay to explore the tidal flats. Just keep an eye on where the tidal edge is and don't go out terribly far. Anywhere along the coast, be wary of places where the rising tide may force you up against a cliff as the water deepens. Ask locally for tidal schedules.

Perhaps the most comprehensive trail guide for the whole province is the recently updated *Hiking Trails of New Brunswick*, by Marianne and H. A. Eiselt. *The New Brunswick Trails Council Trail Guide*, which is bilingual, is quite general and covers multi-use trails only. To find out more about the New Brunswick Trails Council, go to www.sentier nbtrail.com.

Nova Scotia and PEI

Since much of Nova Scotia and nearly all of Prince Edward Island are privately held, there are few large national parks. Provincial parks are many but small, and are found mainly along the coast. This means that long, isolated trails for backpacking are rare, but there's plenty of fine day-hiking to be done. If you go in midweek you'll have the trails mostly to yourself.

Here in the Maritimes the coastal walking is terrific. In many places it's possible to walk between B&Bs in the small "outport" towns, all of which were once linked by footpaths.

Nova Scotia has a lot of geological variety along the coast, making for interesting rock underfoot and diverse ecology in the surroundings. While there is no equivalent to the West Coast Trail of Vancouver Island or the East Coast Trail of Newfoundland, you'll find seaside hiking possibilities everywhere. Some are proper walking trails, built to high standards and well maintained, while others are rough paths.

On average, you'll have rain a couple of days out of seven. Watch out for weather changes. When the fog rolls in, the temperature can drop quickly into the single digits. East-coast fog is pea-soup fog. You can get lost in it. Squalls and storms can also appear suddenly, with accompanying wind and cold precipitation. Carry a warm layer, plus a rain jacket and rain pants, tuque and gloves. Be prepared for hurricanes, which are infrequent but quite dangerous along the south and east coasts of Nova Scotia. Along rocky shorelines, be wary of waves. People can be lured out on the rocks, which look safe enough as normal waves come in—then a large wave sweeps someone away. Peggy's Cove is notorious for this.

Inland PEI has the Confederation Trail, which is pleasant but used heavily by cyclists. It passes through farmland rather than wildland, so be prepared for a rural experience rather than a wilderness adventure. In Nova Scotia, Kejimkujik National Park—the only inland national park in the Maritimes—sits in the centre of the island southwest of Halifax, protecting wooded hills and lakes popular with canoeists. There's also backpacking here, and more in Cape Breton Highlands National Park at the northern tip of the province, where you'll find the highest, roughest terrain in Nova Scotia. And the worst weather. These parks maintain their trails and backpackers' campsites to national standards. Black bears are around, but they're very reclusive. Check locally for precautions to take when storing food overnight.

In this region the hiking season begins in late April, although somewhat later on Cape Breton. As elsewhere beside the Atlantic, expect moderate temperatures—summer highs in the mid-20s—and fog, especially early in the season. Away from the sea the temperature can climb into the 30s in midsummer, with high humidity and plenty of bugs. Blackflies are at their worst early in the season. You may want a head net. The mosquitoes come out later and stay all summer. By August things are cooling off and the bugs are less trouble. Fall colour is at its best in early October, and the hiking season ends soon after that.

Low shoes are popular for day-hiking in Nova Scotia and PEI, as are walking poles. You may want long pants to combat the bugs, and likewise a light tent with tight netting. Poison ivy is found here and there. Night-time temperatures are fairly warm, often above 10°C, but cold storms can make for chilly nights. In late August you should plan for frost and bring a three-season sleeping bag.

Michael Haynes has written all three of the currently popular Nova Scotia guidebooks: *Hiking Trails of Nova Scotia*, *Hiking Trails of Cape Breton* and *Trails of the Halifax Regional Municipality*. I'm looking forward to seeing a comprehensive guide to hiking in PEI. In the meantime, check locally.

East coast of Newfoundland

Way out on the eastern edge of North America, where the icebergs drift by, the Avalon Peninsula of Newfoundland offers the long and beautiful East Coast Trail. It stretches north and south from St. John's for over 200 kilometres, with more under construction. You hike beside the sea, sometimes close to the waves, and elsewhere overlooking the water from rocks and cliffs. The trail takes you through stands of evergreen forest, some of them dwarfed, and across open areas of low-growing but surprisingly lush vegetation shaped by salt spray and ocean wind.

You're at the mercy of the elements here. One moment you can be sweating in the heat, then the breeze gets brisk, or the rain starts, or a cold fog rolls in. Be prepared for anything and everything.

The season along this part of the Atlantic coast begins late, in mid-June. Spring arrives all at once, as the wildflowers bloom and the birds and sea life return en masse. By mid-July the daytime highs are reaching well into the 20s, with nights cooling down to around 10°C. A hot day can hit 30°C; a cool, drizzly, classically maritime day will keep the temperature in the single digits. A favourite time for hikers is fall, meaning September and October, when the days tend to be bright and mild and the season's colours are very beautiful in the long light glancing off the ocean. By mid-November the snow is flying.

Rain is definitely something to prepare for here, but on average five days out of seven will be sunny enough for pleasant hiking. Morning fog is thick and common but local; you pass in and out of it as you move from bay to headland. Thunderstorms and deluges aren't common. Rather, bad weather is typically showery, windy and rapidly changing.

Mosquitoes and deerflies are a minor nuisance. The wind is practically constant, and it has a way of keeping these insects down around your knees instead of up in your face. However, the blackflies will go for you anywhere they can reach your skin, and they can be bad early in the season. Long pants and tight cuffs are recommended. Zip-offs allow for easy changes into shorts when conditions allow. Overall this is a rather damp place, so you'll need outer clothing that repels moisture and dries quickly. Synthetics work well. Try a fleece jacket under Gore-Tex.

There are stretches of this coast that are wild enough for true backpacking, complete with trailside camps, but many people hike from outport to outport, from B&B to B&B. An average day's walk is on the order of 10–20 kilometres. Along the way you'll almost certainly see eagles, caribou and seals, perhaps even whales, and certainly thousands upon thousands of seabirds. Black bears may be around, but they haven't been reported for some time.

The hazards here are peculiar to the coast. People sometimes overestimate their endurance in walking this trail, which is generally easy with few major ups and downs, but it takes a winding route along the irregular shoreline, and the climbs and descents add up. That cape in the distance might look close, but you'll be a long time getting there. Plan accordingly, and carry plenty of food and water. Set aside enough time to reach your goal without exhausting yourself by having to hurry. You'll want yet more time for exploring the many side trails that lead to viewpoints and beaches. Pack warm layers to repel the wind and rain. The footing can be wet and slippery, so wear walking shoes or light hiking boots with good grip. Walking poles or a hiking stick will help. Be careful when picking berries along the cliffs. People have fallen off. And watch out for big waves.

The East Coast Trail is fairly new (begun in 1994 and officially opened in 2001), so the world hasn't discovered it yet. Even on a long weekend, once you get away from St. John's you may encounter few other hikers. Every metre of this route is steeped in Newfoundland's long seafaring tradition, part of which is to chat with strangers and show kindness and hospitality found nowhere else. Prepare to meet some wonderful people.

Trail guides to this and other routes in the area: *Trails of the Avalon*, by Peter Gard and Bridget Neame, and *Hiking the East Coast Trail*, a growing set of volumes by Peter Gard and Libby Creelman. Detailed maps are available. For more info, go to the East Coast Trail Association's website, www.eastcoasttrail.com.

Interprovincial trails

Not just one, but two across-the-country trails are under construction in Canada: the National Trail and the Trans Canada Trail (see map on page 313). Both have been forced to use roads as interim routes for some sections until true trails can be linked or built throughout.

The Trans Canada Trail is currently farther along than the National Trail, with 10,000 of the proposed 18,000 kilometres operational in 2007. A single route from Newfoundland to Alberta, the Trans Canada Trail splits in two in Calgary, with one leg heading northwest to the Yukon and the other heading west to Vancouver. It's multi-use, accommodating wherever possible five different recreational activities: walking, bicycling, cross-country skiing, riding horses and driving snowmobiles. All-terrain vehicles are permitted in certain places. Thus far, six official guidebooks by Sue Lebrecht have been produced to cover segments in various provinces. These are titled *Trans Canada Trail Newfoundland*, *Trans Canada Trail New Brunswick*, etc.

The National Trail is more restrictive, limiting use to self-propelled activities only (hiking, biking, skiing). Of the 10,000 kilometres planned,

Peter Gard

East Coast Trail

about 3,800 kilometres are in place. The National Trail follows a more northerly route through Alberta and British Columbia, reaching the west coast at Bella Coola instead of Vancouver.

For more information on these two great projects, check their web-sites: www.nationaltrail.ca and www.tctrail.ca.

APPENDIX

Hiking in the high ridges in Dune Za Keyih Provincial Park, northern Rockies of BC

Twenty essentials for an all-day summer hike in Canada

1. Hat for sun protection
2. Warm layer: sweater or light fleece jacket, tuque and gloves
3. Rain jacket with hood
4. Lighter, kept dry ("waterproof" matches seldom are)
5. Sunglasses, and spare glasses if your vision depends on them
6. Sunscreen
7. Insect repellent
8. Headlamp or flashlight
9. Handkerchief or bandana
10. Pocket-knife and/or multi-tool
11. Toilet paper and small moist towelettes for washing hands
12. Watch
13. Compass and/or (better) GPS receiver
14. Topographic map
15. Whistle. To bring help, blow it three times. Do this over and over.
16. A large, plastic garbage bag, one of those bright-orange ones. Should you be needing rescue, this will make you more visible.
17. Small first-aid kit (minimum: Band-Aids, blister pads, space blanket, pencil and a couple of note cards, list of basic first-aid steps as per page 130, whatever meds you normally need)
18. Water bottle. The best beverage to carry in a water bottle is plain water.
19. Water-filtration device or disinfection kit
20. Food

Suggested extras: rain pants, trail guidebook (to save weight, bring a copy of just the trail descriptions you need), natural-history guide, cell phone in case of emergency.

Suggested clothing, equipment and food for summer backpacking in Canada

This is a general list for the whole country. Depending on where you are, certain items won't be needed.

Important: on a week-long outing, your pack will be heavy with food for the first few days. You'll enjoy the trip more if you go as lightly as possible. Here is a good rule to follow:

"When in doubt, leave it out."

Clothing

- [ ] Usual underwear, plus lightweight long underwear to put on if the weather is unusually chilly
- [ ] Socks. Wool recommended (usually fewer blisters than with cotton) or whatever you're used to. Bring a spare set.
- [ ] Hiking boots: lightweight or moderate-weight and broken-in. Boots made entirely of leather, and well waterproofed with Sno-Seal or some other wax treatment, will be warmer in wet, cold conditions than leather-and-fabric models. Wearing Gore-Tex socks over your regular socks also helps a lot.
- [ ] Neoprene wading shoes, or moccasins or sandals of synthetic material for fording streams, if on the program. Can also be worn around camp.
- [ ] Long pants. Good choice: nylon ones with zip-off lower legs. Cotton jeans aren't recommended. They tend to get wet and cold, and they take a long time to dry.
- [ ] Short pants, if not wearing zip-offs
- [ ] Gaiters, for keeping stuff out of your boots when wearing shorts
- [ ] Long-sleeved shirt, nylon recommended
- [ ] Lightweight fleece jacket or wool sweater, bearing in mind that wool takes longer to dry than fleece
- [ ] Light insulated jacket. Down-filled, synthetic-filled or heavy fleece. Can be put in your sleeping-bag stuff sack and used as a pillow.
- [ ] Waterproof rain jacket with hood. Waterproof and breathable fabric (Gore-Tex, etc.) is popular, but after an hour in the rain, Gore-Tex is just as non-breathing as cheaper, lighter, coated fabric.

- [ ] Waterproof rain pants
- [ ] Poncho, if not bringing jacket and rain pants. Ponchos are light, but they don't protect the lower legs in wet brush, nor do they protect the lower body in wind-driven rain.
- [ ] Gloves. Recommended: pile or synthetic knit gloves, which dry quickly.
- [ ] Cap with brim for sun protection
- [ ] Tuque (knit cap) or hat with earflaps for chilly conditions. Also good for wearing in your sleeping bag.

Pack

- [ ] Internal-frame or external-frame backpack with capacity of at least 60 litres. Should have a comfortable padded hip-belt and should fit properly, so weight can be transferred to hips.
- [ ] Fitted pack cover or large plastic bag to cover your pack in the rain
- [ ] Sitting pad of sleeping-pad foam sized to slip down the inside, next to your back

Sleeping

- [ ] Summer-weight (warm to 0°C) down-filled or synthetic-filled sleeping bag, in stuff sack
- [ ] Plastic bag in which to put your sleeping bag, in its stuff sack, to make sure that it stays dry
- [ ] Foam pad. An inflatable type, such as the Therm-a-Rest, is the most comfortable. Closed-cell foam is cheaper and lighter. Ordinary air mattresses aren't recommended (heavy, cold, likely to leak).

Personal essentials

- [ ] Small plastic bowl, insulated plastic cup and nylon spoon. You can skip the bowl and eat from the cup.
- [ ] Strong stuff sack to use as a food-hanging bag, large enough to hold all food, soap, etc.
- [ ] Small carabiner for attaching food sack to rope or cable
- [ ] Strong plastic bag for packing out garbage
- [ ] Lighter, kept dry. "Waterproof" matches seem rarely to light very well.
- [ ] One-litre plastic water bottle or bladder-type water container

- [ ] The means to make drinking water safe (pump filter, some other device, chemicals, etc.)
- [ ] Small first-aid kit. Minimum: blister pads and Band-Aids. (See page 129 for a more complete kit.)
- [ ] Any medications you require
- [ ] Foam earplugs, if you're sensitive to the sound of people around you snoring
- [ ] Sunglasses
- [ ] Sunscreen rated SPF 30 or higher
- [ ] Insect repellent. Recommended: any brand with 20%–50% DEET, in a small pump-spray bottle.
- [ ] Cloth handkerchief and/or large bandana or small towel
- [ ] Pocket-knife and a light multi-tool. Large knives aren't recommended.
- [ ] Small flashlight (two-AA-cell type), or better, a headlamp. The new LED-type lamps are very light and compact. Be sure the batteries are fresh or bring spares.
- [ ] Comb/brush
- [ ] Toothbrush
- [ ] Extra glasses/extra contact lenses if your vision depends on them. Glasses are better as spares. They'll always work, even if you develop an eye problem that precludes wearing contacts.
- [ ] Toilet paper, sanitary napkins, moist towelettes, etc., in a zip-lock plastic bag, plus an extra bag to carry used items to the next point of disposal
- [ ] Compass and/or (better) GPS receiver, plus a topographic map
- [ ] Whistle, to bring help
- [ ] A couple of extra brightly-coloured plastic garbage bags

Recommended personal extras

- [ ] Walking poles. Nearly everyone who tries these likes them. (A single walking stick is not nearly as effective.) Poles make the hills easier, they provide better balance in awkward spots, and they're great for wading streams. Using rubber tips on walking poles reduces annoying clacking in rocky spots.
- [ ] Camera and plenty of film, or if the camera is digital, extra storage media and extra batteries

- ☐ Binoculars of the compact type, 6 x 15 to 8 x 24. Large binoculars are too heavy.
- ☐ Chemical water treatment, as personal backup for a group pump filter or other disinfecting device
- ☐ Small bottle of biodegradable camping soap
- ☐ Notebook and pencil, perhaps a sketchbook and coloured pencils
- ☐ Field guide to plants, animals, geology, etc.
- ☐ Paperback for reading on a rainy day

Group Gear

* You could share the equipment listed below with one to three other people, to save weight.

- ☐ Lightweight mountain tent. The better designs pitch with few or no stakes. All seams should be sealed to prevent leaks. The fly should cover the whole tent.
- ☐ Lightweight stakes of aluminum or nylon
- ☐ Small sponge, to sop up water from unexpected leaks
- ☐ Light backpacker's tarp, for shelter while cooking and standing
- ☐ Lightweight camping stove, preferably one that uses isobutane/propane fuel cartridges. Or a naphtha-fuelled (white-gas) stove.
- ☐ Fuel. Allow 50 grams of isobutane per person per day, or 0.1 litre of naphtha (white gas).
- ☐ Light cookset. One or two pots, pot-lifter and plastic scrub pad.
- ☐ Light backpacker's water bag—not a heavy canvas water bag—for collecting from stream or lake and carrying to camp
- ☐ Water-purification filter or other form of treatment
- ☐ Plastic trowel for digging individual poop-holes if necessary
- ☐ 15 metres of light camping cord to tie between trees for drying wet clothing and sleeping bags
- ☐ 15 metres of heavier cord if needed for hanging up food at night

☐ Pepper spray to use in case of bear trouble. One or two dispensers per group provide peace of mind, although a party of six or more persons is considered to be attack-proof. A group in which each member carries pepper sprays is extra prepared. Be sure the spray is instantly accessible, not in your pack. And remember that you can't bring it on the airlines.

Food: Try for minimum weight and maximum nourishment

☐ Suppers based on dried foods (pasta, Japanese noodles, beans, rice) or freeze-dried meals

☐ Hearty breakfasts that are more than just instant cereal (my current favourite: instant black-bean flakes mixed with instant rice, plus a little cheese, corn chips and salsa mixed in)

☐ For lunch and snacks: granola bars, dried fruit, jerky, sausage, cheese, trail mix, crackers, cookies, candy

☐ Remember that you'll need one fewer breakfast and supper than you'll need lunches, because you'll eat breakfast before you leave and supper after you get back

Heard in the wild . . .

"It's never actually around the next corner."

"When you're on the trail to the pass, what goes down must come up."

"Everything is horrid when there's honey in your hair."

"All the animals out there are way smarter than we think they are. Especially bears, raccoons and blackflies."

"My dog won't come into the tent with me. Maybe I'd better wash."

"Freeze-dried onions keep their fragrance far longer than they ought to. If you catch my drift."

"Canadian water still thinks it's ice."

"That zipper? That zipper will never work again."

"The sunsets in this country go on forever."

"The weather's here. Wish you were beautiful."

"When I was 30, this trail was a lot easier."

"The reason you didn't hear any snoring last night is because you were the one doing it."

"Mommy, wake up! My teddy bear is floating!"

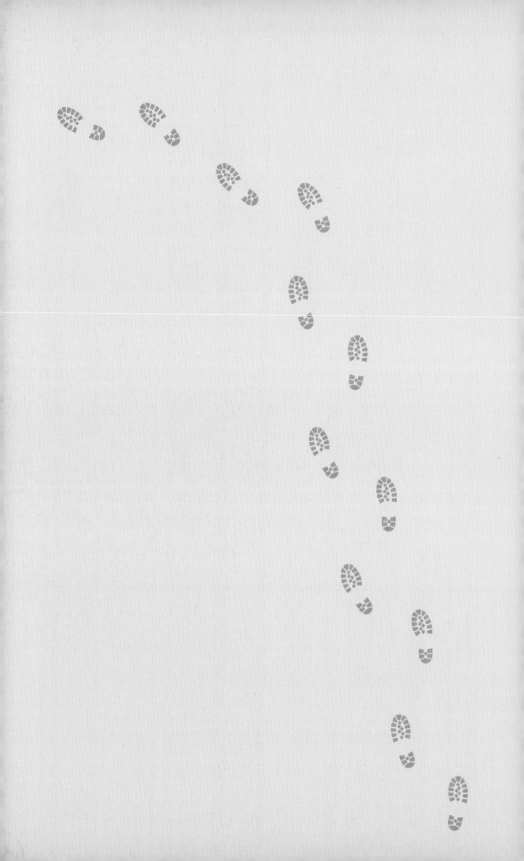

Index

A

accessories for packs • *72*

Achilles tendon • *40*

alcohol

  as stove fuel • *96*

  effects in camp • *127*

  swabs • *130*

all for one, and one for all • *200*

Allison, Leanne • *319*

altimeter • *117, 119, 227*

anaphylactic reaction to insect sting • *305*

anecdotes

  bad blisters • *32*

  Conrad Kain on walking • *10*

  falling asleep • *111*

  heard in the wild • *356*

  knife-thrower • *79*

  spiders in tent • *77*

  Will Gadd on being hungry • *148*

animals

  danger from • *295*

  observing • *221*

  protecting food from • *190*

ankle, sprained • *232*

antibacterial hand gel • *107*

Appalachian Trail • *339, 341*

approach shoes • *31*

art (sketching) • *127*

artificial respiration • *130*

asthma • *177, 292*

athletic drinks • *149*

Audubon Expedition Institute • *145*

B

backpacking

  choice of group members • *156*

  in selected regions of Canada • *311*

musical instruments for • *127*

off-trail • *270*

on the cheap • *138*

story of a trip • *163*

why we go • *2*

with children and dogs • *262*

bags, bum • *73*

ball cap • *60*

Band-Aids • *129*

bandages • *129*

bandana • *109*

barometer • *119*

bathing and swimming • *239, 280*

bean flakes • *145*

beans and rice for breakfast • *196*

bear-bells • *135*

bear-pole • *190*

bear-proof container • *145, 300*

bears

  attacks • *297*

  avoiding • *225*

  black • *296*

  encounters with • *228*

  grizzly • *202, 297*

  polar • *300*

  protecting food from • *189, 190*

  repellent spray • *133*

  shouting to warn • *136*

beavers, danger from • *302*

becoming separated and lost • *286*

Beers, Don • *2*

behavior matters • *156, 178, 234, 240*

Being Caribou • *319*

bells, bear • *135*

belt, choosing • *49, 52*

Benadryl • *111*

benighted • *288*

beverages • *149*

Notes